BIG TECH
TECH
MUST GO!

Martin Andree teaches media science at Cologne University in Germany. He has been doing research on the dominance of Big Tech for more than 15 years. Leading German media (including public German television and leading German newspapers) and conferences (including the Digital Summit of the Federal German Government) regularly call on his expertise for contributions on this subject. In 2020, he published the *Atlas of the Digital World,* which has a strong reputation. He received the Günter Wallraff Special Award for Press Freedom and Human Rights for the book *Big Tech must go.*

Verena Bönniger is a communication designer and creative director at Delicious Layouts Visuelle Kommunikation.

MARTIN ANDREE

Digital Giants are Destroying our Democracies
and Economies — We Will

Campus Verlag
distributed by
The University of Chicago Press

The original German edition was published in 2023 by Campus Verlag with the title *Big Tech muss weg. Die Digitalkonzerne zerstören Demokratie und Wirtschaft – wir werden sie stoppen.*
The English edition is distributed worldwide outside German-speaking countries by
The University of Chicago Press.
All rights reserved.

ISBN 978-3-593-52115-2 Print
ISBN 978-3-593-46230-1 E-Book (PDF)

All rights reserved. No part of this book may be reproduced or transmitted in any form or by any means, electronic or mechanical, including photocopying, recording, or by any information storage and retrieval system, without permission in writing from the publishers.
Copyright © 2025 Campus Verlag, part of the publishing group Beltz,
Werderstr. 10, 69469 Weinheim, info@campus.de.
Cover design and Typesetting: Verena Bönniger, Delicious Layouts, Hilden
Printing office and bookbinder: Beltz Grafische Betriebe GmbH, Bad Langensalza
Beltz Grafische Betriebe is a climate-neutral company (ID 15985-2104-1001)
Printed in Germany

www.campus.de
www.press.uchicago.edu

CONTENT

Preface of the English Book Release   7

KNOCKOUT: How Big Tech stops 'unwanted' research   9

GAME OVER 2029: The dominance of Big Tech   15

1. Our democracy is in danger   16
2. The 'point of no return': 2029   21
3. The Internet of monopolies   28
4. The victims: Journalism, bloggers, global brands, public service broadcasting   37
5. Fair and free competition has been completely eliminated   47
6. Is it really so dramatic?   49

THE END OF THE FREE INTERNET:
How the tech giants occupied the digital media space   59

1. Stuck in the silos of the platforms   60
2. Media genres are now the private property of companies   68
3. How Big Tech is expanding its monopolies   82
4. Killer acquisitions   89
5. Self-allocation of internet traffic   95
6. Monopoly accelerator: Generative AI   100

HOSTILE TAKEOVER:
How digital superpowers change our entire society   103

1. Death trap: The narrative of weak, vulnerable media   104
2. How Big Tech will take over the economy   110

3. Why politicians will be dependent on platforms in the future   122
4. Mega-media are taking over our society   128
5. Tech giants manipulate traffic   133
6. Spying and policing activities by Big Tech   138
7. The principle of maximum takeover   143

IV.
MONOPOLIES, FAKE NEWS, HATE SPEECH:
Is this actually legal?   149

1. Insufficient legislation against monopolies   150
2. Maximum profits for tech giants without liability   168
3. How we are imprisoned by the platforms' legal systems   177
4. Is the status quo unconstitutional?   181
5. Conclusion: Goodbye, democracy and free media   197

V.
ACCEPT HERE:
Why nobody cares   203

1. California Dreamin': The good beginnings   204
2. Digital Darth Vaders dress up as philanthropists   210
3. The destruction of freedom in the name of freedom   217
4. Promote versus punish: Big Tech's lobbying machine   225

VI.
COUNTDOWN 2029:
How can we liberate the Internet?   239

1. A glimmer of hope: The people do not want Big Tech monopolies   240
2. How can we liberate the Internet   244
3. Seriously?   262
4. A free Europe between US digital feudalism and China's online dictatorship   265

Thanks   276
Notes   278

Preface of the English Book Release

The publication of *Big Tech must go!* (released in August 2023) sparked a huge debate about digital monopolies in Germany—including about one hundred events, interviews on television, radio and newspapers, press contributions, conference talks, panels and reviews. In October 2023, it was selected as one of the Nonfiction 'Books of the Month' (BuchMarkt). In May 2024, it received the 'Günter Wallraff Special Award for Press Freedom and Human Rights'. The book even attracted attention in many countries outside of Germany.

Indeed, one aspect of this book is particularly relevant also outside Germany: The first chapter contains the first holistic measurement of a full country's entire digital media usage. This baseline measurement is particularly interesting because it precisely quantifies the incredible dominance of Big Tech in the various categories and markets. The analysis is based on a scientifically sound, 'court-proof' baseline data measurement. The documented monopolization is NOT based just on surveys, but on the real usage out in the various markets.

Despite the fact that this analysis only shows the dramatic situation in Germany, we can assume that the level of concentration and dominance would be more or less identical in other Western democracies. For this reason, the following chapters, with their full interpretation of the implications for our media systems and our democracies, will be useful internationally. Also of interest for and potential use by international readers is the comprehensive set of solutions proposed in the last chapter to restore media pluralism in the digital world and to reestablish competition and fair access across digital media.

After the overwhelming success of the book, I received dozens of requests from many countries outside of Germany—including to give about 50 international conference talks and interviews. In parallel, the hostile and surreptitious takeover of our free media by Big Tech has drastically accelerated. This book has correctly predicted, back in 2023, that Big Tech would inevitably extend its dominance into the political sphere too. This is exactly what has happened—with Musk and Big Tech now being part of the new US government. Due to the global state of emergency, I have reacted as quickly as possible:

I have first translated the website for this book ...
☞ *www.bigtechmustgo.com*

... and also the website of the underlying scientific data measurements ...
☞ *https://www.atlasderdigitalenwelt.de/en*

... plus I have made a video of an English conference talk available online ...
☞ *https://www.youtube.com/watch?v=IBjLYwJ0hj8*

    In addition, I have now translated the entire book as quickly as possible to make its content available internationally. I would like to thank Campus, my German publisher, which, in cooperation with The University of Chicago Press, ensured that this English edition has been published so swiftly. I hope that it can make a contribution to save our free media from being taken over by Big Tech monopolies in the digital sphere. It's time that Western societies wake up and act—before it is too late and Big Tech has destroyed our democracies.

KNOCKOUT:
How Big Tech stops 'unwanted' research

If you 'get into trouble' with Big Tech, you will not forget it in a hurry. In October 2020, I experienced the very real threat of Big Tech at first hand. Our 'Atlas of the digital world' had just been published. It is the first baseline measurement of digital media usage (information can be found at *www.atlasderdigitalenwelt.de/en*). Such measurements are important for our society. They show precisely the extent to which the Internet is already dominated by digital corporations. And here already a quick reveal: We actually measured a level of dominance that was so incredible that, at first, we could not believe our eyes (☞ I.3–4).

Previously, there had been little reliable scientific information on this simple question. It is very time-consuming to carry out such data analyses. You have to measure millions of domains. You have to evaluate usage on different devices such as smartphones, desktops or tablets and analyze huge samples. Just the research equipment for such a study costs millions of euros. But, in the end, we achieved what had seemed impossible for many years. The idea was to publish this atlas periodically on the basis of the scientific data model we had developed. The plan was to provide society with information—which would be always up-to-date—on the digital basis of our democracy. The digital companies did not like our idea at all. One of them immediately took action and put a stop to it. Within a few days, the whole initiative was brought to a halt. In order to protect partners, I cannot lay out more details. But the message was clear: Leave this field of activity.

This experience changed my life. The incredible power of Big Tech or "GAFAM" (i.e. Google, Apple, Facebook, Amazon, Microsoft),[1] which we had just scientifically measured, also encroached on my personal life during that period. I realized that the huge domination of Big Tech that our data analyses had revealed was not just a theoretical construct. Big Tech is actually using its dominant power in our society to suppress the publication of 'unwanted' information. As we will see, my experience is not an isolated case. Over and over again, Big Tech abused its power to prevent scientists and journalists from publishing 'unpopular' information (☞ V.4).[2]

This experience made me realize that the digital giants can already do whatever they want in a country like Germany. They are already so powerful that they can rely on scared partners, dependent companies or institutions throughout our society to push through their interests. The presumptuousness of this approach surprised me at the time. I would not have expected that an American tech giant would dare to actively use its dominant market position to prevent future scientific research at a public university and to stop the publication of 'unwanted' data and studies in a free country like Germany. But it clearly shows the unscrupulous manner in which the digital corporations are already operating in our country.

There was one small consolation. After all, our data analysis had already been published. So this time, Big Tech had missed the boat. There is one pretty cool side effect of the seemingly uncool knowledge unit called 'a book': once it is published, you cannot delete the information any more. You cannot push toothpaste back into the tube.

When these strong reactions to our measurements came from behind the scenes, I initially asked myself: Why is that? After all, the Big Tech companies are constantly being criticized anyways. We already know about plenty of evil things they have done to our societies. The most important topics under discussion include:

- Intentional breaches of the law and active abuse of regulatory loopholes
- Spying on users and usage of their data in digital surveillance capitalism
- Passing on personal data to government security authorities
- Manipulation of elections (Cambridge Analytica)
- Division of society through 'echo chambers'—people mainly see opinions on platforms that confirm their beliefs
- Fake news and algorithmic preference for radical and emotional content, as this maximizes the attention of users
- Exploitation of cheap labor and creation of precarious working conditions
- Accumulation of profits plus consistent refusal to pay appropriate taxes in the respective countries of business

How can this strong reaction to our seemingly harmless scientific data measurements be explained? The answer is actually quite simple. As we know from many studies on digital corporations, they ultimately have only one goal: the accumulation of the maximum amount of power, money and domination. They see themselves as pioneers of a new, digital world that will replace the old and outdated analog world. And in this new, 'better' world, everything will have to dance to their tune. With regard to digital companies, there is ultimately only one question of interest: What can halt their unstoppable march to power?

If we look at the above criticisms of digital corporations, they all have one thing in common. Although all of these issues concern areas that are extremely harmful for the Western world—such as the division of society, social imbalance, threats to security—they are basically irrelevant to digital corporations and their efforts to grow. No matter how critically these issues are viewed, in most cases they only generate image problems or marginal penalties for Big Tech. The tech giants set aside budgets for the many ongoing legal disputes, which they can easily finance from their booming profits. For them, the cost of legal disputes is, in other words, peanuts. They can invest gigantic budgets in lobbying and PR to counter such image issues. It is no problem for them to manage it. Apart from that, the products of the tech giants dominate the market as monopolies in many cases. Bad press is annoying, but ultimately irrelevant, because most people do not feel like they have a choice anyway. They may not like the digital companies, but they still continue to use Google, WhatsApp and Instagram.

Moreover, most of the points mentioned 'only' concern ethical aspects. These can be discussed wonderfully on talk shows or at political hearings. The digital companies are regularly invited here and are allowed to speak at length. They keep repeating their supposedly good intentions, admitting mistakes, vowing to do better, and so on. We have observed this method for decades: Regrets, promises and then nothing happens.

In contrast, our topic leads right to the heart of the problem: the ongoing takeover of our media system by digital corporations. As we will see (☞ I.1–4), the tech giants have already gone a long way with this. What could really stop their progress? We can only devise measures to counteract them if we get to a broad public awareness of how dangerously far they have already progressed with their hostile takeover. The ethical issues mentioned above are ultimately negligible from the digital companies' point of view. But these questions on media dominance take the social debate into completely different spheres, also in terms of possible penalties and sanctions. When we talk about Big Tech eliminating our democratic media landscape and destroying our economy, we are taking the discussion to an entirely new level. Then we are talking about antitrust penalties amounting to many billions of euros or even scenarios in which these companies are broken up.

This was precisely the reason why our measurement of the enormous market concentration based on solid scientific models had caused such trouble behind the scenes. The GAFAMs were aware that the issue of a hostile takeover of the Internet can quickly unite parties and groups that are often quite politically divided—if they understand what is really going on. It is obvious once you look at our data: We are *all* being cheated on by Big Tech, whether we are rich or poor, left or conservative. We are all victims of these monopolies. The digital corporations are the mortal enemies *of the left and of free market capitalism alike*. Because *they destroy political and economic freedom at the same time*—the freedom of our pluralistic media system as well as the freedom of our pluralistic market economy.

For as long as we keep getting caught up in specific aspects and only argue with each other about fake news, surveillance or populism, we are failing to realize that we are all fundamentally affected by the hostile takeover of the Internet, regardless of whether we are progressive or conservative, whether we are arguing on the side of culture or the economy, whether we are artists or entrepreneurs.

The status quo harms all of us. If we would recognize this together, it would be easy to overcome the blinkered thinking in our political debates. Together, we could reclaim the wonderful Internet that the digital giants have stolen from us users. We could make sure that it is not only the Big Tech companies that make big money out of the Internet, but that all creators, publishers and bloggers get a chance to monetize their content in a fair way. We could revitalize the digital sphere that is currently occupied by 'colonialist' digital giants. We could make sure that our children still live in a pluralistic democracy, with a pluralistic, open media system and a pluralistic, open economy. We just have to notice the massive problem that is on the one hand so obvious, yet on the other hand seems so difficult to recognize.

As a media researcher, I have written several academic books and a handbook. In this book, I have decided to write in a more accessible way so that everyone can understand what the analyses of our data means, how our media system is doing and how far Big Tech has already succeeded in its hostile takeover. And to show how endangered our democracy is and what we can do to prevent it from collapsing.

This book is not about the usual criticisms of the digital world—that gaming is addictive, that young people's self-esteem is being damaged by Instagram consumption, that hate speech is increasingly poisoning the way we live together, that our data is being monitored, that fake news and populism are on the rise and so on. It would be just as wrong to just look at the latest technological advances (ChatGPT et cetera) without analyzing the fundamental underlying problem. This book has a purely positive relationship with the digital world. It doesn't claim that the 'good old analog world' was better in any way. I work in the digital industry and fortunately spend most of my life working on digital matters. My book is therefore strongly *in favor* of digital media.

The issue is that the digital world has been stolen from us. And yet we still have power in our hands. We can free the Internet from the domination of digital corporations (☞ VI) and return it to the purpose for which Tim Berners-Lee originally conceived it: a democratic and anti-hierarchical means of mutual human connection, understanding and networking. The most burning issue of the digital transformation is not its much-discussed side effects. The most burning issue is its main effect: that tech companies are exploiting the digital revolution to take over ever larger parts of our society. We need to recognize and tackle this problem. Then we have a chance.

I have presented these often complex relationships in as simple and entertaining a way as possible. I am extremely grateful that I was able to partner with the fantastic graphic designer Verena Bönniger for this project.

I dedicate this book to my two children and sincerely hope that they and their families will one day be able to live in a free media democracy, even if the chances are unfortunately slim.

Further content 'bonus tracks', updates and potential corrections can be found on the accompanying website *www.bigtechmustgo.com*. Simply scan the printed QR code to enter it.

GAME OVER 2029:
The dominance of
Big Tech

1. Our democracy is in danger

In a hundred years from now, people will look back on our era and rub their eyes in amazement. How on earth did a handful of digital giants take control of our democracy and our free economy at the same time? Did we fail to notice because of the huge amount of attention focused on the climate crisis, the corona pandemic and the war in Ukraine? How did Big Tech get this far with its hostile takeover of our media system, in broad daylight, without us noticing and without us mounting any kind of defence?

Everyone is talking about A.I. right now—but in retrospect, generative AI will probably be seen as 'merely' finishing off our current media system (☞ II.6). When millions of machine-generated texts and posts flood social media, the massive devaluation of online content that has been progressing for decades will reach its final stage. Digital companies will then probably 'finish the job'. Journalism and editorial media do not have the slightest chance of surviving in their current form.

This hostile takeover of our media system by Big Tech has been going on for two decades. Our media system will no longer be under our control in just a few years. But there are few if any signs of any concern or alarm. Sure, people are discussing the opportunities and risks of generative AI. But the looming takeover of our democratic public sphere by Big Tech is not an issue, despite the fact that the media are the basis of our democracy. They inform people, they enable citizens to form political opinions, they keep a check on the politicians, they keep an eye on the rich and powerful.

With the rise of digital media, we are experiencing one of the greatest technological revolutions in human history. The ever-increasing replacement of traditional information services by digital platforms is like open-hear surgery being performed on our democracy. We have known since McLuhan ("The medium is the message") that media are never 'innocent'.[1] They form the basis of our social thought patterns, attitudes and behavior. A massive change in our media landscape will have massive consequences for our democratic society.

Of course, digital companies play a central role in this process. As our holistic baseline measurement of all German internet traffic has shown conclusively, the tech giants already own large parts of this future public sphere via their dominant positions. They will own the new digital basis of our democracy in a few years. GAFAM will take over. We can assume that the situation will be identical in the other Western democracies.

This extreme dominance of media control is alarming. Under no circumstances should individual forces be allowed to gain command of our media system, regardless of whether they are political parties, the government, powerful individuals or digital corporations. If this happens, the freedom and independence of our media will be lost and our democracy will be severely damaged.

Are you surprised that this danger is not currently a topic of social debate? If so, you are right. Are you wondering if I am exaggerating or even scaremongering? Unfortunately not. We have measured the entire web traffic and our data analyses deliver crystal clear results: we will soon pass a tipping point. Beyond it, there will be no turning back. Our media system, which is the basis of our democracy, will fall into the hands of the digital giants simply due to the dynamics of the digital transformation. Let us start with the most important key points to explain this:

▶ It is a truism already that digital media will replace analog media.

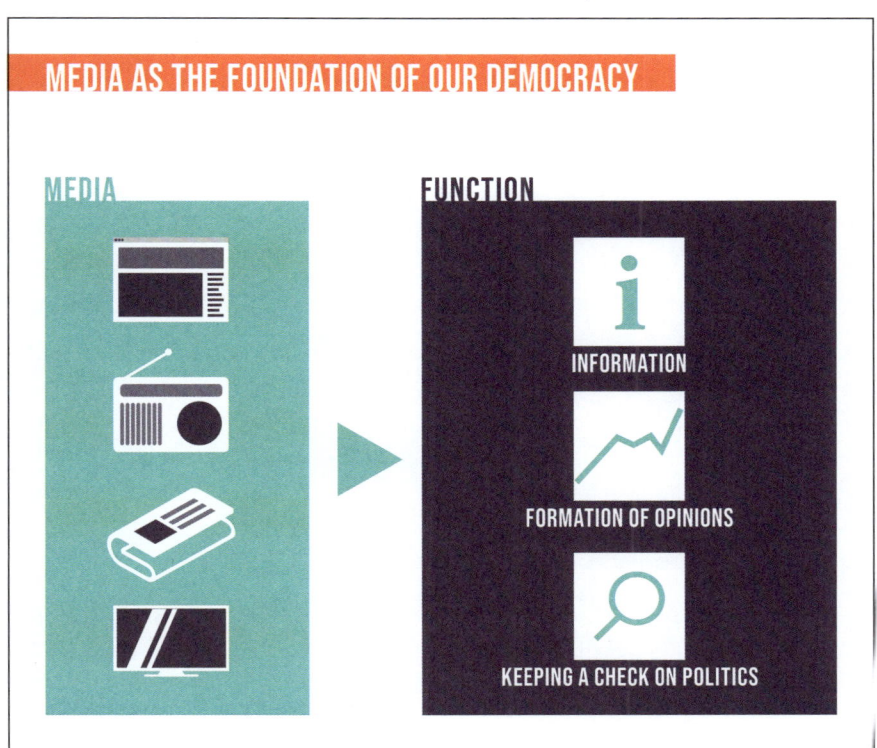

- What few people realize is that this transformation is already at a very advanced stage. Digital media have already overtaken analog media and are now the leading media.
- Soon, in 2029, analog media will have fallen below a 25 percent share. For the analog world, that will mean: GAME OVER. The political discourse will then be in the hands of the platforms.

One key question is how quickly this transformation will take place. Another question is: what will happen if the media-based democracy as we know it is lost? How will it affect our lives? I guarantee you that the consequences for people will be very tangible (see text box at the bottom of the page).

FUN FACT: Digital media have been the leading media since 2020.

Dominance by Big Tech—six dangerous consequences

1. Editorial media and journalism will continue, inexorably, to become less and less important and to melt away.

2. This does not only strengthen phenomena like fake news. In the future, the tech giants will be able to determine which citizens receive which news via the platforms. They are already manipulating traffic to suit their interests. Neither science nor politics have access to these processes. People are becoming increasingly disempowered.

3. Political expression and influence are increasingly controlled by the platforms.

4. The editorial media have always exercised played a role as a fourth estate, a check on other powers. Through the media, citizens have been able to publicly denounce issues or abuses, for example corruption in business or politics. Editorial media have been able to report on crime until the State prosecutors

What happens when we reach the tipping point?

A handful of digital corporations have succeeded in stealing our wonderful democratic Internet from Western societies using aggressive methods and unfair tricks (☞ II.2). By taking over large parts of the Internet, they have managed to exploit the digital transformation for their own purposes. They have already made a lot of progress in that endeavour. In the subsequent pages, we will scientifically demonstrate how much progress they have made. Unfortunately, we have protected our democratic order against all kinds of attacks—against antidemocratic parties, against overthrows, against violent attacks from the outside. But we currently have no effective defense mechanisms against the acute threat posed by digital corporations (☞ IV). And technologies such as generative AI will only massively speed up this takeover.

There is one crucial question: At what point will the dominance of the digital corporations have progressed so far (also as a result of the ongoing digital transformation) that the resulting momentum will be irreversible? From the existing data, we can see that this point will be reached in around five to ten years at

intervened. In the future, this function will be taken over by the platforms. These digital companies will be able to set the agenda in society, i.e. select the topics that are widely discussed by the general public. They will be able to actively control the so-called 'agenda setting' in our society—the selection of topics that are widely discussed.

5. Governments and politicians will also do a large part of their communication via platforms in the future. They will become increasingly dependent on the digital corporations. In the future, the tech giants will be able to decide at will how much attention (traffic) the various political messages receive. Only they will have access to the machine room of digital media and the distribution of messages online. And they will aggressively exploit this access to their own advantage.

6. Any kind of resistance to the digital elite of the tech giants will be pointless, because they have gained power over our public sphere. Our political discourse will be controlled by them.

the most. After that, it will be almost impossible to stop this dynamic, because the democratic media and the systems that are still available to us will no longer work. The total 'share of voice' of the shrunken editorial media will be too small to strike back against the supremacy of the platforms. When they were still big and powerful, they did not protest. Beyond the future tipping point, any protest will be meaningless.

We can hardly underestimate the consequences: What if the domination over large parts of our society falls into the laps of the tech giants? What if the free market economy itself falls victim to this dynamic? What happens if the digital corporations replace our pluralistic, free economic order with their monopolies? What if our democracy is damaged forever?

2. The 'point of no return': 2029

When we talk about the takeover of our media system, the key question is: Exactly how big is the threat? Let us first get a holistic overview. The media landscape currently consists of two fields. On the one hand, there are the traditional, analog offerings such as newspapers, radio and television, the editorial media. And then there are the digital media, which have been on the rise for decades, such as social media, video-on-demand (e.g. YouTube), search engines (e.g. Google), including the digital extensions of journalism and editorial publishers.

We all know that we are currently in the middle of a transformation process. Digital media are replacing analog media. It makes sense to briefly outline this process over time. The starting point of this development was in 1989. Tim Berners-Lee invented the World Wide Web during his stay at CERN in Geneva. At the time of his invention, the relative share of digital media in terms of total usage was exactly 0 percent. By coincidence, it was the same year when the Berlin Wall came down. Back then, the analog media accounted for 100 percent of usage.

We all know that digital media are taking over. We know anecdotally that young people are already using digital media almost exclusively. We know that the older generations are also becoming increasingly digital. But when it comes to determining exactly how far this transformation process has progressed, most people have no clear answers at hand. After all, it makes a difference whether the media that form the basis of our democracy are 10 percent digital, 50 percent digital or 80 percent digital. In fact, it is not at all easy to identify reliable answers. If we wanted to get scientifically sound knowledge, we would have to 'track' a very large number of people using one and the same monitoring methodology. In other words, we would have to measure their exact media consumption across all various channels and formats down to the minute and the second.

No such study exists. It is far too complicated to measure the various forms of media consumption. Just imagine the research equipment that would be needed just to measure exactly how many minutes a day a person reads a newspaper. But don't worry, there is an answer to our simple question about the importance of digital media. We will just take a small detour and look at another question: in which channels (analog or digital) are companies spending how much money on advertising?

Digital media have been the leading media since 2020/21

Why does this detour via investment in advertising make sense? Well, all media bundle the *attention* of large audiences. It does not matter which channels are used to attract this attention, whether it happens on the radio, on TikTok or when reading a magazine. But the combined attention of all media is then sold to advertising companies.

Naturally, advertising companies think very carefully about where they should invest their valuable money on advertising. They have hundreds of measurement methods at their disposal to determine exactly where to invest: Where do I get the most attention for the money I pay? An entire industry of market research companies and agencies earns hundreds of millions of euros every year by analyzing the selection of these channels for advertising companies.

This is precisely why advertising investments provide a wonderful indicator of the relative importance of the various channels. And the figures here are more than clear. We can set the 'tipping point' for Germany in the year 2020 or 2021 (depending on the data source). Since this tipping point, *advertising companies have invested more in digital media than in all other analog media combined.*[2]

This insight comes as a surprise for many people. Most users would estimate the share of digital media to be lower. But, in fact, analog times are over.[3] If you look at advertising as an indicator of bundled media attention, it has been true for several years: *Digital media are the leading media.* Analog media are now only of secondary importance. And they will continue to melt away. At some point, digital media will take over. And one thing is clear: it won't be long now.

There are a lot of explosive implications behind this finding. This is because many stakeholders in the media, business or politics still pay attention first and foremost to what happens in analog media. If you were to ask an editor at *Der Spiegel* (a leading political magazine from Germany) about his competitors, he/she would certainly point to *Focus*, *Die Zeit* or *FAZ* (other leading German print publications).

He probably would not say that Facebook and Instagram are the most dangerous competitors for *Der Spiegel*. But that's exactly the case. Let us think a few years ahead. If we ask which company could one day take so much attention away from *Spiegel* that it would be a matter of survival for the editorial team, then it is certainly not *Focus* or *Die Zeit*—but the competition from digital platforms.

Platforms are destroying the financial basis of journalism

There is another reason why it is interesting to analyze advertising investments. Advertising may be annoying and irritating for many media users, but they forget that the same advertising serves a 'good purpose' for our democracy. After all, it is the same advertising that enables media companies to finance editorial offices, create films, hire journalists and carry out research (see illustration on previous page).

This also gives us a first impression as to how the digital basis of our democracy could look in the future. After all, as we all know, the platforms' business model is based on 'user-generated content'—in other words, content that users create for them. The platforms commonly do not pay any fees, do not maintain editorial teams, they do not spend time and resources on research. They do not conduct interviews, analyze topics or investigate. They merely offer users a digital forum where they can disseminate their content as they wish. The only difference is that users do this work for platforms free of charge and receive no financial reward for it.

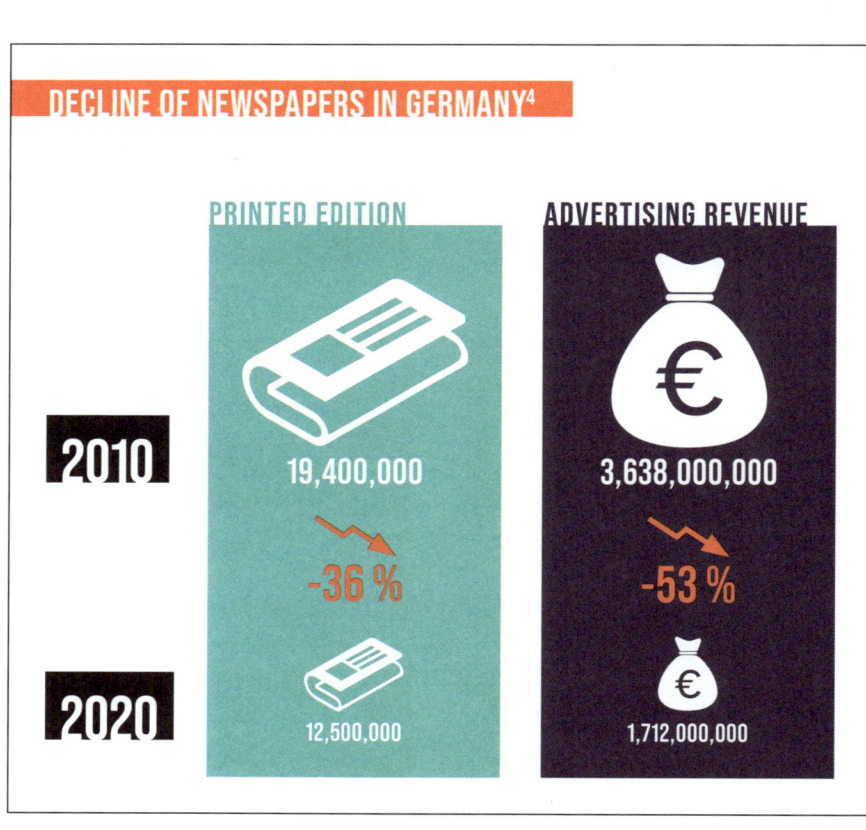

Anyone who thinks that it is not worth analyzing such advertising investments is mistaken because the privately organized media are dependent on this advertising, regardless of whether it is *RTL* or *Pro7* (Germany's biggest private broadcasting channels), *Der Spiegel* or the *Süddeutsche Zeitung* (large German print publishers). If advertising investments continue to migrate to platforms, then the analog and editorial media will inevitably 'dry up'. This is precisely what we have been observing for years and for decades: newspapers are dying, jobs are being cut in editorial offices, publishers are constantly restructuring, journalism is dying.

When will the editorial media collapse?

The question is at what point the analog media will have melted away to such an extent that they reach a second 'tipping point'. After all, in such processes of stagnation, the decline from a certain point onwards is no longer linear, but dynamic. This is the case with many economic business models. After a certain threshold, it is no longer economically viable to maintain a factory, for example. It is no longer profitable because the costs of production exceed the income. At this point, the owners will stop the business and close the production facility.

As we have seen, it has taken digital media more than three decades to achieve their current level of dominance. We can safely assume that the speed of their growth will advance in the future. We can see from the published predictions that digital media will probably bundle three quarters of all advertising investments in Europe by 2029 (in 2024, they were already at 63.3 percent). In contrast, the relative share of analog media will fall to less than 25 percent in 2029.[5]

This will be critical for analog media in three aspects. First, they will lose relevance for society as a whole. Second, many media companies will no longer be able to sustain themselves profitably. Closures, mergers, job cuts and restructuring will accelerate the erosion process. However, the third consequence is the most significant one. The loss of relative share of attention will mean that the editorial media will no longer be able to defend the media system against the hostile takeover of the platforms.

They never had the slightest chance in this battle. As we will see later (☞ II), this hostile takeover by the digital corporations was carried out using unfair methods. Due to a regulation that massively privileged the platforms, all digitalization offensives by analogue media were doomed to fail from the outset. The only problem in 2029 will be that they will no longer have the necessary significance in society to publicly denounce this issue. Their 'share of voice' will then be too small.

Beyond the year 2029, corrections or changes of direction will be virtually unthinkable: GAME OVER.

One question is still open in our analysis: what exactly does this mean? Replacing analog media with digital media could also be a great thing. Incidentally, I am a 'digital addict' myself, and ten years ago I would probably have replied in a discussion on such topics:

"That's great! That's just part of progress—new ideas come, old ones go. What's wrong with that? Why do we still need analog media? Just bring on the cool new platforms and get rid of the old stuff."

But as we will see, it is not that simple. What exactly happens if we switch our our current democracy based on analog media to one based on digital media? What are the consequences if the platforms become the foundation of our democracy?

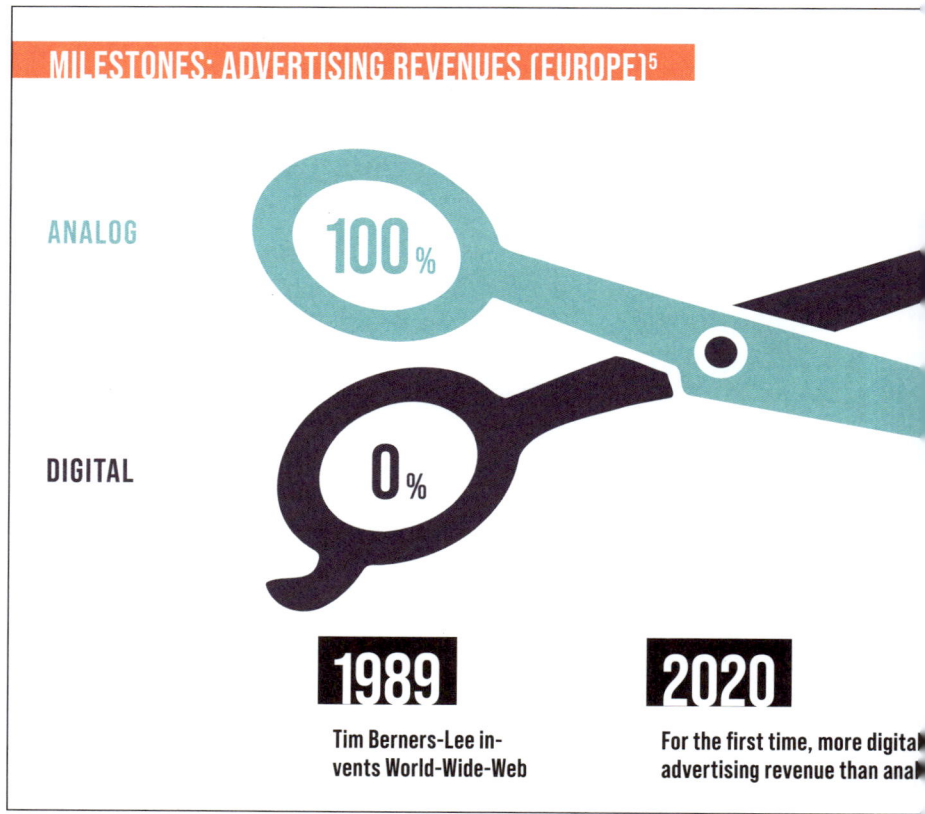

MILESTONES: ADVERTISING REVENUES (EUROPE)[5]

ANALOG 100%

DIGITAL 0%

1989 Tim Berners-Lee invents World-Wide-Web

2020 For the first time, more digital advertising revenue than analog

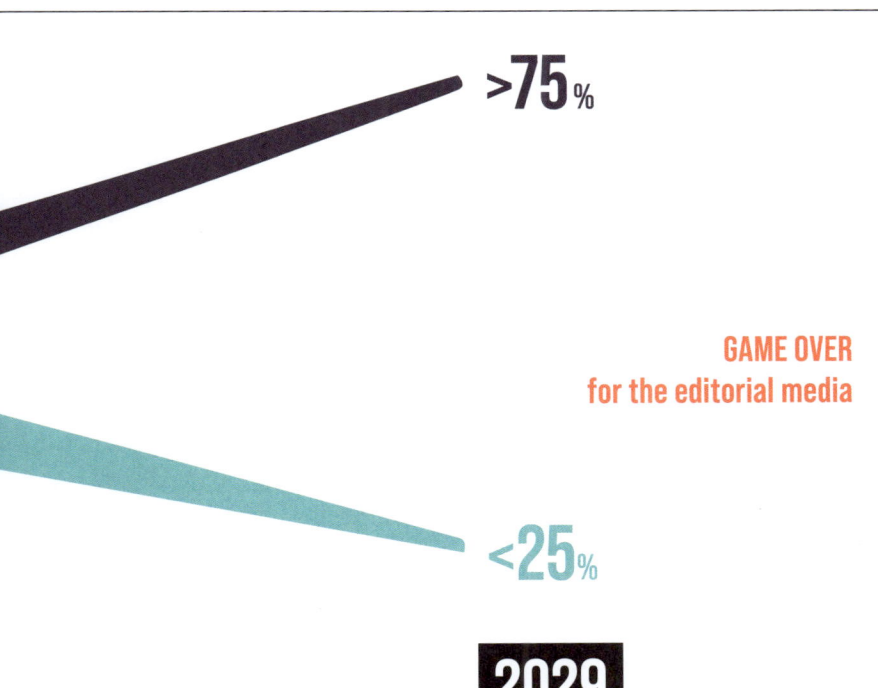

>75%

GAME OVER
for the editorial media

<25%

2029

Three quarters of advertising revenue is digital

3. The Internet of monopolies

We know that the media are the basis of our democracy. We can only form public opinion via mass media. This enables political parties to develop their programs and to take positions. We also know that digital media will replace analog media. In the last resort, it is also irrelevant whether this transformation will take another five, ten or twelve years. The key question is: What will this purely digital world look like in the future?

We can answer this quite simply with a thought experiment, namely by switching off all analog media:

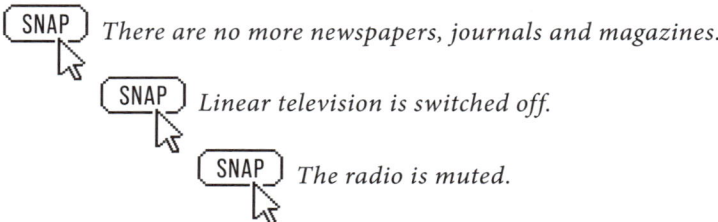

There are no more newspapers, journals and magazines.

Linear television is switched off.

The radio is muted.

As the predominantly digital media future is just a few years away, all we have to do now is to get a clear picture of the current digital situation. From this, we can precisely determine what our digital media world will look like very soon.

We have such a scientifically founded cross-section thanks to a research project at the University of Cologne. Here, we have performed the first such baseline measurement for a full country in very comprehensive data analyses. It shows the entire digital usage of the German population on all 16 million domains based on the real usage of all devices (smartphone, tablet, desktop). We analyzed many billions digital bits of attention (called 'views' or 'impressions') for this study.[6]

When we saw the results for the first time, we could hardly believe our eyes. We initially thought that our calculations must be incorrect. Why? Because the supposed diversity of content on the Internet is an illusion. The huge, colorful Internet actually turned out to be a gigantic graveyard of unused content. Almost all traffic is generated by just a few gigantic platforms, namely the offerings of digital corporations such as YouTube, Facebook, Instagram, Google and WhatsApp.

From this status quo, we can deduce what our media landscape will look like in a few years' time: After the further meltdown of newspapers, television and radio in five to ten years, our media world will belong to a handful of US digital corporations. GAME OVER.

Platforms destroy provider diversity

The destruction of provider diversity by the digital monopolies is astonishing. Why? Because the reality of digital media usage is the exact opposite of the colorful and dynamic 'Robin Hood' world that had been promised to us by digital evangelists for decades. Wasn't the Internet the universe of the cool underdogs? Wasn't the web supposed to give to the poor and take from the rich?

This beautiful and misleading fairy tale is mainly based on a book by Chris Anderson, *The Long Tail*.[7] It is one of the most popular bestsellers about the web ever written—and probably one of the most dangerous ones, as the exact opposite is true. But Anderson's theories still shape our idea of a pluralistic and diverse digital

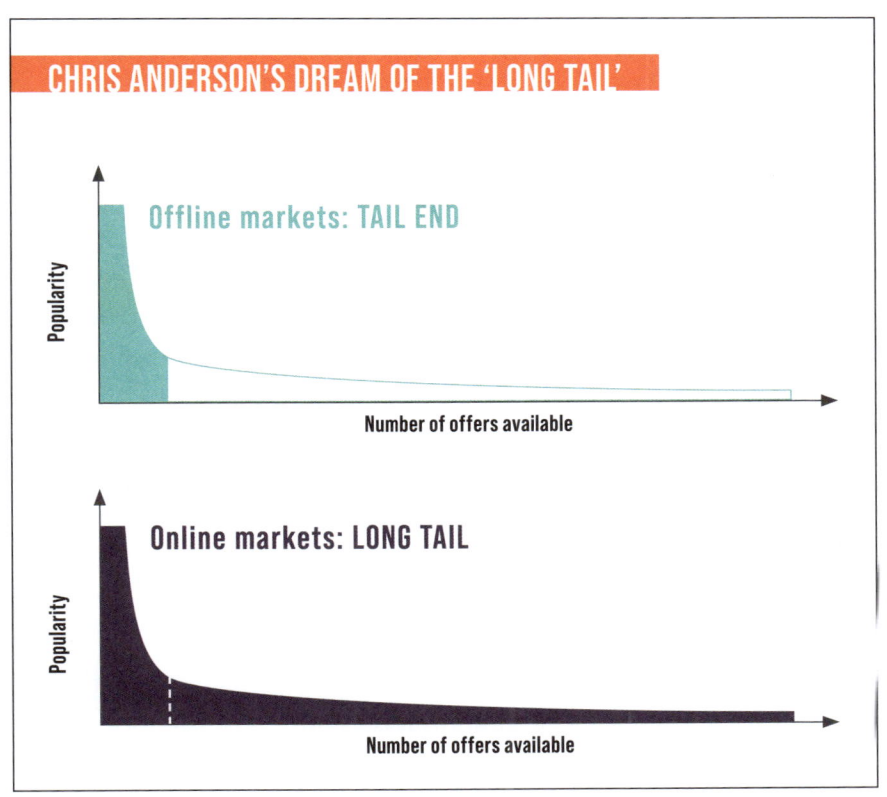

world in which smaller challengers can successfully compete with big players. This misconception consistently leads politicians, companies, bloggers, creatives and users in the wrong direction. It is important that we analyze this in depth. This is the only way for us to debunk one of the most fundamental misconceptions about the Internet.

The dangerous thing about Anderson's point is that it is so convincing at first sight, even though it is so fundamentally wrong. Anderson says that new digital technologies lead to a *multiplication of the supply of content*. He illustrates this using the example of a bookshop that can only keep a few tens of thousands of books on stock, simply due to limited shelf space that is available to the seller. By contrast, Amazon can offer millions of titles. If we take a superficial look at other markets, we see the same result: there are hundreds of different programs on television and millions on YouTube. There are thousands of newspapers, but millions of blogs. A CD store could only offer thousands of CDs, Spotify many millions of titles, and so on.

So what is wrong with Anderson's claim? His point is correct in terms of the quantity of content *offers* available out there. But this reveals nothing about the main question: which of these offers are actually *used*? If offers are not used at all, it is just as if they did not exist. The variety of the content offered is then just a dazzling illusion that actually conceals a gigantic graveyard.

However, it is very difficult to assess the diversity of existing digital offerings at the level of all websites and apps. Why? Because three requirements must be fulfilled in order to deliver a scientifically reliable answer:

1. You have to measure the *entire* Internet. Only if you know the size of the whole thing is it possible to recognize the relative significance of the individual offerings, for example by calculating market shares. There are currently around 16 million active domains in Germany, and you would have to measure every single one of these offerings.

2. Surveys or measurements of reach (how many people use an offer) do not deliver answers to our question. You have to determine the *actual duration of use* for every person and every domain. This is the only way to find out the total (aggregated) attention per user at the level of the individual offers. Which in turn means: you have to measure usage continuously, 24 hours a day, seven days a week.

3. Because users today are on very different end devices, all devices used (smartphone, desktop, tablet) must be measured separately, and all single impressions have to be merged at the level of each individual person.

Because we carried out such a baseline measurement for the first time, we were also able to fundamentally clarify the question of the 'Robin Hood' Internet. As we measured the entire net, we can also show the entire German traffic in a single diagram. The diagram shown on the following page is an aggregation of hundreds of millions of impressions. In fact, it would be possible to derive all the key messages and outcomes of this book from just this one overview. And we can already reveal in advance: our measurements definitively disprove Chris Anderson's dangerous myth about the Internet.

The digital universe: a handful of giants and a huge graveyard

It is absolutely vital that we get a full understanding of the following illustration in detail to recognize the extent of the massive problem we are facing in the digital world. The diagram you see on the next double page is nothing more than a *ranking* of all content available on the internet—i.e. websites, platforms, apps, web stores and so on. On the vertical Y-axis, we see the total aggregated usage time achieved by each individual offering in Germany. On the X-axis, we can see the rank that the respective service occupies, from 1st place to 131,993rd place.

When I show this diagram at conferences, there are sometimes listeners who cannot recognize the line of the graph at first sight. They think the diagram is empty because the line is missing. This is because the curve is largely congruent with the Y-axis and then merges with the X-axis. You do not have to be a math geek to understand what this means: the traffic on the Internet belongs to only a few providers, on the very tiny space directly next to the vertical Y-axis. The offerings of the four leading providers (Alphabet, Meta, Apple and Amazon) account for around 45 percent of all traffic on their own. This is an unimaginable dominance when you consider that this overview combines very different 'markets' (i.e. video-on-demand, e-commerce, social media, banking, gaming, email, messenger and so on)—in other words, everything that is used digitally on end devices.
On the other hand, you can see that, beyond the digital giga platforms, the line approaches zero virtually immediately. The top 100 offerings generate 71.8 percent of total traffic. Rank 101 to 500 only manage a weak 14 percent, then not much more happens in terms of traffic.

If you work your way from the other side, from right to left, you can see that all listings between place number 10,000 and 131,993 only attract around 2 percent of the total traffic.

A HANDFUL OF PROVIDERS ARE DOMINATING THE INTERNET [A]

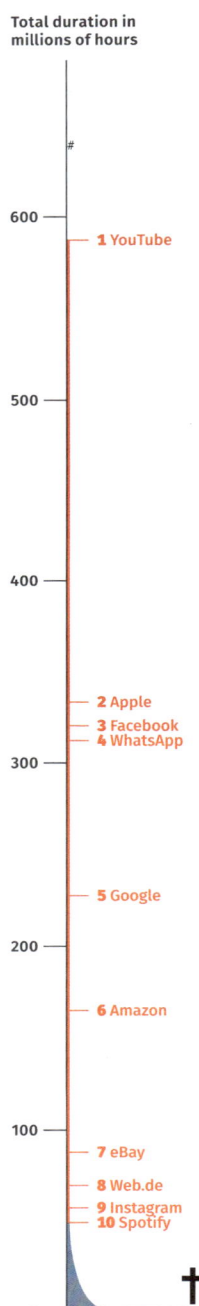

An outlandish concentration of digital traffic

If you have truly taken in how huge and empty this graveyard is, you should be a little dizzy by now. But it is actually much worse than you think. When I show my diagram at public talks, there are sometimes very attentive listeners who interrupt me here. They point out to me that there are a total of 16 million domains in Germany (.de). The owners of the domains even have to pay money for the registration. Thus, the likelihood is high that they are active. Moreover, many people in Germany also use other domains (.com, .org) or visit foreign websites. Have we measured all 16 million or just the displayed 131,993 websites and apps?

The question is more than legitimate and once again shows the incredible concentration of digital traffic. Our measurements actually record every single domain accessed over a period of three months. This means that if just one person in our panel spends even a few seconds on a single page (for example, briefly checking the opening hours of a dental office), the use of this page is counted.

However, our measurements over three months on all end devices only show traffic on 131,993 websites and apps. That is correct. Which in turn means: more than 99 percent of all domains (i.e. around 15.9 million domains) show *no traffic at all*. ZERO. Actually, all these domains should also be shown on the X-axis. But then we would have to extend the horizontal line on the X-axis by a factor of 121—i.e. let it run about 42 meters (!!) further over the edge of the book to the right. If you understand what this means, the feeling of dizziness should now be accompanied by genuine shock.

Let us go back to our overview, which 'only' shows the 131,993 websites and apps used. We can now mathematically calculate the concentration, i.e. the uneven distribution within these 131,993 offers. You can compare it to the distribution of wealth, a common exercise of economists. On a scale, the value 0 would represent an equal distribution (all people in this country would own the same amount) while the value 100 would represent the maximum conceivable unequal distribution (in this country, one person owns everything, everyone else owns nothing).

The uneven distribution of German online traffic is indeed hair-raising. The value is an incredible 98.8 (mind you: this calculation does not even include the 15.9 million unused domains!). The majority of traffic is bundled by the platforms of digital corporations. Very few companies own almost everything, the rest almost nothing. From a purely mathematical point of view, we are therefore only a smidgeon away from a purely monopolistic Internet (see figure below).

GAME OVER.

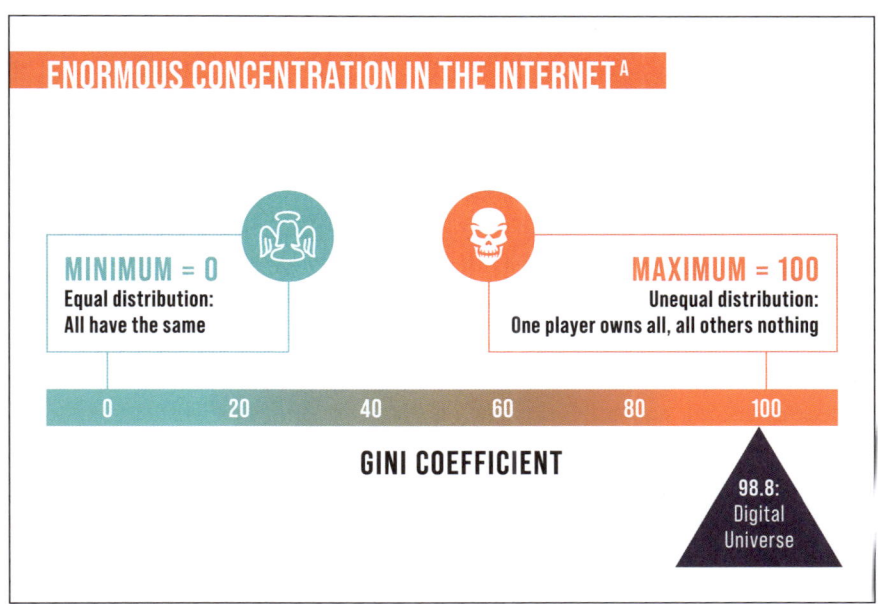

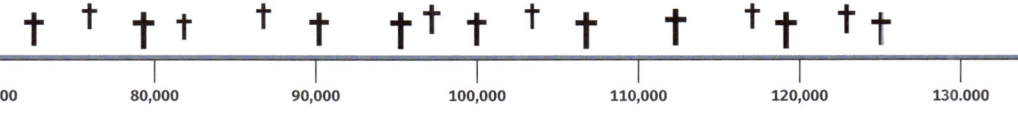

What will our purely digital media world look like in the future?

In our thought experiment, we have switched off analog media and are now only looking at digital media usage. Which in turn means that we can precisely compare what it will mean if we fully switch to digital media in a few years' time. We are looking directly into the future of our media democracy—if it is still a democracy.

It should be mentioned right now that this catastrophic state of digital media is not a problem of the digital sphere itself. It is entirely caused by our own regulatory mistakes. We have regulated the Internet in such a way that a huge desert has emerged. The abundant water is only available to a handful of platforms, whose oases are flourishing and thriving—and the rest of the world is dying of thirst. It is our own fault: we have allowed the Internet to be stolen from us by a handful of tech giants. Nothing and nobody has to stop us from reclaiming the Internet for our society (☞ VI). Because the current situation is desolate.

If we do nothing, the future will look like this: We are exchanging a previously flourishing landscape of diverse and pluralistic media providers for half a dozen monopolies or near monopolies. Legal experts would argue that we can only speak of a monopoly if no other provider exists. However, we are arguing here from the perspective of media usage. Here we can also speak of monopolies if there is practically no alternative usage of existing offerings. This is the case with search engines (Google), social media (Facebook and Instagram as offerings from the same company), messengers (WhatsApp, also from Meta) or free video-on-demand (YouTube).

This dominance of the tech giants and the simultaneous total elimination of healthy and fair competition is apparently the consequence of a platform economy regulated the wrong way. Among the offerings of the top 10 in Germany, which already bundle 50 percent of traffic, nine of them are platforms. Only one service on the list (web.de, a German email provider) is not a platform and also originates from Germany, but it only accounts for 1.5 percent of total usage time. While our traditional media system consisted of 100 percent editorial media, the future of the media will undoubtedly belong to the platforms and their business model of 'user-generated content'.

So what will happen if analog media use continues to shrink over the next few years and is replaced by the use of digital media? Once again, a look at advertising investments offers us major insights. Remember the tipping point discussed above, according to which more than half of all advertising spending is already invested in digital media? Let's now take a closer look at this purely digital universe to find out: Who will actually earn the money on the Internet in the digital future?

From various publications, we can now specify the share of the Big 3 (Alphabet, Meta, Amazon) of the current total digital advertising revenues. The values vary somewhat depending on the country and study. For the countries of the Western world (excluding China), the values are within a corridor between 80 and 90 percent. Industry insiders estimate the share in Germany at 80 percent, whereas in the USA it is already at 90 percent. On average, these top 3 companies therefore absorb around 85 percent of advertising revenue—whereas hundreds of thousands of content providers have to survive with the remaining 15 percent[8] (see below).

Where will the money be earned in the future?

Do you remember our hypothesis from the introduction? That the concentration of media usage on very few providers will inevitably destroy the editorial me-

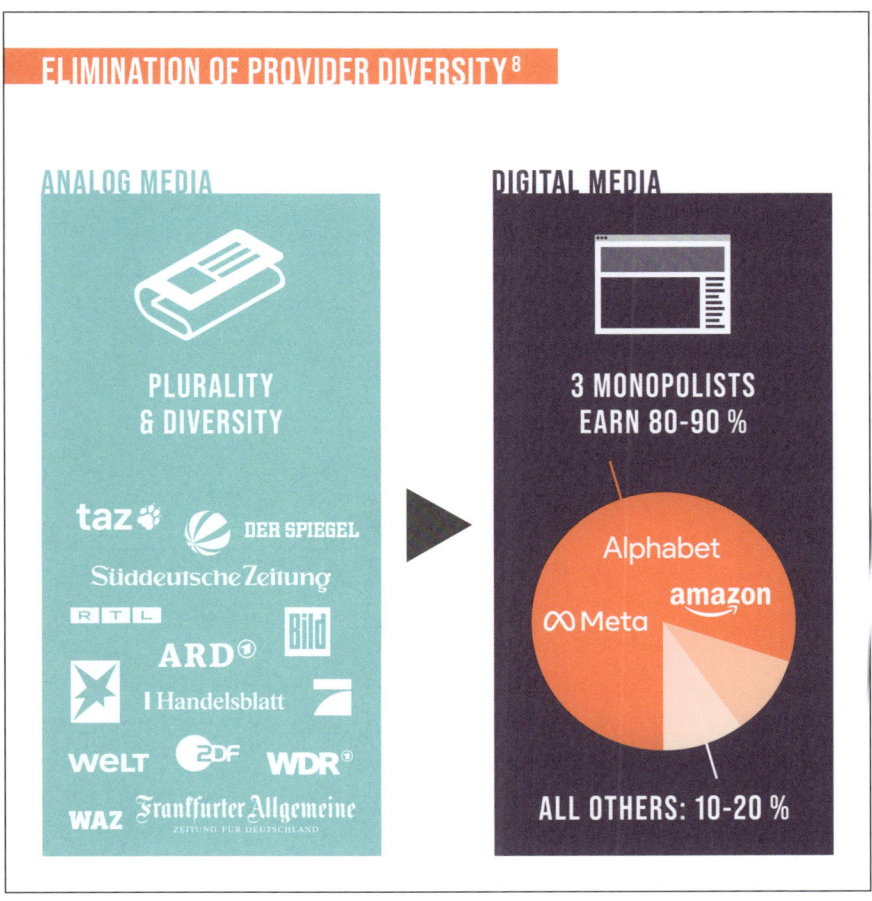

dia, which after all have been the foundation of our media democracy for several decades? Our review of the distribution of advertising investments provides an important acid test from other, independent data sets. In fact, the imbalance in monetization is even more significant than in the media usage we have measured.

At the moment, it is almost only the digital companies that earn a lot of money from Internet traffic, while the others are left more or less empty-handed. The platforms of the digital corporations therefore work like black holes with an irresistible pull, attracting more and more traffic. Thus, they are systematically draining the remaining Internet of traffic. We feed the platforms with our attention (which they monetize through advertising) and our data. On top, we also provide them with the content that fills their feeds for free. We do all the work—and they make all the money.

4. The victims: Journalism, bloggers, global brands, public service broadcasting

The threat to our society described at the beginning is now becoming visible: digital media will form the future basis of our democracy. But in just a few years, this very basis will belong almost entirely to a handful of tech giants—which means we will lose control of our democratic public sphere. If digital corporations own our media, they will automatically control our democracy.

We have looked at the extent of dominance from different perspectives and have kept coming to the same conclusion. The supposed diversity of providers on the web is an illusion. This is because traffic is concentrated on just a very small number of offerings. It is so important to repeat this insight again and again because it is in such blatant contradiction to the obvious fact that there is so much different content spread all over the web. Just think of the many hits we get on banal Google searches. For example, the search engine returns 2 billion 420 million hits for the query 'Internet Statistics' (query Dec. 4th, 2022).

This is the root of what is probably the worst and most dangerous misconception about the reality of digital media. Our old concept of digital diversity is purely an illusion. And this illusion of diversity is similar to mechanisms that can be observed in the way in which autocrats have entrenched their regimes. Today, the autocrats are so successful in many countries precisely because they do not present themselves to the outside world as a evil dictators or tyrants, but rather throw on a colorful robe of different parties, institutions and currents. In this way, purely dictatorial systems constantly create new phantasies of diversity and pluralism. They even stage elaborate elections, even though the winner is always known in advance.

Why do I mention this example? Because we have learned to consistently reject such illusions of diversity by dictators as bullshit. When autocratic regimes orchestrate such scenarios, we understand immediately that we are fooled. When Google shows us millions or billions of results in response to our search queries, we should also be skeptical. We cannot check whether these offers even exist anyway. But we do know one thing for sure from our measurements: nowhere is demand more concentrated among fewer providers than on the Internet.

JOURNALISM/NEWS: TOP OFFERS [9]
Relative significance

Total duration in millions of hours

As our ranking of all measurable offerings on the web shows, the platforms have completely eliminated any form of healthy and fair competition in the digital media universe. It is therefore completely irrelevant whether providers still place content on the 16 million registered domains. The platforms have emptied this potentially diverse digital universe of traffic. We are dealing with a completely dead desert landscape.

This digital meltdown has massive consequences for everyone who is active in this market. Let's take a closer look at this for a range of sectors.

Journalistic offerings have no chance

Remember our experiment: we switched off all analog media and are now looking at what people are currently doing in digital media. Now we also want to find out: How much time will people spend consuming news under purely digital conditions?

To this end, we created a category that includes all forms of news and information usage.[9] Fortunately, the reach is huge. Virtually all online users in Germany are consuming such offers. But even the usage time of all services combined is very low, amounting to a tiny seven hours a month—which corresponds to less than 14 minutes a day.

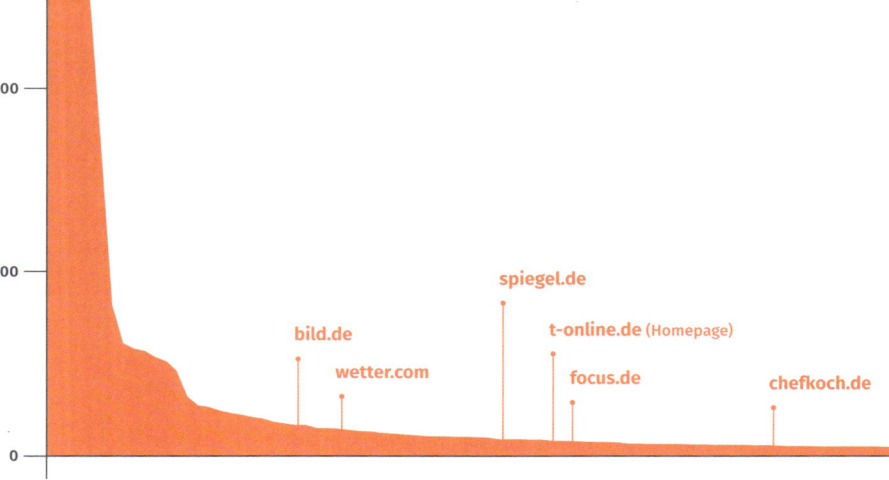

The figure shows that no existing offer manages to compete with the platforms and the huge amounts of traffic that they accumulate. And this even though we only show the best of the best here. Let us take a look at spiegel.de, one of the most successful journalistic offerings in Germany with an impressive reach (49 percent, i.e. around 29 million users). The problem is the low usage time: readers spend just 18 minutes here—not per day, but per month! Or in other words, about half a minute a day. This is precisely why spiegel.de is only on rank 45 of all offers in Germany (see figure). And that is already one of the strongest journalistic offerings we have. Let's take a look at *Süddeutsche Zeitung* (a leading German daily newspaper), on the other hand: The offering once again manages a good reach among users (25 percent), but only just under 9 minutes a month (17 seconds a day). The total collapse of journalism in digital conditions becomes visible when we compare these figures with the way people consume a traditional analog newspaper. Research suggests that people spend nearly 40 minutes a day, or around 19 hours a month reading their newspaper (and here we are only talking about a single print media being used!).

On closer inspection, the total digital consumption of news and information is even lower than it appears at first glance. This is because the 14 minutes of use per day (all offers added together) includes a lot of content that we would not classically count as journalism—such as wetter.com (a weather forecast site), 'Chefkoch', a website for cooking (see figure), or the starting pages of webmail providers.

So if we switch off analog media, journalism in the digital world will have largely disappeared from our media usage.

GAME OVER.

BLOGS: TOP OFFERS [11]
Relative importance

Total duration in millions of hours

Bloggers have no chance

Let us once again recall Chris Anderson and his message of the good Robin Hood Internet, which would take from the rich and give to the poor. Back in those days, many people were still dreaming of the democratic potential of the Internet.[10] This was supposedly being unleashed by exactly the same dynamics. Anyone who had something to say could publish it directly online, bypassing the hierarchies, institutions and gatekeepers that had previously decided about their publication—in the case of journalism, publishing houses or editorial offices.

The industry was excited about the arrival of a new era in which bloggers could communicate their ideas directly to an audience of millions. People were thrilled about a completely new form of collaborative and participatory journalism, also called 'citizen journalism'.

Since then, tens of thousands of bloggers have followed the various digital promises and published articles and content online. It is therefore an interesting exercise to perform a reality check after at least two decades in order to assess the situation: How are these activities doing? Have bloggers succeeded in using their domains to build up a relevant public sphere of their own that forms a counterbalance to the editorial offerings of digital publishers on the one hand and the platforms on the other?

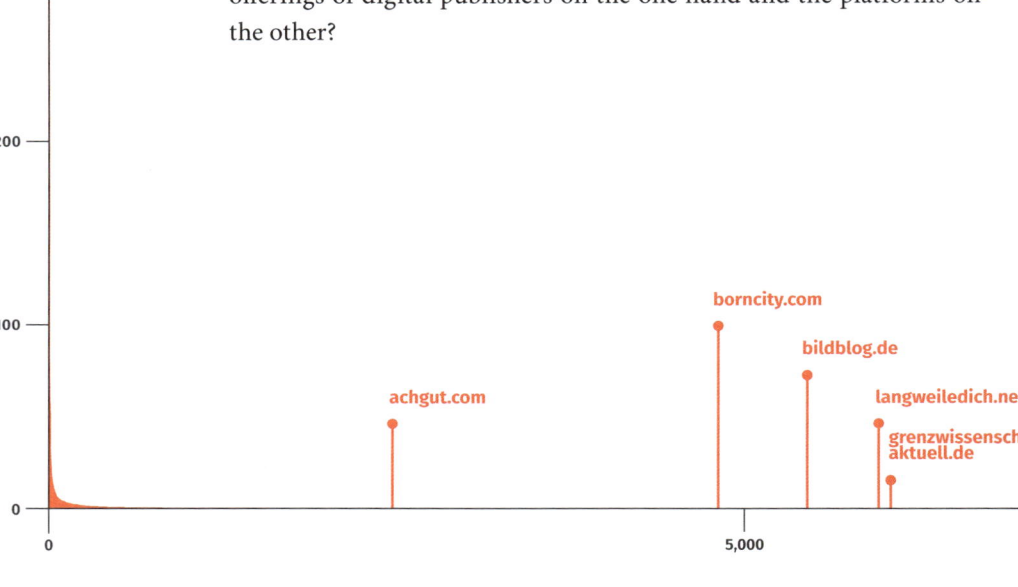

In our research, we collected hundreds of the most successful German blogs and measured the whole bundle.[11] The results are again shocking: even over a three-month period, only five blogs achieved a net reach of more than one (!) percent. The usage times are even more disastrous. Among the largest blogs in Germany, there are just six where the users spend more than one minute a month (!!) on site.

Our measurements show that there is a huge number of blogs. But in the reality of media use, they play almost no significant role. The total aggregated usage time of all blogs in Germany amounts to around six thousandths of a percent of total digital media usage. And the net reach of all blogs in Germany over a period of three months is only 14 percent—which, conversely, means that the vast majority of all Germans, namely 86 percent, never read blogs.

Critics may object: The successful bloggers today are on YouTube or Instagram. They are right—they have been forced to move there because the digital companies have sucked the traffic into their platforms. And that is where the digital companies are now earning most of the money with their content.

GLOBAL BRANDS: TOP OFFERS [12]
Relative importance

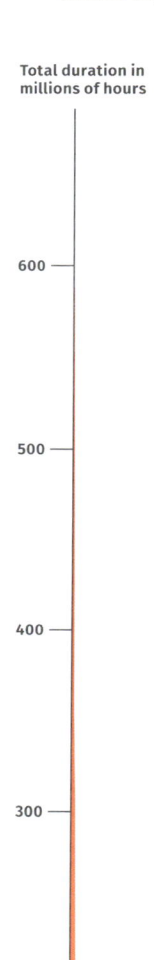

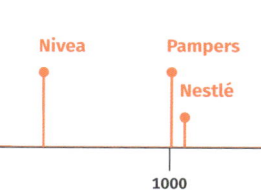

Global brands have no chance

You might think that bloggers are typically idealists with hardly any financial resources at their disposal. No wonder that their offers are doing so badly. But we will see that this is not the problem. Our next example shows that even very financially strong global companies have no chance of competing against platforms, which are like black holes in space, sucking in most of the traffic.

Globally active brand corporations and FMCG manufacturers had become aware of the huge potential of their own brand pages certainly by around 2000. That makes sense. First, it was already clear twenty years ago that the future of the media was on the Internet. Engagement on their own brand websites enabled brands to achieve nothing less than a form of free advertising. This 'touchpoint' does not have to be paid for by the manufacturers. Every visit to these sites by consumers provides close contact with the target group without having to spend money on advertising. What could be better for a consumer goods company than free advertising?

On top of that, the brand manufacturers also had an unbeatably strong starting point. First, their brands were already well known. There was no need to educate users about the name and performance of the product. Second, the companies were in direct contact with tens of millions of consumers every day through the sheer use of their products. This is precisely why they started to advertise the names of their own domains on the back label of their products from early on ("more information can be found at *www.brandname.de*"). In addition, digital advertising could be directly linked to the company's own websites. And they could also integrate references to their own domain in TV advertising.

It was precisely this motivation that led to the birth of 'content marketing'. The approach can be summarized as follows. The basic assumption here is that old-style advertising annoys people anyway. In the new digital channels, users now have the power to decide for themselves what pieces of content they want to watch. This is precisely the difference between streaming and television, for example. On TV, you were always forced to endure annoying commercial breaks if you wanted to watch the rest of the program.

The promise of content marketing was from the beginning: relevant content. The plan is as quite simple. You attract users to your domain with free, relevant content. And only by responding to their interests and by answering their questions in a professional manner you carefully guide them to your own products in the second or third step. We can assume that all major consumer goods companies have pursued this strategy since around the turn of the millennium. We have analyzed all the major branded goods websites and show the most important ones in Germany here.[12] The larger companies in this overview will have invested many hundreds of millions of euros over these two decades just in Germany in order to establish their own strong online presences.

If we look again at the best of the best of those brand websites, their achievements look more like a joke considering these huge investments. Only two domains (the ones of Nivea and Nestlé) achieve more than 10 percent of net reach. The intensity of usage is even lower. The few people who visit such sites only stay for a very short time. Only six brand domains in Germany achieve a usage time of over two minutes—per month! This is why the most user-intensive offer (Nivea) only gets to 840th place out of all the offers (see figure).

FUN FACT: Even financially strong global corporations don't stand a chance against the platforms.

Again, this usage is microscopic, considering further that many advertising companies link their online advertising to these sites. And despite millions in

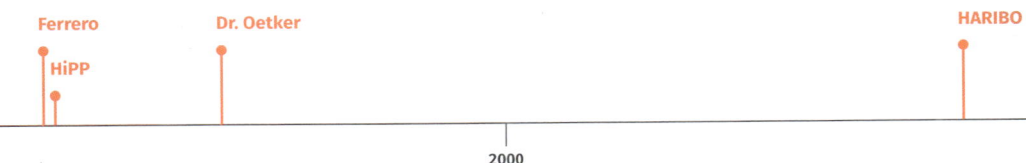

investments, despite decades of efforts, despite concentrated digital expertise and cooperation with excellent partners and leading agencies, even global brand groups achieve virtually nothing.

Is it not bizarre? The websites of billion-dollar corporations are just as insignificant on the Internet as those of the bloggers. The deadly dynamic of traffic concentration affects everyone—regardless of whether they are rich or poor.

Public service broadcasting has no chance

In the digital world, we love 'disruption': new innovative ideas that take over the market and replace old ones. The bloggers represented just such a disruption of the classic journalistic business model. They were digitally skilled creatives with fantastic ideas and execution. They did not have to deal with massive costs for staff, offices, production or manufacturing paid by their analog competitors, the established editorial players. The bloggers were high-performance digital machines, startup-style: fast, innovative and extremely cost efficient. But as we have seen, their assault on the news media failed to produce a truly sustainable alternative digital segment.

But it wasn't just disruptors like bloggers who quickly understood the digital dynamic and took it seriously. The same also applies to the various established market players out there. Since the turn of the millennium, it was clear that the analog business models that had been considered crisis-proof for decades were now under digital attack.

We have highlighted two categories so far, the news media and the consumer goods industry. We can be sure that both news media and brand corporations alike have put an enormous amount of investment and organizational resources into building successful online presences for two decades. But they have not achieved impressive successes.

As we will see, the situation for public service broadcasting is exactly the same. That is regrettable, as it is of particular importance for our democracy. Our German 'dual system' of private and public service broadcasting is even legally secured through a series of rulings of the German Federal Constitutional Court.

Based on our measurements, we can now aggregate all digital offerings run by the national German public service broadcasting services.[13] These include the ARD offer with a reach of 17 percent (usage time: around 43 minutes per month), ZDF with a reach of 26 percent (usage time: around 18 minutes per month) and tagesschau.de with a reach of 29 percent (usage time: around 20 minutes per month). Accordingly, the situation is similar to that of the news media, bloggers and brand corporations. If these largest public service broadcasting offerings were included in our overall ranking, they would also rank far behind the traffic giants of the platforms, coming somewhere between 30th and 40th place.

If you combine the largest video-on-demand offerings of public service broadcasting and compare the total usage time with the total of all digitally used video streaming offerings (the largest providers here are YouTube, Amazon Prime and Netflix), all public service broadcasting content combined only achieves a share of around 4 percent.

This finding is dramatic. The effects will be immediately understood if we compare this figure with the share of public service broadcasting on German television. In the same time period, all public service broadcasters combined achieved a share of 48 percent, almost on the same level as private broadcasters.

The conclusion is very worrying. According to mainstream media policy arguments in Germany, public service broadcasting plays a central role in the formation of political opinion for our democracy. But it only plays this role under analog conditions. If we follow the conditions of our thought experiment and switch off all analog media in order to understand a purely digital media reality, we see that public service broadcasting will have practically disappeared. In the digital sphere, its offerings only account for a microscopic 4 percent of media-on-demand (the share of total digital media usage is logically even much lower, at only around 1 percent).

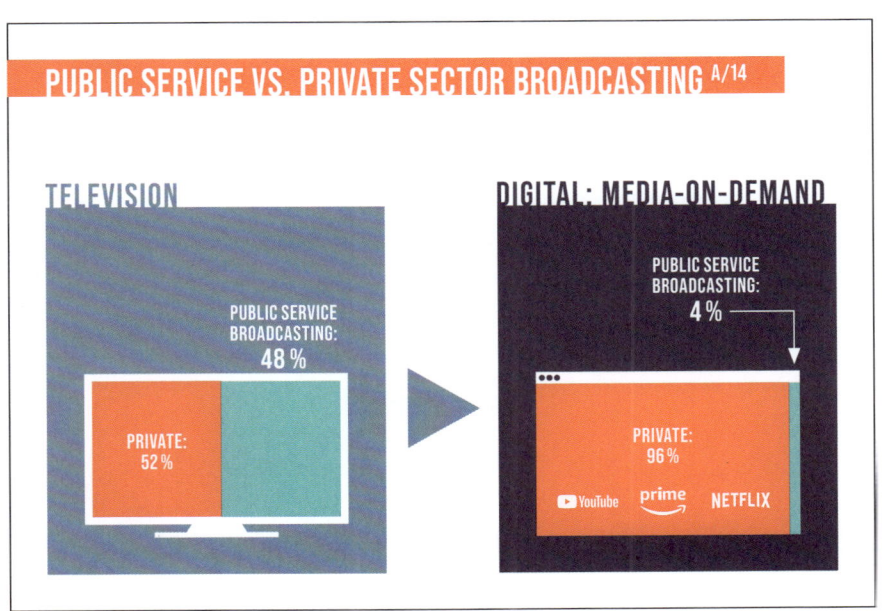

> **FUN FACT:** As a result of the platform economy, public service broadcasting is being digitally eliminated—Germany's 'dual system' is being nullified.

Again, one might argue that the content of public service broadcasters can also be seen on platforms such as YouTube or Instagram. But firstly, the low number of views will not drastically change our finding that the content of public service broadcasting plays only a marginal role in the digital world. But for all the public service broadcasting content visible on platforms such as YouTube, we need to consider that the editorial teams of the public service broadcasting services are effectively working for the platforms. Unlike the bloggers or the private publishers, this content for the platforms is directly financed by the broadcasting fees paid by the German people.

5. Free and fair competition has been completely eliminated

The uniformity and consistency of our findings is alarming: the news media are failing, as are the bloggers, global brand corporations, public service broadcasters. All of them are unsuccessful in digital conditions. Despite hundreds of excellent companies and thousands of brilliant minds that have been applying expertise and investment to this task for many years, no one seems able to make it. There is no single exception to the rule.

We could add other categories or sectors and would always come back to the same conclusion: No player is able to sustainably overcome the pull of the monopolies (details see 'Atlas of the Digital World'). Of course, our measurement results only apply to the German digital universe. But we could look for examples beyond Germany's borders and would find out: Nobody makes it in the USA either. Nobody in Great Britain or Australia. Nobody in France, nobody in Italy, nobody in Spain.

The only logically compelling conclusion is obvious: free and fair competition has been completely abolished in the field of digital media. The competing companies in this market do not have the slightest chance against the dominant positions of the tech giants. It does not matter whether they are innovative or offer better products or services: For competitors against tech monopolies, every single race is always lost before it has even begun.

Monopolies must be a taboo in the field of media

We are not talking about a minor defect that should be 'critically reviewed', as our inactive authorities and bureaucrats would probably phrase it. *The complete meltdown in the field of digital media has already taken place.* This digital media system is currently dominated by a handful of monopolists. You do not have to be an expert to know for sure that such monopolies damage our society as a whole. After all, we are not talking about a trivial market just for consumer goods. In the case of cookies or soft drinks, consumers could either grudgingly accept the ridiculous prices of a monopolist or easily switch to other categories. But in contrast to such exchangeable goods, our media are not an arbitrary commodity. The media constitute the foundation of our democracy, they shape our public sphere. Citizens in our country inform themselves here on every conceivable topic in order to develop their attitudes and political opinions.

This is precisely why dominant market positions must be an absolute taboo in our media system. *No private company should ever be allowed to gain dominant access to key elements of our public sphere.* Where such dominant positions exist, they must be consistently broken up by liberating and opening up the affected category of the media to competition. For this reason, legislation such as the classic German media law holds a clear anti-monopolistic position (☞ IV). It is legally irrational and damaging to democracy not to implement this philosophy just as consistently in the field of digital media as we would do in the analog sphere.

6. Is it really so dramatic?

When I present the current dominance of tech platforms at public talks, many people in the audience are often surprised at how strong GAFAM's positions already are. Most listeners understand the basic problem. They grasp that our entire media system will fall into the hands of the tech giants as a result of the ongoing digital transformation. Doubts are sometimes expressed in two directions. Some experts refer to other scientific studies that are not so alarming with regard to the aspect of market concentration. Others are skeptical as to whether the transformation will really take place as quickly as described here.

The first argument is very valid. In fact, the field of digital media concentration is difficult to understand even for media scientists. The reason for this insecurity is as simple as it is tragic: almost all published studies are based on surveys. Surveys often only cost a few thousand euros. In contrast, measurements of real media usage such as those we have carried out here are extremely expensive and require a massive investment of time and resources. Of course, every survey may serve its own purpose. But surveys are of no use at all when it comes to assessing market concentration.

Why? First of all, surveys are unreliable. According to surveys, people read a surprisingly large number of books and watch surprisingly little porn. Applied to our topic: In surveys people typically state that they inform themselves about politics primarily through high-quality journalism. The only strange thing is that, despite their statements, journalistic content on the Internet hardly attracts any traffic.[15]

Misleading studies show diversity that does not exist

Second, such studies typically analyze reach, and only on the basis of subjective assessments (how many people said that they used an offering). However, we can see that the reach measured by surveys is often many times higher than the real reach of media. Here is an example: The German 'Working Group for Media Analyses' (agma) regularly publishes figures on the supposed reach of analog newspapers and magazines. According to these surveys, *WELT* (a German newspaper), for example, should reach 850,000 readers. But we know that the print circulation of *WELT* sells only about 85,000 copies.[16]

You can only understand these results if you carry out such surveys yourself. Users often say things about themselves that are simply not true. Of course, it is extremely problematic that such large figures sound great. 850,000 readers sounds much better than 85,000, doesn't it? Now put yourself in the difficult position of the media industry, which has been fighting against continuous erosion for many years. In the short run, its very survival depends on looking good to advertisers. It is understandable that media companies love to do surveys. And then such figures are often used in public debates. In our measurements, however, we do not show subjective assessments from surveys, but real usage. This is the real, 'hard' currency. But here's a fascinating surprise: even with real usage measurements, it is misleading to analyze reach. *The single one decisive indicator for assessing pluralism or concentration is the aggregated duration of usage.*

Why? Because also a short visit of just a few seconds counts as reach. However, you can only tell the real strength of an offer in terms of how competitive it is by its ability to capture the attention of users over a longer period of time. This aspect is also known as 'stickiness': how long do users 'stick' with the content, how much time do they spend on these domains? This leads us to a very important finding of our research: many of the stronger offers beyond the platform giants have considerable reach, but the usage time is very short. We have already seen it above with the example of spiegel.de (German online news journal): 29 million users is impressive—18 minutes a month is frighteningly little.

Here is a fascinating finding: We can illustrate this problem using our own data in a compelling way. For example, we can show a ranking of the 100 strongest offers, once by aggregated usage time, and once by reach. It is important to note that both graphs rely on exactly the same measurements! The only difference is that the aggregated usage time includes *both* aspects, meaning: How many people use an offer, and how much time do they spend there?

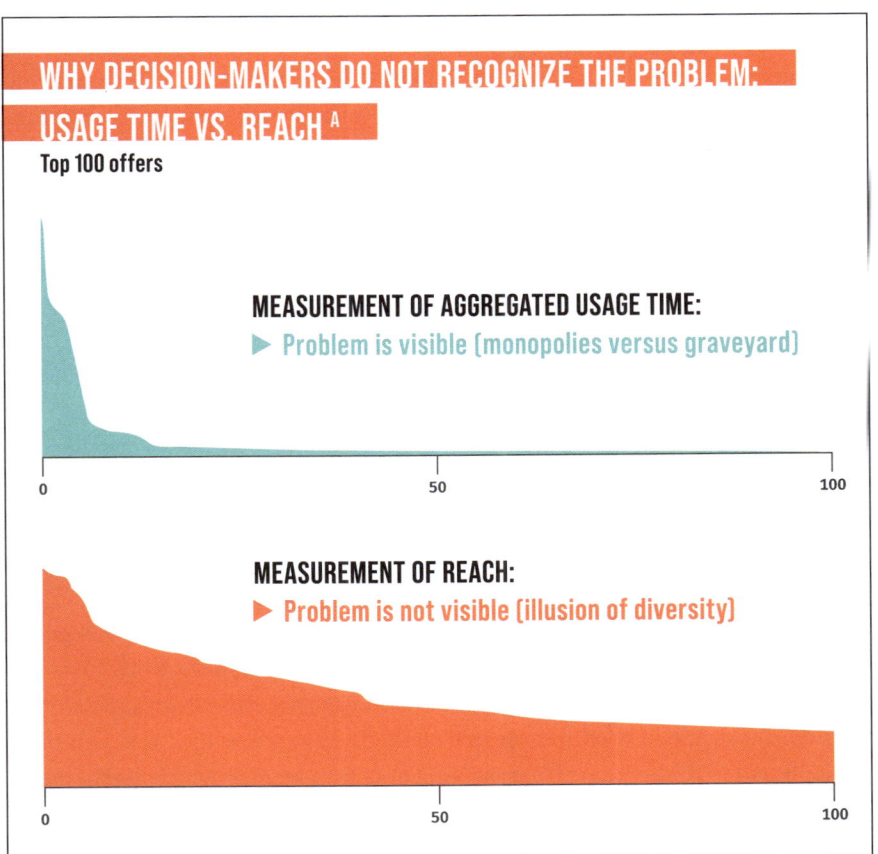

The huge difference is visible immediately. And now put yourself in the shoes of a decision-maker, such as a politician dealing with media policy. As long as you only look at reach, you will not even realize that there is a problem anywhere. Everything looks great. The fact that it is not just a problem, but a huge catastrophe, can only be recognized by evaluating the aggregated usage time.

It is immediately clear that most offerings look much better than they actually are when you look at their reach. However, it means absolutely nothing if a large number of people visit a service but hardly spend any time there. And tragically, almost all existing studies are based on analyses of reach. And remember: Subjective reach based on surveys will again look much better than the real reach shown in the diagram above.

The data collection method is therefore not a matter of scientific quibbling. The method determines what can be discovered in the research results in the first place. And now ask yourself a few questions. Put yourself in the shoes of any content provider (not a tech giant) who is commissioning a study. If you were taking the decision on a study in such a company, which method would you choose? The very cheap method (survey) that makes you look awesome? Where everything comes across just great? Or would you choose an extremely time-consuming and expensive method that reveals that your own offerings are completely insignificant? Which also sheds bad light on you and your organization in terms of public perception? So that you have to justify yourself in all directions?

Political decision-makers are being misled

Finally, let us consider the massive political implications. How are politicians, authorities and institutions supposed to take educated decisions when they have hundreds of such misleading studies at their disposal? How should they identify the central problem if the chosen methods of market observation are not even suitable to answer the question? How would decision-makers know that they see a phantom diversity of providers in such studies—even though in reality, this diversity is an illusion?

In fact, it is tragic: The people responsible for our media have full calendars, many commitments and short attention spans. They are not experts in digital media research and empirical methods. None of them has time to deal with the tedious and complex details of scientific research methods. How are political decision-makers supposed to come to a realistic assessment of the extent to which digital media is already dominated by quasi-monopolies? And in the end, the same applies to us users: how will society ever find out about the catastrophic state of the Internet?

This is probably another reason why our measurements met with the resistance of digital monopolists, as I explained it at the beginning. Since then, dozens of new, survey-based studies have been published. In these studies, the problem does not appear, simply because it cannot be captured by the chosen research instruments. The facts we have measured will therefore very soon disappear in this intoxicating feed of ever new studies in which the problem is not visible, until it is too late and we can no longer do anything about the Internet takeover.

Is the transformation really happening so quickly?

At public conferences, people often ask me another question: will the takeover of our media system by digital corporations really happen so quickly? The tipping point mentioned above (2029) is based on a comparison of advertising investments between analog and digital media. The assumption is that analog media will be too insignificant once their relative weight is below a quarter of the total media attention. The figures used are based on current and published statistics. However, there are three reasons to believe that we will see this tipping point arrive even earlier than described here. This additional dynamic is driven by two population groups that could not be more different: the very young and the very old.

Let us start with the young population. Our measurements show that the concentration of usage on just a few apps and domains is massively *stronger* among young users than among the population as a whole. Looking at young users also provides us with insights into the future of media use. We can see: in addition to the higher online share, digital usage will also be much more concentrated on just a few platforms.

A second dynamic is caused by older user groups turning to digital media at an advanced age [A]—we can assume that this applies to around 1 to 1.5 million people per year in Germany. These new digital 'immigrants' are of course primarily going to the big players—Google, Facebook, WhatsApp or Amazon—and less to more remote niche offerings. And this is why an additional dynamic is being built up at the other end of the demographic pyramid, again reinforcing and accelerating the tipping point in favor of the digital companies.

First acid test: Advertising companies invest in digital media

Do you remember how we initially determined the importance of digital media based on advertising investment? This gives us a good confirmation that the massive concentration we have measured is correct. Otherwise, we would have to ask the question: Why, for goodness sake, would advertising companies be so stupid and invest so much money in digital channels? And why would they spend about 85 percent of this money on the big three digital giants Alphabet, Meta and Amazon?

The answer, of course, is that they are not stupid. They simply invest where the audience's attention is. Advertising investments are a 'hard' indicator because experience shows that people and decision-makers think more intensively when they decide to spend large amounts of money.

Second acid test: capital markets invest in digital media

The accuracy of our findings can also be confirmed from the perspective of the capital markets. Would financial analysts and venture capital funds invest gigantic amounts of money in booming digital companies if enough 'attractive' companies from the analog media sector were available at much lower prices? The capital markets, whose rational way of thinking is usually several years ahead of the present, made up their minds years ago and have long since written off analog media. A simple example shows just how dramatic the situation is. Alphabet generated a profit of 67 billion euros in 2021. Bertelsmann (the leading German mass media company) achieved 2.3 billion (this also includes RTL), while other German media companies achieved figures well below 1 billion euros (ProSieben Sat.1 0.5; Axel Springer 0.4; Holtzbrinck 0.3; Gruner & Jahr 0.1).[17]

Let us look at an important incident that also took place in 2021. The long-established Hamburg-based media group Gruner & Jahr (with print magazines such as *Stern*, *Brigitte* and *Geo*) was acquired by the mass media group Bertelsmann (respectively RTL) for a price of 230 million euros. Let us put this into a digital perspectives. Alphabet, Google's parent company, made a total profit of 67 billion euros in 2021—in just one year! This means that Alphabet could easily buy almost 280 media groups the size of Gruner & Jahr from its sheer operating profits—every year!!

Of course Alphabet would never do that. It is not at all interested in Gruner & Jahr. From the capital markets' point of view, these are companies that have been languishing for years without any future prospects. This explains the restructuring that Gruner & Jahr went through afterwards: Many print offers were stopped, massive layoffs followed. Alphabet, on the other hand, is investing in products and technologies with which it can further expand its dominant market positions and monopolies in digital media (☞ II.4).

The key factor for investors to measure the value of a company is the so-called *sales multiple*. In other words, how much higher (or lower) is the value of a company in relation to the turnover it generates each year? This value provides a good indication of how positively (or negatively) the capital markets assess the future potential of a company. The higher the value, the more optimistic the financial markets judge the future of the respective company.

Let us take a look at our example. In 2021, Alphabet's valuation was almost 2 trillion US dollars (1,917), with revenues of 257 billion (257.64). Accordingly, the sales multiple is around 7.4 or, to put it simply, the company was worth more than seven times its annual revenues.

Let's take a look at Gruner & Jahr, on the other hand: RTL paid 230 million euros for the group and took over a turnover of around 500 million euros in return. This means that the sales multiple is actually no longer a multiple at all. Gruner & Jahr was only worth less than half of its annual turnover. Direct comparison: Alphabet = 7.4, Gruner & Jahr = 0.46.

This is not about badmouthing analog media. Rather, the sales multiple as a 'hard' indicator of financial evaluation once again confirms the results of our analyses. These valuations are only rational if the vast majority of market participants assume a rapid takeover of our media system by the digital giants. Analysts and investors in the financial markets think very carefully about where they invest their money. Accordingly, the capital markets are obviously taking a drastic approach to the superiority of Big Tech. From the point of view of the financial markets, the editorial media are already gone.

Third acid test: Ranking of media groups

We can see the same picture if we simply look at the ranking provided by media researcher and journalist Lutz Hachmeister. It shows the largest media groups in the world—once for the year 1995, once for 2020 (see page after next). We see that in 1995, three German and five other European companies were still among the world's top 20 media companies.

In 2020, the picture changed completely. We are mainly dealing with US corporations. Five of the top ten are platforms. German or European companies play almost no role. Bertelsmann, still the world's second-largest media group in 1995, comes 19th and there are only two other players from Europe. We can easily extrapolate this development into the future: European companies are disappearing from the market in relative terms. The editorial model is dissolving and US platforms will take over the European media market.

New technologies such as ChatGPT will massively speed up this development. After all, any generative AI is only ever as good as the corpus of texts, images and videos with which such self-learning systems are fed—which can then automatically generate millions of new content pieces and posts at the push of a button. And who has the largest existing data volumes—thanks to our active support and cooperation? The platforms, of course. How are alternative competitors supposed to stand the slightest chance against this superiority of Big Tech? All the digital companies have to do now is to finish the job and take over completely.

THE DECLINE OF EUROPEAN MEDIA COMPANIES[18]
Top 20 ranking of the largest media groups (worldwide)

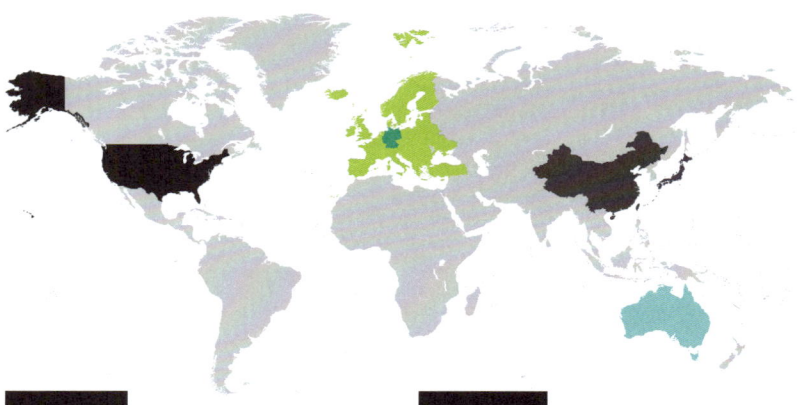

1995

1.	TIME WARNER INC.	USA
2.	BERTELSMANN AG	D
3.	THE WALT DISNEY COMPANY	USA
4.	VIACOM INC.	USA
5.	THE NEWS CORPORATION LTD.	AUS
6.	SONY ENTERTAINMENT	J
7.	HAVAS P.A.	F
8.	ARD	D
9.	NIPPON HOSO KYOKAI (NHK)	J
10.	LAGARDÈRE GROUPE	F
11.	POLYGRAM N.V.	NL
12.	TCI COMMUNICATIONS INC.	USA
13.	REED ELSEVIER	GB
14.	MCA INC.	USA
15.	ADVANCE PUBLICATIONS INC.	USA
16.	ASAHI SHIMBUN	J
17.	REUTERS HOLDING PLC	GB
18.	GANNETT CO. INC.	USA
19.	NBC	USA
20.	KIRCH-GRUPPE	D

2020

1.	ALPHABET INC.	USA
2.	COMCAST CORPORATION	USA
3.	META PLATFORMS INC.	USA
4.	TENCENT HOLDINGS LTD.	CN
5.	THE WALT DISNEY COMPANY	USA
6.	APPLE INC.	USA
7.	CHARTER COMM. INC.	USA
8.	SONY ENTERTAINMENT	J
9.	BYTEDANCE LTD.	CN
10.	WARNERMEDIA	USA
11.	SHANGHAI MEDIA GROUP	CN
12.	MICROSOFT CORPORATION	USA
13.	ALTICE EUROPE N.V., ALTICEUS INC.	NL
14.	VIACOMCBS INC.	USA
15.	AMAZON.COM INC.	USA
16.	NETFLIX INC.	USA
17.	LIBERTY/QURATE RETAIL INC.	USA
18.	NEWS CORP./NEW FOX	USA
19.	BERTELSMANN SE & CO. KGAA	D
20.	VIVENDI P.A.	F

CHAPTER II

THE END OF THE FREE INTERNET:
How the tech giants occupied the digital media space

1. Stuck in the silos of the platforms

A handful of big tech corporations dominate our digital media system and have completely eliminated free and fair competition. This creates a huge amount of damage to our democracy in terms of media and press freedom. We saw in the first chapter how far Big Tech has already progressed. Now we want to go deeper: How did digital corporations achieve this hostile takeover?

Let us go back to the early days of the platforms to understand what has happened since then. We can imagine it as a sequence of individual steps—something like this:

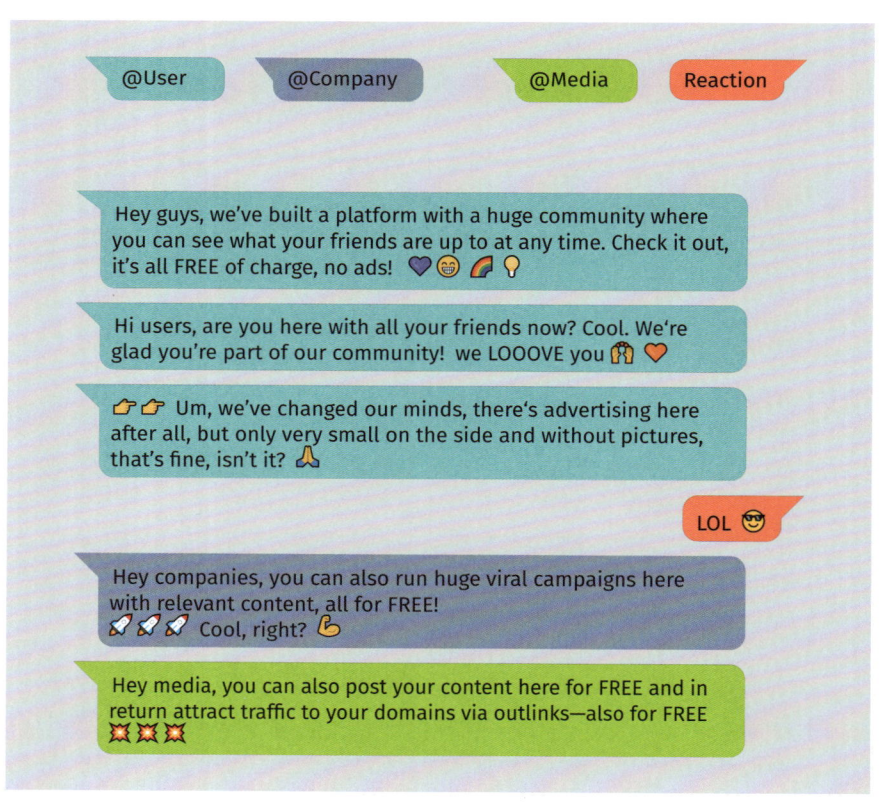

Hey companies, you've now set up huge content marketing departments that create content for us from morning to night? Yay! You rock! 💪

Um, by the way, we'll be putting the ads in the feed from now on. 🙏

Hey companies, why don't you invest in paid advertising, it works great! 🚀🚀🚀

Hey media, are you now fully dependent on our traffic? Super. ✅

👉 Oh users, by the way, we've been monitoring you and collecting your data for some time now—we forgot to tell you that. 😊

👉 Hey users, we're showing you less and less of what your friends are doing. We'd rather show you other cool stuff that we think you'll find interesting, ok?

Oops, media and companies, important side note: We've changed the rules and are now reducing the visibility of outlinks for your posts. Can you just let your content marketing departments know? Thank you. 🙈🙈🙈

Sorry, someone of our people here has been passing on your data to the US secret service agencies for 4 years—hope you are not angry, sorryyyyyy! 😬💅😊

Hey companies, there's no more organic reach for you any more, sorry. We would prefer you to book paid campaigns with us anyway—look how cool the performance is. What should you do with your content marketing departments? Good question, you have to find a suitable solution. 😬🚀💪

Oh, we completely forgot: We have now completely eliminated outlinks in the feed ⛔—sorry, media and companies. 🙏

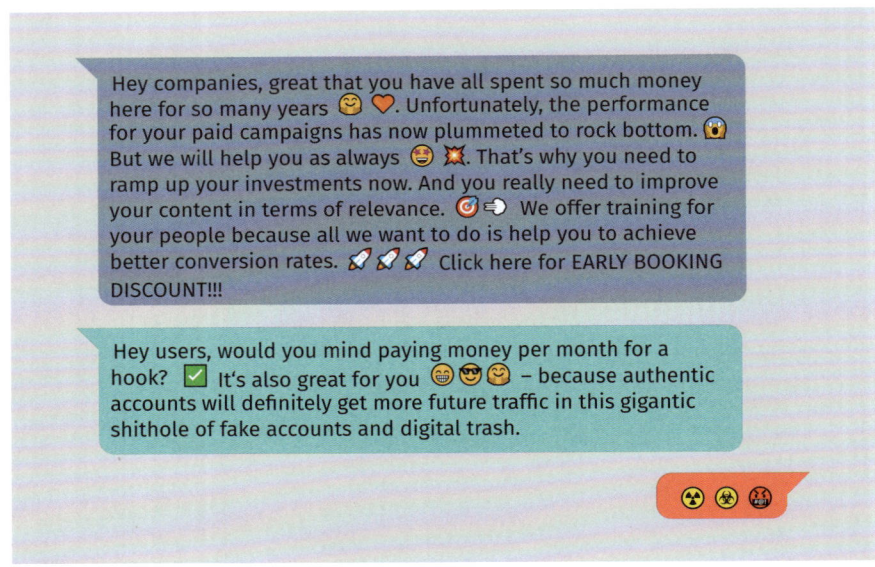

We immediately recognize what is happening here: We all fell right into the trap. The digital companies initially lured us onto their platforms with a series of incentives. As soon as the lock-in had set in and we were trapped on the platforms, they kept changing the rules of the game in order to extract more and more money from us. The platforms operate a kind of mixing desk whose control levers and sliders only they can change at will. Of course, the platforms will always turn the knobs in such a way that they exploit all participants more and more aggressively (the users, the advertising companies, the media). The users have no power to defend themselves, simply because they have no access to the control levers. Cory Doctorow appropriately calls this 'enshittification': The platforms are being flooded with more and more shit—and we're all being screwed by Big Tech.[1] 💩 💩 💩

Already as a college student, Mark Zuckerberg wondered why the platform's users could be so idiotic as to trust him. He called his users "dumb fucks" (see the text in the box). We can be sure that this is exactly what the tech giants think about us all the time—not just about their users, but about all people and institutions who fail to realize that they are continuously being cheated upon, regardless of whether they are politicians, authorities, institutions or experts.[2]

Bearing this in mind, we can completely reject all the fairy tales Big Tech tells us about its own successes. The digital corporations prefer to explain their supremacy through their supposedly superior innovative strength and the unbeatable superbrains of their founders and developers. We have already seen that this argument does not stand up to scrutiny. On the contrary, the tech giants operate in fields that have been almost completely devoid of competition for many years. That's why we have seen only very few real innovations from the GAFAM companies for a long time, also considering the research and development budgets they have at hand.

But how exactly have they managed to render their monopolies and oligopolies so invulnerable? Is it perhaps due to the superior quality of their products (as the tech giants explain it) or did they apply unfair methods? Above all, how for goodness sake did they get away with it? To find answers, we first need to understand how exactly the digital companies have locked us into their platforms. As we will see, they used about a dozen tricks and gimmicks, such as the use of network effects, monopoly abuse, killer acquisitions of potential competitors and many more.

But let's start with a lesser-known example of the methods tech giants use to lock us into their platforms. Imagine going into a department store, wandering around and then realizing at some point that you cannot get out. All the passages, pathways and escalators only lead deeper into the store and the way back out is mysteriously blocked. The situation is very similar with the elimination of 'outlinks' on many platforms. Outlinks redirect users to offers outside the domain they are using. Platforms such as Instagram or TikTok no longer allow outlinks on their normal posts. But even on platforms like Facebook, it is hard to use the outlinks. Why is that? Because around 80 percent of them are consumed on mobile devices via apps. These apps use a so-called in-app browser. They are designed in a way that you do

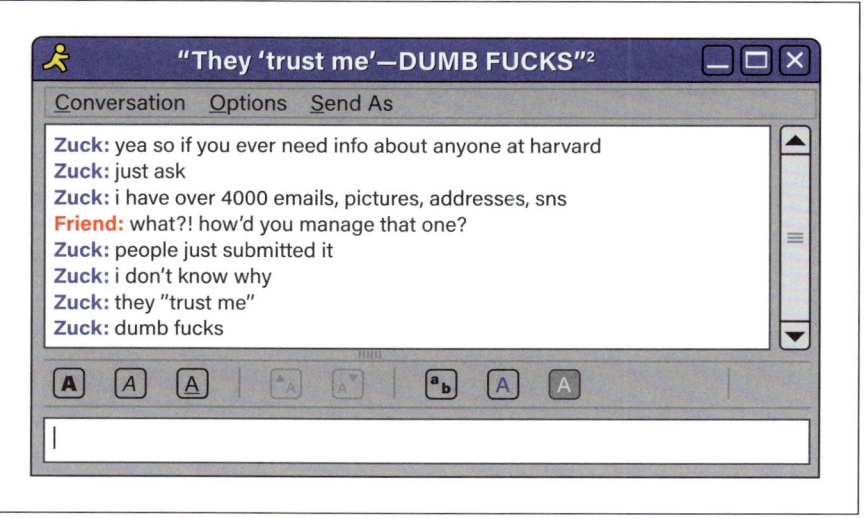

not leave the platform even when you call up the outlink. The external content is called up and loaded *within* the platform's user interface.

The platforms' motives for these blockades and barriers are obvious. In order to earn more and more money, they try to capture as much of the audience's attention as possible. The better and more efficiently they lock users into the platform, the longer the usage times of the individual sessions will be, which they can then monetize in the form of advertising.

If you think that our department store example is exaggerated, try it out for yourself. Go to Instagram and select any post, for example from a major digital publisher such as *New York Times* or similar. The publishers post their content for free on platforms such as Facebook or Instagram. Why do they do this? As we saw in the first chapter: Because the vast majority of web traffic is on the platforms.

The situation for publishers in the battle for traffic is desperate: If they want to secure tiny crumbs of traffic for themselves, they have no choice but to display short teasers of their content on the platforms, to lure people to switch to their own domain.

Do the experiment just for fun: take a post from a publisher and try to find your way back to the publisher's original domain. We have illustrated a kind of instruction manual for this on the following double page.

These barriers to the outside are just one of the many obstacles and tricks that the tech giants have invented to lock us users into their platforms. Of course, users still have the freedom to leave the app completely, open their normal web browser and call up any domain they wish. But this is hardly viable in the reality of digital media usage. The consumption of digital media is characterized by very short sessions, hundreds of impressions and huge floods of content. Users scroll down platform feeds at breathtaking speed. It is difficult enough for any text, picture or video to stand out in the digital ocean of content, stopping the swiping thumbs of users (this is called 'thumbstopping' content). In the digital media reality with its highly competitive, tiny attention spans of tenths of a second, the barriers and detours constructed by the platforms ("link in bio!") are almost insurmountable walls.

Thus, our department store comparison is by no means exaggerated. Interestingly enough, such barriers would of course not be permitted in a store. In Germany, 'forcing' people to consume something (even indirectly) would violate the so-called 'Unfair Competition Act' (UWG).

As a non-expert, you immediately think: that's monopoly abuse. After all, the tech giants are using their dominant market positions to virtually lock users into the platforms. A clear case for the German Federal Anti Trust Office, right? Wrong. Surprisingly, neither this nor any other state authority would be responsible for the specific case of digital outlinks in Germany. In contrast to other countries, such practices of unfair competition have been removed from the jurisdiction of the public authorities. In Germany, the Unfair Competition Act (UWG) is enforced through possible legal action initiated by competitors or private associations. But who should bring about legal action? Perhaps TikTok, which has itself abolished outlinks? Or publishers' associations that are completely dependent on the digital corporations? The fact that State authorities in Germany cannot directly intervene in such cases is fatal. We are not dealing with an ordinary market here (soft drinks, socks, etc.), we are dealing with our media system. The basis of our democracy is at risk. And yet this dubious practice is beyond the direct control of supervisory authorities in Germany.

Because the platforms have reduced the outlinks so much, a new digital trend called 'zero-click content' has emerged. In this specific way of using digital media, there are no more clicks required, which means that the traffic remains entirely on the platforms. You already know this from Google 'snippets'. In search queries, you see excerpts from websites, for example with images, price information or rating stars, as a graph or as a list of important bullet points. Google encourages content factories to design the source code of their pages accordingly. A study by search engine expert Rand Fishkin found that, in 2021, two out of three search queries ended with Google itself and led to no clicks at all.[3] This must be a disaster for anyone who creates content. You provide all the content, Google makes the money. 'Native', as it would be called by marketeers, practical, and great for Google. The traffic remains entirely in the silo of the platform.

As we will see in the following chapter, outlinks are just one of about a dozen unfair, questionable practices that digital companies use to protect their monopolies and eliminate free competition. Remember the many different victims we analyzed in the first chapter—digital publishers, bloggers, brand corporations, public service broadcasters? They are all having their traffic taps turned off by the same mechanisms. Their opportunities to attract users to their own sites with relevant content continues to diminish.

TRAPPED IN PLATFORMS—EXAMPLE: INSTAGRAM

If you read an interesting article on Instagram from a publisher and try to get to the article itself, your path will usually go through the following steps:

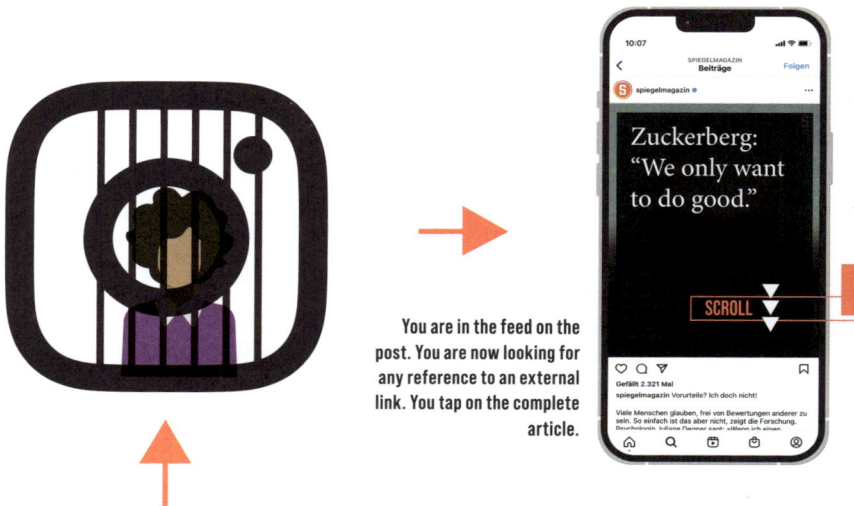

You are in the feed on the post. You are now looking for any reference to an external link. You tap on the complete article.

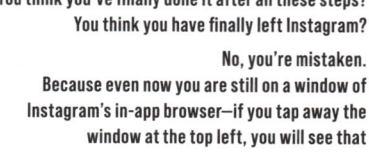

With other providers, you are now sometim[es]

taken to a new intermediate page w[ith] a list of links from ot[her] articles as thumbnai[ls] and a button "Visit u[s at] xyz.de" (correspond[s to] the link highlighted i[n] red here).

You think you've finally done it after all these steps? You think you have finally left Instagram?
No, you're mistaken.
Because even now you are still on a window of Instagram's in-app browser—if you tap away the window at the top left, you will see that you are *still* inside Instagram.

Finally, we have arrived at the publisher's embedded website (spiegel.de).

In our example, we are forwarded directly to the spiegel.de homepage.

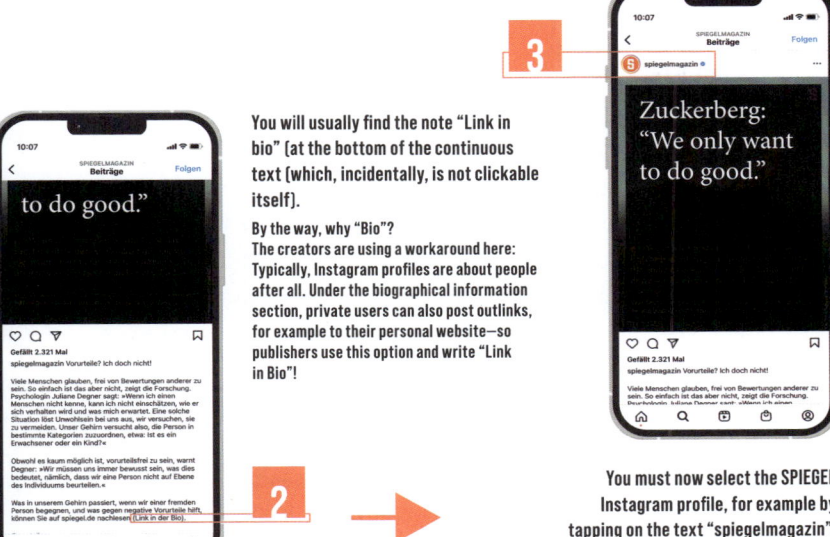

You will usually find the note "Link in bio" (at the bottom of the continuous text (which, incidentally, is not clickable itself).

By the way, why "Bio"?
The creators are using a workaround here: Typically, Instagram profiles are about people after all. Under the biographical information section, private users can also post outlinks, for example to their personal website—so publishers use this option and write "Link in Bio"!

You must now select the SPIEGEL Instagram profile, for example by tapping on the text "spiegelmagazin".

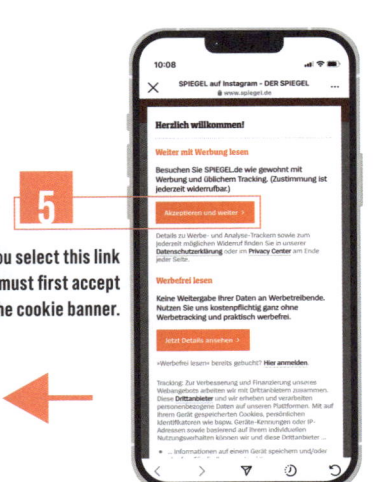

You select this link and must first accept the cookie banner.

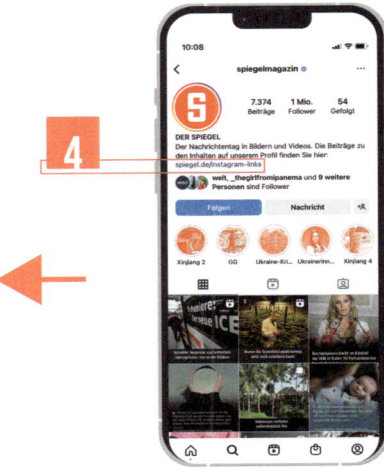

The profile of "spiegelmagazin" opens. Below the information in the fourth line you will find a link (spiegel.de/instagram-links)—which is highlighted in color and clickable here (in contrast to the non-clickable information in the article).

2. Media genres are now the private property of companies

Imagine if, in the 15th century, Johannes Gutenberg had found an evil trick to fully control all access to his movable letters by making use of clever network effects. Even today, the descendants of Gutenberg would still be making money from every single application of his innovation. His company, 'Gutenberg Inc.', would have risen to become the largest and most powerful global corporation in the Western world.

No matter what we did, wherever information was exchanged, it would always run through this giga-corporation, which would therefore also make money on virtually anything: school books, street signs, newspapers, menus, websites, banking transactions, product packaging, insurance, contracts, banknotes, house numbers, administrative processes, signposts, stickers, license plates, labels, bread bags, stickers, and so on—because everything would be used with the Gutenberg Inc. lettering system.

Everyone in society would be caught in a lifelong stranglehold by Gutenberg Inc. We would all be condemned to continuous, hard labor for this terrible company. Because, with every use of Gutenberg's idea of standardized letters, we would always have to pay Gutenberg Inc. 10 percent here, 30 percent there. With every transaction, with every use, no matter how small, we would be forced to do whatever this company demanded from us. This mega-corporation would forever be free of any competition and could charge us whatever prices they wanted. In addition, Gutenberg Inc. would also decide which of our documents would be published and printed and how many people would receive the content.

If we complained to Gutenberg Inc. that this practice was unfair, they would always reply in the same way: "Look how useful and beneficial the standardized letters are. We have invented them to create a better world and kindly shared them with all of you. Completely new forms of interaction and participation have become possible as a result." They would explain that we users are the root cause of the problem. Because we are the ones who constantly use these standardized letters, an invention that unfortunately belonged to them. That this was all our own, free decision. That we were free to find own solutions beyond the scope of their letters any time. We could carve pictures on potato stamps, for example, or simply use handwriting, whatever. That this problem was not caused by the wonderful

Gutenberg Inc. and their outstanding product. The issue was simply the result of our laziness, incompetence and lack of innovative spirit.

As we can see from this comparison, all types of media generally tend to have strong network effects. This applies to both the printing press as well as YouTube. Network effects always occur when the benefit for an application increases disproportionately with the number of users: The more people have a telephone connection, the higher is the value of the telephone network.

This also applies to areas beyond the media. For example, it makes sense for many companies to agree on a standardized format for a railway network. The more people use it, the greater are its benefits. Or to put it the other way around: It makes no sense to allow many different competing formats of rails, because then the locomotives and wagons could not be used by everybody, they would not be interoperable. In the same way, it makes sense for everyone to use the same telephone standard. We will see that this also applies to YouTube or WhatsApp.

What does this mean for media and their network effects? If everyone uses the same media format, then we cannot simply come up with a new one. Once established, these media turn into standards, which is why we are not free to choose any more. We are virtually condemned to use these media for the rest of our lives. Interestingly enough, this has hardly ever been a problem for conventional analog media, for a simple reason: the media themselves were typically available to everybody for free and without constraints.

In the past, users often paid for a connection, either a network access (for example in case of the telephone) or for a device (for example in case of a radio or CD player). Or users paid fees for content, such as for a newspaper subscription. But we never had to get a license or fee *for the medium itself*, for a simple reason: These media were typically not 'owned' by anyone, which is why nobody could claim usage or license fees.

How has Big Tech gained control over the media?

Let us put ourselves in the position of someone who has just invented a new media technology. Let us assume that this inventor has a plan to make as much money as possible with the new idea. Let us imagine such a 'Darth Gutenberg'. His objective would first be to get everyone in society hooked to use his standardized technology. Second, he would try to ensure that they would have to pay him and his descendants for the use of his idea, ideally for all eternity. What options would he have?

In fact, the options for our 'Darth Gutenberg' are very limited. The only way for him to capitalize on such an invention would be to claim intellectual property.

Today, an inventor would typically apply for a patent. In the 15th century, Gutenberg did not yet have the modern option of registering a patent to protect his own intellectual property.

But in any case, it is questionable whether it is such a good idea to protect your invention by a patent if you want to establish a new media channel. After all, the key objective for the inventor would be to convince as many people as possible to use the new type of media. User fees and patent protection would be quite counterproductive here. In fact, patent protection could hardly be used at the very beginning of the implementation of a new media technology. And then the introduction of new media would take several years or decades, at least in the pre-digital era. By the time a general use would have become established in a society, patent protection would always have expired. This is because all patent protection is limited in time, of course for a very simple reason: The legislator wants to enable *competition* under any circumstances and ensure supplier and provider diversity. Otherwise, patents could also be protected for an unlimited period of time and create unwanted monopolies.

In the history of the media, there have always been cases where inventors of media technologies have in fact registered such patents. But they often made them openly available to everyone. In the case of photography, Daguerre made his patent freely available for use (he received a pension from the French government in return). The invention of the telephone is particularly instructive, because Alexander Graham Bell and AT&T had actually applied for strong patents. But at the time, the US government was convinced that the new media technology was a common good, a 'public utility'. For this reason, it intervened resolutely and engineered an agreement that made Bell's invention freely available to competitors.

> *"Society has never allowed that which is necessary to existence to be controlled by private interest."*[4]
>
> Theodore Vail, President of AT&T

Fortunately, the managers at AT&T also saw it that way after some initial struggles. Big Tech could take them as an example. We recognize: Since prehistoric times, human beings have used media as tools to communicate with each other. But throughout human history, the inventors of media technologies have hardly ever had a way to protect their inventions in a way that would enable them to claim intellectual property permanently and thus control their media technology forever. In cases where media freedom was endangered, governments typically found arrangements with the patent holders to make the media available to all. In this sense, media have always been public utilities, common goods or 'commons' up to the present day. Media have always been goods of general and public interest.

The platform economy has fundamentally changed this situation. The large platforms that represent our media of the future are now owned and operated by private companies. These platform monopolies often encompass entire media genres. This is a significant difference to the past. We noticed what happened when Elon Musk bought the Twitter network as a private individual. Twitter is now owned by a person, who has been restructuring and redesigning the network to suit his own interests ever since.

In the history of the media, all kinds of protective rights have existed. In the case of book printing in particular, there were State privileges. But these limitations usually cared less about the rights of the inventor. They evolved from the other 'Dark side of the Force', such as State control and censorship. The State also often played a central role in electronic mass media such as radio or television. For these media technologies, high levels of investments were usually required at the beginning. But the State here only provided the infrastructure and (ideally) did not control the content. Of course, there have been cases in the past where State power has been *abused* by interfering with the media, such as under National Socialism. But this is precisely the case that *should be prevented in all conditions* in a democratic understanding of the media.

Under conditions of democratic freedom, the State must maintain absolute neutrality in the field of media. If the State has the power over such infrastructure, it should use it under democratic conditions, for example by ensuring balanced programming or by enabling pluralistic licensing, as was the case with private television.

Throughout the history of their existence, the media technologies themselves were therefore generally not 'owned' by anyone, neither by individuals nor by single companies. And the media of the past were only created through *useful* network effects: Telegraph, radio, phonograph, radio, television, CD, telephone, fax machine, cell phone and so on. They all developed their real social benefits only when they were widely used. It is also difficult to imagine how media could have become established in our society without this general and open distribution to all. To this day, everyone benefits from the many media that innovative pioneers once invented—without these media being owned and controlled by private individuals or companies.

It is now interesting to look at the current situation of the platforms. Facebook and Instagram, YouTube, Google and WhatsApp obviously occupy the space devoted to the main media genres of our time. Should we not question the current situation? Is it a good idea that it is now legitimate for persons or companies to 'own' media genres that are used by the entire population in our digital age? Is it acceptable that these owners have full control over these media genres?

With regard to the analog media of the past, we would intuitively reject the idea that a single person or company could own or control them. To this day, nobody owns television or radio. But this is precisely the case with platforms. In contrast to the analog media of the past, the digital networks are owned by private companies. In fact, the *network* also represents the actual value for these companies. Big Tech executives openly admit that, in the words of Andy Rubin from Google: *"We don't monetize the thing we create [...]. We monetize the people that use it."*[5]

The right of ownership gives Big Tech far reaching rights to determine the terms and conditions of usage of their media channels (☞ IV.3). They therefore have full control over the content, up to deleting and blocking disliked content or users.

Digital takeover: How open standards have been replaced by closed standards

We immediately recognize how Big Tech has taken over the Internet when we look back at the original media technology of today's digital culture, the *World Wide Web*. Tim Berners-Lee and the idealistic inventors of the World Wide Web were still acting on the principles of public utility media technologies that were not 'owned' by their inventors and were freely accessible to all people for all time. We can discover these principles when we look at the long and painstaking development of Internet standards. These are standards that define for all participants how data should be structured as it flows through the network. They are *open standards*: they apply to all market participants and enable data to circulate freely. Because they are available to all players, they enable a free market of many competing providers. This is because open standards create full interoperability: users can easily switch from one provider to another.

These open standards for the Internet include the 'Internet Protocol' (IP) which defines the structure of the IP address, the 'Transmission Control Protocol' (TCP) which defines the processes of data exchange, the 'Hypertext Markup Language' (HTML) as the format for the browser's web content and so on. Up to this day, the 'Internet Engineering Task Force' (IETF) is a non-profit organization that keeps a close eye on these and other open Internet standards.

This free nature of the Internet was, nevertheless, attacked and destroyed after the turn of the millennium by the emergence of a new generation of platforms. The logic was malicious: what if you built platforms with massive, irresistible network effects *on top of* the open nodes of the World Wide Web? What if you managed to suck the traffic out of the democratic, open web, upwards into the traffic silos of these new platforms?

The move was literally a hostile takeover of the Internet—take*over* because these new media are *super*imposed *over* the structures of the old free web. Of course, a platform like *www.facebook.com* is still located on a specific domain. It uses a specific address (URL) on the Internet, i.e. it occupies a specific node in this network. But it only uses the network as an *under*lying infrastructure.

The cunning trick in taking over the Internet was to break with the philosophy of open standards and to rely on closed standards instead. It was a particularly clever move as this crucial difference was *not even recognizable to the people who were using the new networks*. They came disguised as open media—and they were also free to use, just like the World Wide Web and the media technologies before it.

The free offers of the new platforms seemed open and altruistic, thus quickly bringing huge numbers of users flooding into the respective network. By this trick, they achieved a wide distribution in a very short time and thus also created the desired network effects. However, this was only a camouflage that disguised the fact that users were locked into these platforms without knowing it. People only rarely realize how trapped they are in these closed standards—for example when they want to leave a platform and lose all their content, all their followers, all their traffic and have to start from scratch again on another platform.

In contrast, open standards can always be recognized by the fact that switching from one company to another is not a problem. Open standards create diversity and competition by default. We can quickly demonstrate this using the Internet as an example: Anyone who has a website and is no longer satisfied with their web hosting can easily switch to an alternative provider. The open standards ensure that they can simply transfer the entire website to the new hosting supplier. There is no risk of losing any of the traffic that has been built up on the domain over the years.

Also in the case of email, a so-called open protocol had been established already in the early 1980s, SMTP ('Simple Mail Transfer Protocol'). This was a format that was freely accessible to all competitors. All emails were 'packaged' into it, which explains why (to this day!) the same form of communication (email) is used by completely different providers, but also by completely different business models (email programs, webmail or freemail from email providers, etc.). Although many corporations compete with each other, they do so on the basis of a standard that is openly available to all participants. And here, too, we find a large number of providers and fair competition.

In contrast, the large social media offerings rely on *closed* standards in order to eliminate competition and to keep users locked into the platforms. For example, while you can send an email from Microsoft Outlook to Gmail and then to yahoo.com, this is not possible with social media platforms. You cannot send a message from your Facebook profile to someone on LinkedIn, or comment on, share or even view posts across networks. This prevents other networks from competing with Facebook, for example, on the basis of the same open protocol.

Interestingly enough, we can clearly see the connection between open standards and positive effects on competition in our own scientific measurements of online traffic: Among the huge monopolies, the market for email service providers is a welcome exception. Here, strong local German providers such as web.de or GMX have been able to compete with Gmail for years (which is almost a miracle, as Gmail massively benefits from the strength of the other Alphabet/Google offerings through cross-platform network effects, ⟹ II.3).

Closed standards therefore lead to one market participant defining its own proprietary standard and actively excluding other market participants from it. The intention is to systematically create monopolies. This in turn has particularly serious consequences in the field of media, because these monopolies damage our fundamental rights to freedom of expression and freedom of the press. In these sealed-off traffic silos, the 'feudal lords' are in control and no longer the people who produce the media items.

In the past, the managers of the tech giants have even openly admitted that their aim is to systematically eliminate competition and deliberately create media monopolies. Big Tech cannot even be accused of acting secretly. In fact, the digital companies themselves know best of all the deadly impact of network effects on free competition in media markets. The obvious proof of this is provided by Facebook's acquisition of WhatsApp in 2014 for the widely known amount of 22 billion US dollars. Why, for goodness sake, would a digital company be so idiotic as to buy a very banal technology that could easily have been copied for a few hundred thousand dollars—especially as Facebook had already operated its own messenger service since 2011? In addition, Facebook already had well over a billion users in 2014.

It is hard to imagine a better starting position for Facebook at the time, because Facebook could have simply converted all its own users to an own messenger service. But under the conditions of network effects, there is only one factor that is decisive: who will be the first to succeed? In this case, it was WhatsApp. And as soon as the network effect takes hold, nobody has the slightest chance. Not even a company with the power and financial strength of Facebook at the time. There is only one goal in such a case, and that is to take possession of the media monopoly at any price—literally *at any price*. That is exactly why the acquisition was the right move from a business perspective. Unfortunately, the consequences for our democracy are catastrophic because Meta is now a monopolist in two media categories (social media and messengers).

After thousands of years of media evolution, we are now experiencing a decisive paradigm shift. Never before in the history of mankind have commonly used media genres belonged to individual, privately owned companies that have very extensive control over their channels and content through their ownership rights. This fact alone leads to a considerable erosion of media freedom. After all, media freedom does not only mean independence from State censorship, for example. At its very core, media freedom has always meant that media were never owned by individuals or companies, but always had to be a common good, a public utility: they belonged to the communities that created them in the first place by their usage.

Now, however, this has changed. The tech giants have stolen free media from Western societies through their closed standards.

The end of free media

What will the future bring us if our media are largely digitized in just a few years? Let's take a quick look first at the 'analog' channels:

- No one owns the newspaper media genre—and there are a large number of competing publishers.

- No one owns television—there are private broadcasters, public service broadcasters and clear rules that ensure diversity.

- The radio media category is not owned by anybody—there are private broadcasters, public service broadcasters and clear rules that ensure diversity.

Thus, none of the existing analog media genres have a central owner with controlling access to the full content. In all of these media, there is a strict economic separation between the transmission channel and the transmitted content. Let us now compare the situation in the era of platforms:

- There is mainly one search engine (Google), which is owned by a tech giant (Alphabet), with a usage share of about 90 percent in Germany.
  There is no serious competition.

- There is mainly one free video-on-demand service (YouTube), which is owned by the same tech giant (Alphabet), with a usage share of about 80 percent in Germany.
  There is no serious competition apart from TikTok.

- There are two relevant offerings for social media (Facebook and Instagram), both of which are owned by the same tech giant (Meta), with a usage share of about 85 percent in Germany.
  There is no serious competition.

- There is mainly one messenger service (WhatsApp), which is owned by a tech giant (Meta) that also dominates social media.
  There is no serious competition.

- There is a duopoly for audio-on-demand (Apple Music and Spotify).
  There is hardly any serious competition.

All of these digital media genres are owned by single, privately owned companies. Thanks to their rights to define terms and conditions, the owners of the platforms have nearly unlimited control over all content (☞ IV.3). In future, they will be able to decide at will on the visibility of people and their content contributions in the media ('boosting' versus 'dimming', we will come back to this later, ☞ III.5).

This can all be written down in a few seconds, but the implications are huge. First of all, we allowed Big Tech to abolish the free internet before our very eyes. Tim Berners-Lee and his peers had created an independent structure that had provided an open, free platform for an infinite variety of offerings.

Every piece of content on the Internet used to be basically equal. In the words of Tim Berners-Lee: "Every node, document—whatever it was called—would be fundamentally equivalent in some way".[6] This is exactly what is illustrated by the core metaphor of the network (*net* or *web*). In a network structure, all nodes are situated on the same hierarchical level. They are linked together by a multitude of connections. On the Internet, you could enter this network of offers at any point, find hyperlinks that you could select at will to move on to the next node, and on and on—a navigational movement that used to be called 'surfing'.

Even the analog media were and still are free because they were never 'owned' by anybody. And in this sense, the internet was perhaps the last free media structure. The Internet itself is still not owned by anyone, which is why the Internet is not a company, does not generate billions in revenues, does not have a CEO and we do not have to accept any terms and conditions of use. As the highest supervisory body, the 'Internet Engineering Taskforce' (IETF) decides on the open internet standards. To this day, it is an open group of volunteers without a legal form. 'The Internet Society' (ISOC) deals with infrastructure issues and is a non-governmental organization. The central body for the distribution of domain names and IP addresses, the 'Internet Corporation for Assigned Names and Numbers' (ICANN), is a non-profit organization. In the words of Berners-Lee: "There was no central computer 'controlling' the web, no single network on which these protocols worked, not even an organization anywhere that 'ran' the web".[7]

We now have a deeper understanding of the massive consequences of digital network effects and can repeat our experiment from the first chapter: Let us switch off the analog media again—the television remains black, the radio turns silent, there are no more print media.

Now, we have a world of digital media that is dominated by platforms. Let us remember: the top ten offerings (which are in the hands of just seven corporations) already bundle more than 50 percent of German web traffic. Of these top ten, nine are platforms based in the USA. Only one offering (web.de) is not a platform, is based on open standards and originates from Germany (is it really a coincidence that these three factors apply all at once? I don't think so...). However, this one exception only accounts for 1.5 percent of the total digital usage time. The other nine offers combined account for around 49 percent of aggregated usage time.

The nine platforms with closed standards mentioned above are characterized by the fact that in most cases they monopolize one type of media genre. They no longer compete in a market—*they themselves constitute the respective market*. Through their rights to define terms and conditions, they have full control over the respective media genre.

We can see what this means if we imagine that the same was the case in the analog media. It would be as if individual corporations owned entire media genres. One company, DARTH, would own all television (public service broadcasting would not exist any more). A second company, FAT, would own the radio. A third company, EVIL, would own all the newspapers and magazines.

It is obvious that we would no longer have free media in this scenario. It would also be completely absurd to ask whether that would be a bad thing at all: "The people from DARTH, FAT and EVIL are super cool and always fun at parties. DARTH, FAT and EVIL only have good intentions. They always say they want the best for everyone." You could just as easily assume that a censor or politician trying to control the media has only good intentions (as Franz Josef Strauß probably did in Germany when he had police officers march into the editorial offices of *Der Spiegel* in 1962, arresting journalists).

Any situation like this is unacceptable. It breaks completely with the democratic principles of free media. The key issue is that these companies have full control over the respective media genres. Elon Musk's takeover of Twitter is just one example of how easily such platforms can control media content. Perhaps this is at least one positive effect of Musk's acquisition of Twitter: it is now obvious for anybody what the future holds for us. Our digital media system is controlled by individuals and companies who can largely do what they want with it.

Oh dear, how we have all boycotted the platforms! Ever since GAFAM took over the Internet, there have been repeated boycotts. The boycotters were concerned with issues such as the placement of advertising in the context of fake news, hate speech, discrimination (especially with #StopHateForProfit), the terrible working conditions of Big Tech employees, the disclosure of user data to US government agencies or other third parties, the surveillance of users, racist content, and so on. Just this short list shows the complete moral rottenness of the Big Tech companies.[8]

There was a big rebellion on the web in the wake of the takeover of Twitter by Elon Musk. A huge wave of outrage swept through the web. Opinion leaders allegedly left the network en masse and switched to the open source alternative Mastodon. Unfortunately, it had no effect, just like the many previous digital boycotts. After a supposed 'mass exit' lasting weeks, it turned out that hardly any users had really disappeared from Twitter. A study could quantify that. A tiny number of

140,000 users had threatened to leave Twitter—and only a microscopic 1.6 percent (!) of these 140,000 did actually leave.⁹

This is hardly surprising. You can perhaps boycott individual media content (for example, you can decide not to watch the soccer World Cup). On the other hand, it is almost impossible to boycott key media genres themselves—unless you want to destroy your own social existence. Digital platforms are the media of our time. A boycott is therefore about as easy as taking a vow of silence. And that is precisely why all boycotts of digital media are hopeless in most cases.

This also means that we users cannot be blamed for the digital catastrophe because we could supposedly 'use alternatives'. That is exactly what we cannot really do. As all our friends and contacts are tied to the platforms, we are all stuck in these digital media together. This is one more reason why media should be treated as public utilities and common property.

BOYCOTT!

It is impossible to boycott media

FAMOUS BOYCOTT ATTEMPTS 2017-2022

- **Twitter-Boycott**: End of 2022; after takeover of the platform by Elon Musk
- **Social-Media-Boycott**: Beginning of 2021; by Premier League clubs
- **Facebook-Boycott:** 2020; *#StopHateForProfit*
- **Amazon-Boycott:** Beginning of 2020; *#MakeAmazonPay*
- **Amazon-Boycott:** Mid 2019 on Prime Day
- **Facebook-Boycott:** Early 2018; #DeleteFacebook after Cambridge Analytica scandal
- **Google-Boycott:** Beginning of 2017; *#AdBoycottYouTube*
- **Snapchat-Boycott:** 2017; #UninstallSnapchat // #BoycottSnapchat

CELEBRITY BOYCOTT ATTEMPTS

- **Elton John, Jim Carrey, Shonda Rhimes and others:** End of 2022; against Twitter
- **Neil Young:** Beginning of 2022; against Spotify
- **Kim Kardashian, Leonardo DiCaprio, Jennifer Lawrence and others:** Mid-2020; against Facebook (#StopHateForProfit)
- **Rihanna:** March 2018; against Snapchat

3. How Big Tech is expanding its monopolies

From the perspective of a tech giant, it is obviously great to control a monopoly. But it would be even better if the monopoly could be extended to other markets. This is why many dominant market positions lead to cross-platform monopoly abuse. There are two negative effects. First, the dominance of the network effect for the original product is reinforced. Second, new, adjacent fields are caught up by the black hole pull of the monopolies once they have been established. There has already been a case of this, back in the early 1990s, when Microsoft succeeded in widely establishing its *Windows* operating system through license deals with PC manufacturers.[10]

As always, the drivers of such effects argue by referring to the benefits for consumers, who in this example no longer have to bother with laborious installations. Here, the operating system is already purchased together with the computer—quite convenient, isn't it? The collective purchase then provided all users with a 'better' and 'cheaper' product.

The desired network effect kicks in immediately. More and more people use something because other people do the same. A product thus becomes a universally compatible standard. Afterwards, Microsoft used Windows as a Trojan horse to conquer other markets. From November 1989, the text processor Word was converted to 'Word for Windows'. It represented a massive disadvantage for the then market leader WordPerfect, which did not have access to the Windows programming interfaces. Thus, Microsoft achieved its triumphant advance in text processors.

After a short period of time, Microsoft began to copy this method for Excel to eliminate competitors such as Lotus123 and Quattro, simply by bundling it with Word at a favorable price.[11] Microsoft followed the same tried-and-tested method of monopoly abuse in the field of Internet browsers by providing its Internet Explorer browser for free as a Windows 'feature', which ultimately led to the demise of Netscape Navigator. A few years later, Windows was bundled with Media Player. Here, too, it was always emphasized that Microsoft was only acting in the interests of the consumer. The bundling of products saved costs and time—wonderful, isn't it? Furthermore, the products harmonized smoothly with each other, the various modules were seamlessly connected, in many cases programs were already pre-installed, and so on. By doing so, closed ecosystems were being created so that the existing products in the market no longer had a fair chance to compete. As a consequence, WordPerfect continued to stagnate due to a lack of compatibility with Windows. To this day, Microsoft Office holds an 85 percent market share in German companies.[12] Microsoft was sued for monopoly abuse in both the US and Europe, but was able to successfully appeal in the US through clever maneuvering. In Europe, on the other hand, it had to pay a cumulative fine of around 2 billion euros over the years—peanuts in relation to the size of the markets it had taken over.

Microsoft had thus developed a successful pattern of taking over digital markets via monopoly establishment and abuse. The digital corporations kept acting as aggressively as possible and simply created de facto situations, paying little attention to possible breaches of the law, willingly accepting possible penalties later on. The only decisive factor was the complete occupation of entire markets. In addition, they exploited regulatory loopholes and the slowness of the regulatory authorities, which are still today completely overwhelmed by the speed of the digital transformation. The legal proceedings, including the possible appeals before the various instances, would often take ten years or longer. It is obvious that this gave Microsoft and its disciples more than enough time to cheerfully kill off their competitors. In parallel, the tech giants spent massive amounts of resources on lobbying and made public assurances that they were always acting in the interests of users and for the good of mankind.

Over time, this led to the digital monopolies continuing to grow in three dimensions: first, the original monopoly was stabilized (here: Windows); second, the monopoly was expanded into new dominant positions in adjacent markets (here: the Office products or Internet Explorer); third, all the different offerings in the respective ecosystem benefited from the ongoing digital transformation, enjoying purely organic growth in line with the booming digital markets. This dynamic led to incredible sales figures and, above all, the skyrocketing profits that we are witnessing nowadays. The stronger a dominant market position is, the more arbitrary is the price that the company can charge for the product. This is precisely why the establishment of dominant market positions created the basis for the gigantic size of today's Big Tech corporations.

The epidemic of monopolies

To this day, all big digital corporations follow exactly the same pattern that Microsoft successfully implemented. Let us just take a look at various prominent rulings by the European Union:

- ▶ In 2016, the EU initiated proceedings against Google for self-preferencing. Among other things, Google search was already pre-installed on Android smartphones. Google had apparently dictated conditions, imposing restrictions on smartphone manufacturers and mobile network operators. The proceedings have been ongoing since 2016 and a fine of 4.3 billion euros is pending.[13]

- ▶ Another legal case was directed against AdSense, a Google product that allows websites to place ads from advertisers. Google had used exclusivity clauses to eliminate competitors. Put simply: A website that used AdSense was not allowed to obtain ads from AdSense competitors. It would mean another massive case of self-preferencing, which is why a fine of 1.49 billion euros is on the table.[14]

- ▶ Proceedings regarding Google Shopping, Google's price comparison portal, have been ongoing since 2017. Google had also displayed its results with the characteristic display of product photos, prices and links in its normal search above the standard results, thereby exploiting its dominant market position in online searches to outdo other price and product comparison platforms; the fine is estimated to be 2.42 billion euros.[15]

- ▶ Since June 2020, proceedings have been ongoing against Apple and the Apple Pay application because of the underlying near-field communication technology ('tap and go'). This communication between the smartphone and the checkout system can only be used by Apple Pay and not by competing service providers.[16]

- ▶ A complaint by Spotify against Apple is also revealing—because Apple keeps 30 percent of the revenue from Spotify subscriptions on the iPhone for itself. This gives its own music streaming service Apple Music an unassailable advantage over Spotify. Overall, there has been a long-lasting debate as to whether Apple positions its own apps in its App Store better than the offerings of competing providers. The complaint was received in March 2019, so the issue had been unresolved for around four years; these days, a fine of 1.8 billion euros was announced. [17]

- ▶ The EU is also investigating Amazon. The company is accused of systematically exploiting the non-public data of its thousands of retailers, who are actually competitors of Amazon on the Amazon Marketplace. Amazon relented at the end of 2022, which is why the proceedings were discontinued.[18]

The methodology is apparently always the same: tech giants use network effects to gain dominant market positions. They simultaneously secure this dominance and transfer it to adjacent or new markets. In many cases, this approach is illegal. The abuse of their own dominant market positions violates applicable law. In addition, Big Tech giants break the law even though they are fully aware that their actions are illegal. The General Court of the European Union, for example, stated "'that Google's conduct constitutes a particularly serious infringement' of antitrust law and is 'intentional'."[19]

Each of these cases involves hundreds of experts and lawyers, and a differentiated assessment at the level of individual proceedings is beyond my expertise. However, one thing is clear: from the perspective of our scientific measurements, the results of the GAFAM efforts can be interpreted as what they are: the systematic and willful erosion of fair and free competition. This is why all these markets are now occupied by monopolies and oligopolies. The hostile takeover of the tech giants has been a full 'success' for them, even if it is a disaster for the rest of society. Our measurements prove this down to the last detail. We can get an even better idea of the extent of the catastrophe if we quantify the cross-platform formation of dominant market positions at the level of individual companies. Let us take a look at the example of Alphabet.

The overview on the following page once again supplements our descriptions from the first chapter and takes us to the same conclusion from a new perspective: any form of free and fair competition has been completely eliminated in these markets.[20] Alphabet has 'succeeded' in building up dominant positions in around ten other markets, using the strength that originates from its core monopoly, the search engine. The only fascinating exception is Gmail. We now also understand why: because the media genre of email is protected against deadly network effects by open standards.

We find a downright obscene situation in Alphabet's 'Ad Tech Stack', the various services that Google offers to different parties for the placement of online advertising. The topic is so complex that even experts often fail to grasp the ramifications. Put simply: In order for advertisers and providers of web content, typically websites, to find each other, both sides need various tools. One example would be an ad server, by which the individual advertisements are played out. Furthermore, a 'Supply Side Platform' (SSP) is required, where a large number of publishers can offer their content, as well as a 'Demand Side Platform' (DSP), on which advertising companies can offer their requirements for online advertising.

Alphabet, in this case its brand Google, holds dominant positions at all levels of these intermediary services. This means that Alphabet controls both sides of the market, demand and supply.

MONOPOLY WORLD CHAMPION IS ... ALPHABET?
Estimated market shares based on available studies[20]

	MARKET SHARE GERMANY	MARKET SHARE WORLDWIDE
SEARCH ENGINE **Google Search**	Desktop 81% / Mobile 97%	Desktop 80% / Mobile 88%
FREE VIDEO-ON-DEMAND **YouTube**	78%	Info not available
ONLINE MAP SERVICE **Google Maps**	46%	Info not available
E-MAIL **Gmail (E-Mail Clients)**	15%	28%
BROWSER **Chrome**	Desktop 46% / Mobile 49%	Desktop 66% / Mobile 65%
OPERATING SYSTEM **Android**	68%	72%
APP MARKETPLACE **Play Store**	Info not available	by turnover 36% / to downloads 78%
AD SERVER FOR ADVERTISERS **Google Campaign Manager, Google Ads**	40–60%	70–90%*
AD SERVER FOR PUBLISHERS **Google AdManager, DoubleClick for Publishers**	80–100%	70–80%*
ADVERTISING NETWORKS **Google Display Network**	80–90%	70–80%*
DEMAND SIDE PLATFORMS (DSPS) **Google Display & Video 360, Google Ads**	60–70%	60–70%*
SUPPLY SIDE PLATFORMS (SSPS) **Google AdExchange, AdMob, AdSense**	60–80%	50–60%*
TRACKING-TOOLS **Google Analytics**	70–80%	80–90%*

*European Economic Area and UK

The situation is so monstrously absurd that I would like to illustrate it here with an equally absurd comparison. Imagine you want to buy an apartment, but most of the apartments belong to a company called IMMOSUCKER. There are platforms for finding apartments, but they are also owned by IMMOSUCKER. The few remaining providers of apartments that exist can also only offer their properties via an IMMOSUCKER platform. And almost all estate agents on the market work—guess what?—with IMMOSUCKER.

I wish you lots of fun buying your apartment ☺. What do you think your chances are of getting a fair deal here? For better or worse, you are dependent on IMMOSUCKER, who is happily cashing in at every turn you make. There is nothing you can do about it. Sellers and buyers alike are controlled at every single stage of these various transactions. This is also the case in the online advertising market: Google controls all aspects of these processes, supply and demand (!) and can "deliberately play all sides of the market off against each other to its own advantage", according to a conclusive study by Thomas Höppner and Tom Piepenbrock.[21]

Anyone familiar with online advertising should be aware that Google can exploit massive asymmetries and scaling effects for itself here, particularly through privileged access to data and many opportunities of self-preferencing. In addition, the relevant systems are so complex that every company concerned will never change the relevant tools without any need (hence the industry's tendency towards 'single-homing').

You think that I am exaggerating and that it cannot be as bad as described here? It is. Please read the Germany Federal Anti Trust Office's "Sector Inquiry into Online Advertising". Here, the complete meltdown of competition in the ad tech market is described in detail in 232 pages. In the conclusion, the weary experts shrug their shoulders and come to the conclusion that Google is able to shape the competitive process in its favor. And nothing happens (☞ IV.1).

For those who think this is not absurd enough, it is worth remembering that the authorities were also investigating possible illegal non-compete agreements between Alphabet and Meta for some time. According to an arrangement called "Jedi Blue", "Google would give Facebook preferential treatment in terms of ad rates, placements and access to data, in exchange for Facebook distancing itself from an alternative programmatic advertising system called header bidding, which would cut into Google's coffers." However, the EU closed the investigation, possibly due to a lack of evidence.[22]

DIGITAL ADVERTISING AND SERVICES— DOMINANT POSITIONS OF ALPHABET

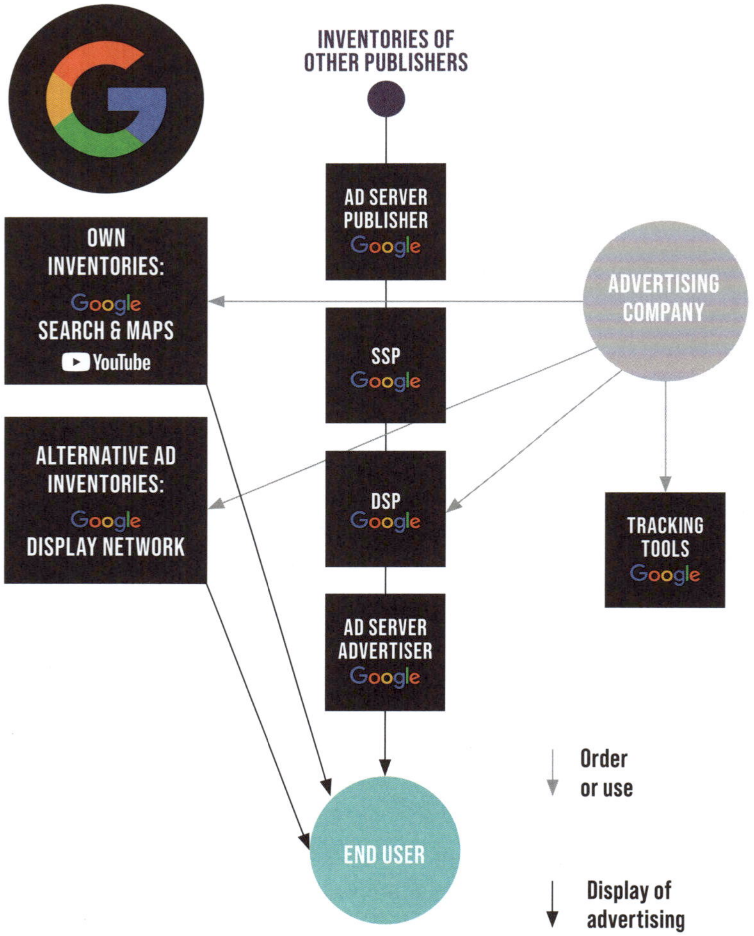

INVENTORIES OF OTHER PUBLISHERS

AD SERVER PUBLISHER
Google

OWN INVENTORIES:
Google
SEARCH & MAPS
YouTube

SSP
Google

ADVERTISING COMPANY

ALTERNATIVE AD INVENTORIES:
Google
DISPLAY NETWORK

DSP
Google

TRACKING TOOLS
Google

AD SERVER ADVERTISER
Google

END USER

↓ Order or use

↓ Display of advertising

4. Killer acquisitions

The easiest way to defend or expand dominant market positions or to occupy new categories is to simply buy existing competitors or technologies through mergers and acquisitions. Such takeovers are also known as 'killer acquisitions'. Big Tech has been extremely 'successful' in this area. The following figures are estimates that have been compiled and aggregated from the various published sources of information, as not all details of many deals are known.[23] After reviewing the available reports, we can assume that GAFAM has bought a total of around 850 companies and invested the astronomical sum of 227 billion US dollars.

If we look at the number of companies acquired, Alphabet and Microsoft are in the lead with around 250 acquisitions each, followed by Apple, Amazon and Meta. Interestingly, a different picture emerges if we break down the shares according to the amount of investment (see overview on the following page). Microsoft is the frontrunner here and is probably responsible for around half of all investments made.

The tech giants often claim that they are innovative inventors. If we examine the acquisitions made by GAFAM, we can quickly debunk this as complete nonsense. Let's take a look at the two lists of the largest and most significant acquisitions, for example. It is immediately apparent that in most cases, Big Tech has simply bought dominant market positions or used them as the basis for its own market conquests. The best known of these are certainly the takeovers of WhatsApp and Instagram by Meta / Facebook respectively. Thanks to WhatsApp, Meta now has a near monopoly on messengers. Thanks to the acquisition of Instagram, Meta holds a near monopoly in the social media sector (around 83 percent share).[24] The acquisition of Oculus VR is likely to be of central importance for Meta's initiatives in the metaverse. This motivation also explains further acquisitions in the field of virtual reality. Overall, most of these acquisitions served the purpose of consolidating and expanding dominance in social media. Finally, Meta's acquisitions in the advertising industry are also significant. One example is Atlas, a planning tool for online campaigns (2013) and the supply side platform LiveRail (2014) which enables publishers to place video ads.

In the early days, Google had a video platform of its own. However, the company was unsuccessful in implementing it. In the final analysis, this was not a problem, as it simply bought YouTube, the platform that today represents a near monopoly for free video-on-demand. Further acquisitions included Android, which provides the backbone for the dominant position in the field of operating systems for mobile devices. The acquisition of DoubleClick gave Google an ideal starting point for its near monopoly in the field of AdTech. Through FitBit, it owns a leading player in the promising field of wearables. On closer inspection, most of Google's 'innovations' turn out to be a combination of various products and technologies they simply bought from outside inventors—such as Google Maps, Google Docs, Google Earth, Google Docs (Writerly) and Google Slides (Tonic Systems).

An important focus of Alphabet has been the systematic acquisition of patents. This was probably also the main motivation behind the acquisition of Motorola. The field of artificial intelligence, where at least 30 companies have been acquired by Alphabet since 2007, is also of central importance for the group's various data-driven business models.

Microsoft acquired the basis for its dominant market position for email software (Outlook) with Hotmail. Furthermore, it bought LinkedIn, the world's leading platform for professional networking. More than half of the acquisitions are in the field of software; other important sectors are cybersecurity and gaming (ZeniMax Media, Mojang, possibly Activision Blizzard). Microsoft also holds shares in OpenAI (Chat GPT).

Amazon acquired a powerful ecosystem in the field of media through a series of takeovers, including Lovefilm, an almost forgotten online video store in 2011, which then formed the basis for the expansion to Amazon Prime. Through the purchase of Twitch it swallowed the leading video streaming portal for gaming. Amazon also acquired the huge film production company MGM (Metro-Goldwyn-Mayer). Furthermore, it expanded its retail empire by purchasing the Whole Foods supermarket chain, further companies such as Zappos (shoes) and other e-commerce providers. Since 2012, Amazon has strongly increased its M&A activities in the area of cloud computing, where it holds a dominant market position.

Apple uses acquisitions to further expand its dominant position in the field of hardware and invests in sectors such as AI infrastructure. Apple was able to use acquisitions in the field of image recognition for facial recognition applications on smartphones, for example PrimeSense. The fingerprint-authenticated payment solution Apple Pay was also made possible by an acquisition (AuthenTec).

GAFAM ACQUISITIONS[23]

COMPANIES (Est.)

Alphabet ▶ 260

Microsoft ▶ 250
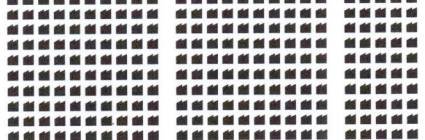

Apple ▶ 130
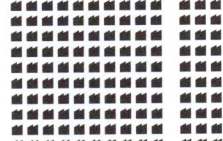

Amazon ▶ 110

Meta ▶ 100

850

INVESTMENTS (Est.)

Microsoft ▶ 110* bn. US $

Amazon ▶ 44 bn. US $

Alphabet ▶ 35 bn. US $

Meta ▶ 28 bn. US $

Apple ▶ 10 bn. US $

227

* excl. Microsoft and Activision Blizzard—announced, but not yet finalized

TOP 10 ACQUISITIONS BY VALUE*[23]

1 Microsoft → 2016 → US $ 26.2 BN → LinkedIn (Social Media)

2 Meta → 2014 → US $ 22.2 BN → WhatsApp (Messenger)

3 Microsoft → 2022 → US $ 19.7 BN → Nuance Communications (AI)

4 Amazon → 2017 → US $ 13.7 BN → Whole Foods (E-Commerce)

5 Alphabet → 2012 → US $ 12.5 BN → Motorola Mobility (Telecommunicati...)

*excl. Microsoft and Activision Blizzard—announced, but not yet finalized

OTHER IMPORTANT ACQUISITIONS[23]

Alphabet → 2008 → US $ 3.1 BN → Double Click today: AdSense (AdTech)

Apple → 2014 → US $ 3.0 BN → Beats Electronic (Hardware)

Alphabet → 2021 → US $ 2.1 BN → Fitbit (Wearables)

Meta → 2014 → US $ 2.0 BN → Oculus VR today: Reality Labs (Wearables)

Alphabet → 2006 → US $ 1.7 BN → YouTube (Video-on-Deman...)

BIG TECH MUST GO!

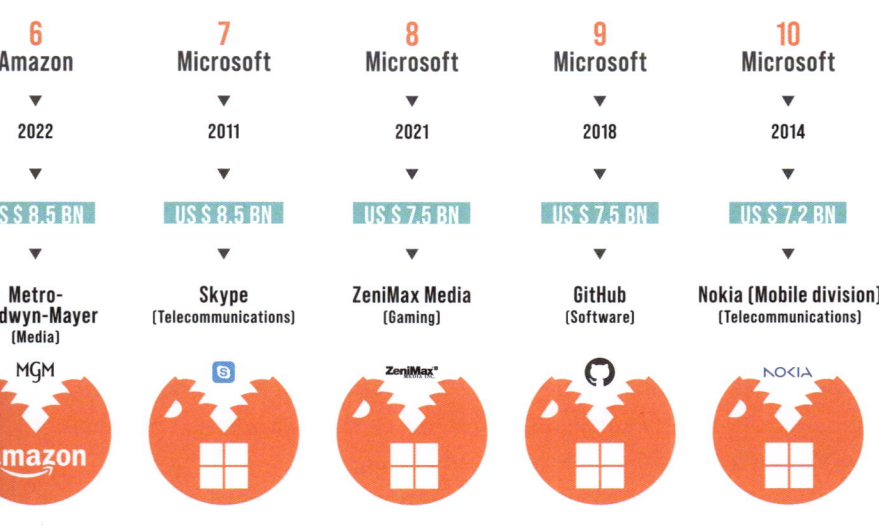

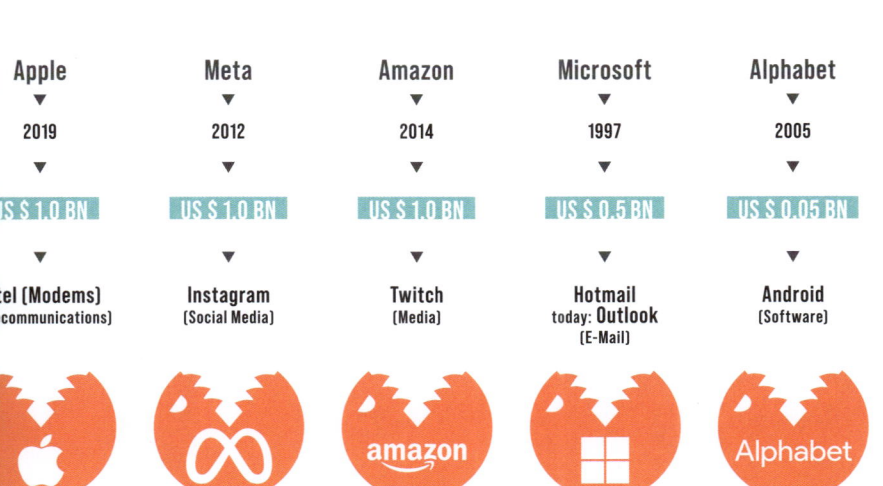

It is quite obvious: Big Tech is not innovating, it is mainly buying innovations. In reality, Big Tech's innovation track record is lousy. But that does not change the status quo, which is particularly depressing because the authorities could have easily stopped most of these takeovers using existing antitrust legislation. If the antitrust authorities had only intervened with a little commitment and determination, it would at least have been possible to prevent monopolistic providers from extending their dominance into a large number of adjacent markets which were just handed over to them without the slightest defense or intervention. Now, in retrospect, there are hardly any legal options to break up the Big Tech companies.

What is particularly fatal about these accumulations is that they lead to a massive self-reinforcing dynamic. The digital giants can now use cross-platform network effects, they can bundle their various products, they can use their own portals and gateways to promote their own products, they can use the data from the various product categories synergistically, they can leverage their user reach to scale their sales, they can boost synergies in terms of costs everywhere, they can combine the expertise from the various categories, they can optimize profitability across various levels of the value chain—and so on.

The diverse and massive leverage and synergy effects are obvious. Any layman can understand that competitors are systematically excluded here. It is hard to imagine how challengers could have even the slightest chance against such superiority. Yet, for decades, the antitrust authorities have been doing nothing to stop this systematic elimination of competition (☞ IV).

5. Self-allocation of Internet traffic

We have used precise analyses to show that there is massive concentration on the internet. We have outlined some of the methods the tech giants have employed to destroy the free media as the basis of Western democracies. Do you still remember our comparison in the first chapter? We said that the structure of Internet diversity resembles the shows put on by autocratic regimes. They feign the existence of competing political parties when you ask them critical questions. They stage free elections. They faithfully explain to the stunned audience that it is simply due to the outstanding successes of their great policies that they always achieve such excellent election results again and again. Clever autocrats will always justify their election victories by pointing to their high popularity, their strong support by the people, their great political programs. They will always claim that they are only concerned about achieving the common good for all. In exactly the same way, the tech giants interpret the dominance of their products as popularity—their services are simply so good that everyone wants to use them.

We would have to catch such actors in the act to prove their harmful actions to the public. We should not just *claim* that autocrats are faking their elections, we would need to measure and prove their wrongdoings with scientific precision. We need *evidence*. This would not be an easy task in elections in autocratically governed countries. For example, you would have to place very courageous researchers in front of many polling stations to ask a lot of people which party they plan to vote for. And they would then have to compare their data with the election results given out by the regime for the same people—in order to prove the election manipulation directly and completely.

As we know, conducting such a scientific study in countries ruled by dictators is almost impossible. The situation is no different for the tech giants. None of the Big Tech corporations would ever allow us to to examine the traffic flows within the black boxes of their own ecosystems. They consistently play with marked cards. In my own life as a researcher, all the requests I have made to digital corporations have always been turned down or simply ignored (which of course does not stop the corporations from talking publicly about 'sharing' or 'transparency' at the same time).

However, despite the lack of transparency on the part of the digital companies, we have managed to provide this proof of traffic manipulation through our own usage measurements. We were able to achieve this thanks to a very complex observation apparatus. I need to briefly explain the basics. It is important to understand that the large platforms play two roles in digital usage behavior. First and foremost, they represent huge accumulations of content that is being consumed by users on the platforms. In this aspect, the platforms are comparable to analog mass media. Television has been replaced by YouTube, for example, print media has been replaced by Instagram or Facebook, and so on. But there is also another aspect that we have to grasp. Through their search functions and links, the platforms also act as gateways. These gateways act as digital distribution points that organize user traffic on the Internet. The Google search engine is certainly the largest of these gateways. Amazon is also increasingly being used as a search engine for products, and large network giants such as Facebook and Instagram are gateways simply due to their huge number of users.

In the first chapter, we established clarity on how unbelievably large the concentration of traffic already is. We can now take an important further step to shed light on the second aspect: the gateway significance of the Big Tech platforms. We need to take this second step as the huge traffic concentrations which we have already shown above are only static: they only show a holistic cross-section of internet traffic. However, our analysis equipment also allows us to display traffic *flows* over time. So we can not only measure how large an offer is at a point in time X—we can also see which offers people are redirected to *after* they have been on a certain app or website. The key question here is of course: So where are they at time Y, *after* using the Big Tech platforms? The results obtained in this regard are even more shocking than the measured market power.

Let us take a look at an example. The chart on the next page shows such a Gephi analysis for the Internet's largest gateway, the Google search engine, again on a representative basis of around 300 million impressions in total.[25] We remember that Alphabet's offerings account for about 18 percent of total usage time—of which around 5 percent is attributable to Google and 13 percent to YouTube.

These values and the values of all other competitors give us a very reliable benchmark. They correspond to the natural preferences that people have *before* they enter the polling booth of the autocratic regime, to explain it in the logic of our comparison. If the autocratic regime was going to distribute the votes fairly, we should be able to assume *that a maximum of about 18 percent of the votes would have to go to Alphabet offers*, while 82 percent should go to the competition.

However, after using the Google search engine, it is not 18 percent, but no less than 35 percent (!) of all users who end up on one of the Alphabet Group's various offerings. Which is almost double the figure we should expect. Mysterious, isn't it? We can also see similarly disproportionate self-allocations if we use YouTube

SELF-ASSIGNMENT OF TRAFFIC-EXAMPLE ALPHABET/GOOGLE[A/25]

Usage time and users per connection

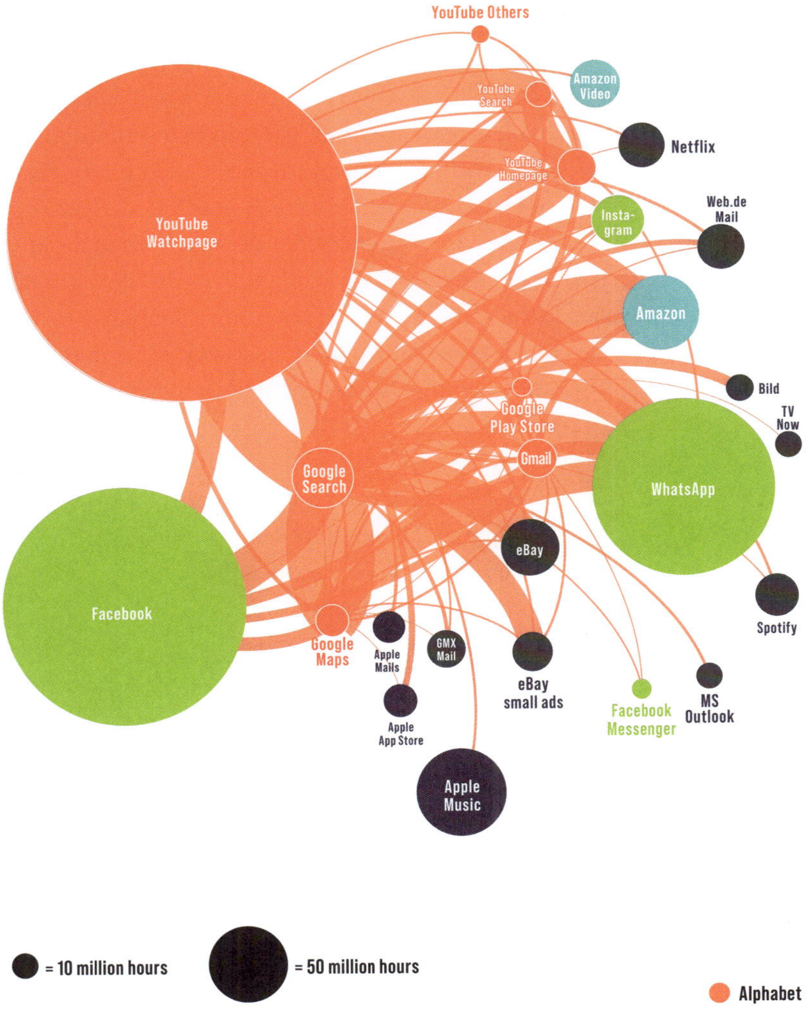

The bubble size represents the total usage time of the offer.
The line thickness shows the number of users.

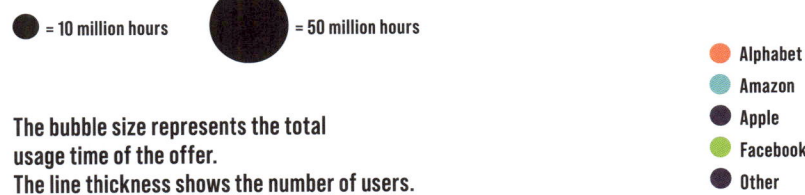

or Google Maps as the starting point for the traffic stream. If we look at the same experimental setup at Meta, we see almost the same results. Meta's share of total online usage here is 16 percent—however, the share of users who are redirected to other offers in its own ecosystem after using Facebook is as high as 36 percent.

Do you realize what is going on here? Let us remember the various victims of the digital monopolies that we mentioned as examples in the first chapter: The digital publishers, the bloggers, the global brand corporations, the public service broadcasters. They are all fully dependent on these gateways. They work hard from morning to night, putting their content online, hoping to gain traffic through the relevance of their posts.

If we look at the results of these measurements, it means that it almost does not matter how relevant their content is. It is relatively irrelevant how exciting their articles are, it hardly matters how attention-grabbing their headline are. They do not have the slightest chance to compete in the long term. Because beyond the already massive network effects, the platforms are also playing with loaded dice. The effects shown here do not show a few percent self-preferencing, but a doubling! This huge, massive detour of traffic cannot be explained by any network effect in the world. Consequently, we must assume that this is a case of deliberate manipulation and pure self-preferencing of traffic.

Do you remember the many cases of criminal monopoly abuse that we described above, using the example of the various antitrust proceedings in the European Union? Where, for example, we talked about self-preferencing in the Apple App Store? We now recognize something important: The practices covered by such court proceedings are only the visible tip of the iceberg. The abuse of monopolies by digital corporations is obviously systematic and probably *affects the entire reality of digital traffic flows*. This is because GAFAM can simply allocate digital traffic to themselves at will because *they have complete control over the gateways*. These are targeted interventions in the traffic flow in order to strengthen their own offerings and actively exclude competitors.

Do you remember how the tech giants have lectured us for decades that our success on the web is simple and just a question of the "relevance" of our content? In Google's own words: "Interesting websites become more popular on their own." It is all very easy, they say. And Google adds: "Useful and engaging content is likely to influence your website more than any other factor [...]. Create new and unique content!"[26] We just need to create great, fascinating and engaging content and the rest will take care of itself? Our measurements show that this is an outright lie, and the tech giants know it. Because they are the ones who simply allocate the traffic to themselves and not to us.

Big Tech has long since destroyed the free internet. Today, it is hard to imagine how we could ever escape their deadly stranglehold. Zero-click content is not a real option, as here we work for free for the platforms. But they also offer us another solution: we can surrender completely, stop running our own domains and go directly to the platforms, which is exactly what the majority of market players have been doing now for years. "No problem at all", the cool autocratic digital rulers murmur into our ears. "Just give us all your content directly. Just move straight into our beautiful, brightly colored cyber prison. Here on YouTube, for example, we have already set up a wonderful cell for you. All your friends are already here—lots of cool people, influencers, bloggers, creators, a super hip community. Put your baseball cap on backwards and be part of our fun gang. Of course, it is clear that you will no longer be free. You will be working for us in the future. But that will have many advantages for you. Because we only have the best in mind for you all."

Normal content providers are being systematically eliminated and 'drained dry' by this dynamic. This development is more than obvious for the many affected media professionals, who have often been barely able to keep their heads above water economically. Without traffic, they die of suffocation. We have been observing this in the market now for many years.

6. Monopoly accelerator: Generative AI

The monopolies of Big Tech are the result of a planned and systematic strategic approach: in an initial phase, millions of users are attracted to create maximum network effects. They are increasingly locked in by the platforms who create barriers to the outside world. These walls are reinforced and become more and more insurmountable. Closed standards and other technological hurdles are created, such as the elimination of outlinks. These actions create a self-reinforcing dynamic. Thus, the platforms fully control all steering mechanisms: They can allocate as much traffic to themselves as they wish by using their own gateways. They can create cross-platform network effects between their various products. There are virtually no limits in terms of exploitation. This turns the platforms into extremely profitable business models. That is why these companies accumulate huge amounts of financial resources that they can invest in acquisitions. These mergers then generate new cross-platform network effects, opportunities for scaling as well as cost synergies. The accumulation of large amounts of data also plays a central role here. The massive increase of usage is flushing ever larger amounts of data into the platforms through the digital feedback channels, which they can interlink and enrich via new layers of the various business models, offers and services.

You can see how hopeless the situation is for new competitors, even if they come up with innovative products or features. The few that succeed are almost always bought up by killer acquisitions (as in the case of Instagram or WhatsApp). And if the owners do not want to sell the business, as in the case of the extremely innovative SnapChat app, all features are simply copied mercilessly by the tech giants over the years. In most cases, this strategy will ultimately bring the competitor to its knees. In most cases, the fight against this multidimensional superiority is hopeless in the long term.

We could mention a number of further aspects. The sheer presence of strong gatekeepers and aggregators is itself promoting concentration, as they typically favor strong market leaders to the detriment of small providers.[27] The result is a self-reinforcing pull towards winner-takes-all markets. Furthermore, a 'cognitive lock-in' takes place through the use of market leaders: The use of an offer becomes a habit, and a change means disproportionate effort for the user. The American media scientist Matthew Hindman has dispelled the myth of supposedly low entry barriers for digital markets and proven that major players invest huge amounts

HOW THE PLATFORMS HAVE DONE AWAY WITH FAIR COMPETITION

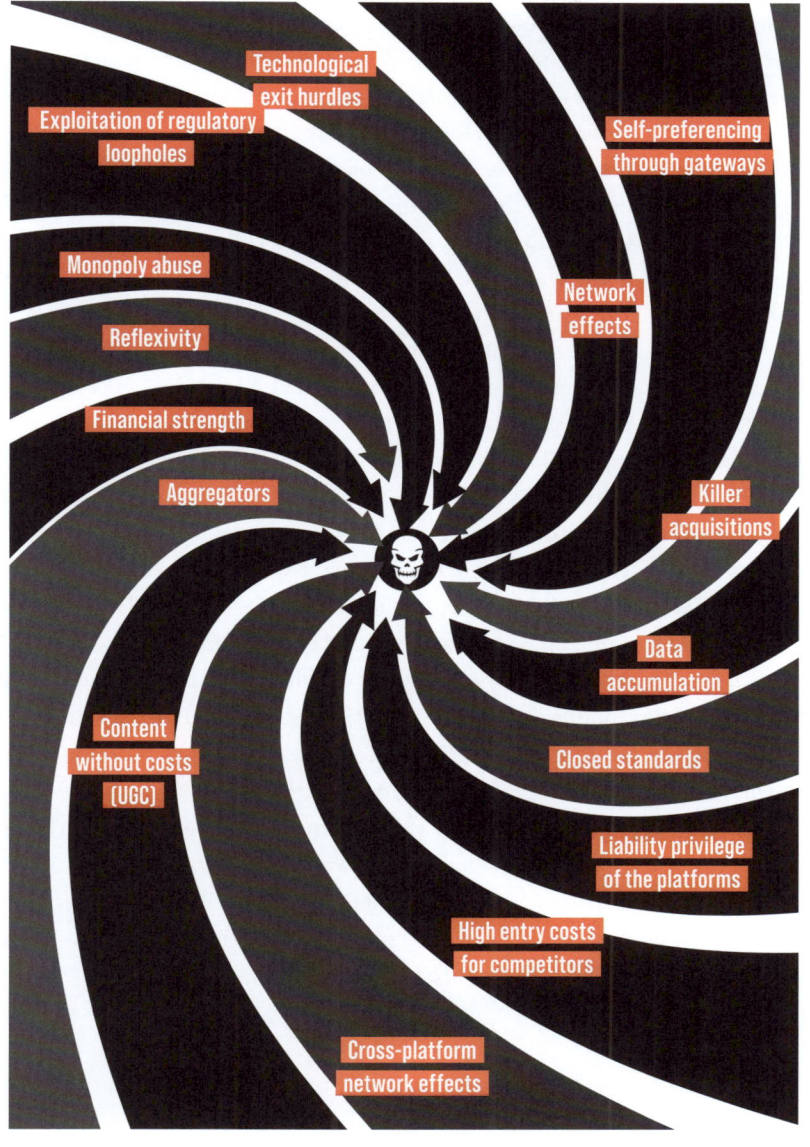

into their technological infrastructure, which often stifles the market entry of potential competitors.[28]

The emergence of generative AI is particularly interesting at the moment, which is why ChatGPT is currently hitting the headlines. Microsoft's involvement shows that Big Tech is also in control when it comes to such new developments. However, one aspect is important: a piece of generative AI can only ever be as good as the content with which it has been 'fed', whether it be images, videos or other types of content. We have seen a tremendous erosion of the value of content over the last ten years due to the rise of platforms. Moreover, we have seen that the structure of this business model reinforces the supremacy of Big Tech by default: they do not have to pay royalties for content, and on top of that, they are exempted from any liability for the very content they monetize. The technologies of generative AI (ChatGPT and others) will further accelerate this dynamic considerably, for a simple reason. With our consent to the terms and conditions of the platforms, we users have granted far reaching rights to the platforms. Thus, the platforms can now exploit this content as they wish. For example, they can train various generative AI applications and services with all this content. The larger the amount of data available for the platforms, the better the performance of the trained AI will be. Once again, the economies of scale of the platforms and the almost unlimited access to data offer an unbeatable starting position for Big Tech.

Fake news, for example, is still created by human authors by the time I am writing these lines. Depending on the content, a human being might need around half a day to produce a fake news article. Generative AI, on the other hand, can potentially create an infinite number of such texts. This future AI will 'not care' whether it produces one fake news article per day or a hundred per second. The feeds of the platforms are already now swamped with posts. Let us imagine a situation in which the amount of all content distributed on social media is multiplied by a factor of, say, ten thousand—and at a cost that tends towards zero. Imagine platforms that can test the impact of these posts in their ecosystems, which in turn continues to 'improve' the performance of each individual post. And don't forget: Platforms can then actually personalize and target each individual post. In a few years, each platform will probably operate its own generative AI technologies, so that the AI can even create personalized posts. And all this without any liability for the content distributed. The future will be exciting, to put it mildly.

CHAPTER III

HOSTILE TAKEOVER:
How digital superpowers change our entire society

1. Death trap: The narrative of weak, vulnerable media

Imagine that, somewhere in Germany, a local or regional government were to take some kind of action against a media operation. Let us assume, a raid were to be carried out on a small local newspaper. Research materials and documents would be confiscated, several journalists would be arrested. Anything even close to such an unlawful attack against our free media by the State, government or politicians would cause a huge scandal. There would be public protests and outcries, calls for resignations of politicians, investigations of public prosecutors. Government officials would immediately distance themselves and promise resolute actions. We can be more than happy that the vast majority of people in our country would entirely reject any attack on the free media today. Freedom of opinion and freedom of the press are protected in our country both by law and by the German people. Fortunately, this was already the case in 1962, when the investigating judge at the German Federal Court of Justice issued orders that led to the notorious police raid at the Hamburg offices of *Der Spiegel* (a major German news magazine) on October 26 on the grounds of alleged 'national treason'. Several *Spiegel* journalists were arrested at the time. The activities of the authorities were triggered by a *Spiegel* report arguing that the German armed forces at the time were too weak to react to possible military aggression from Russia, also due to inadequate equipment. "Conditionally ready to defend" was the title of the article, which also criticized the Secretary of Defense at the time, Franz Josef Strauß.

This intervention created a huge public outcry in Germany. Students and journalists demonstrated on the streets. The German press protested vigorously. When courts and institutions investigated the case, they completely exonerated the *Spiegel*. A large number of political offices and institutions were involved, such as the Federal Public Prosecutor's office in Bonn and the Hamburg Senator of the Interior Helmut Schmidt. The German Chancellor, Konrad Adenauer, also had to explain himself in front of the German Parliament. Several ministers of the Adenauer government protested and resigned from office. Franz Josef Strauß had to leave office, resulting in a government crisis. The Federal Court of Justice acted in favor of the *Spiegel,* followed by the so-called '*Spiegel* ruling' by the German Federal Constitutional Court, which confirmed the importance of the free press for democratic discourse. Further legislative measures were implemented, and so on.

We have already seen that the threat to our media system from digital platforms is not only conceptual or abstract. The hostile takeover of the media system is as real as it is imminent. The facts in the first chapter have been empirically researched down to the last detail, and the dubious methods for systematically eliminating competition in the second chapter have been described just as extensively in scientific research. Why then are we rightly sensitive to possible restrictions on free media when it comes to State intervention? And why are we not at all concerned about the threat to free media posed by the tech giants?

We could even argue that the current threat is much more dangerous compared to what happened in Hamburg in 1962. The scandal of 1962 only affected a tiny part of the media landscape, namely *Der Spiegel*, whereas the advance of the tech giants is threatening our media system as a whole. Even if we fully disapprove of the State's intervention in 1962, we would still have to take into consideration that the responsible authorities of those times acted with democratic legitimacy and in a politically rational way (namely the protection of Germany against a possible military threat from the Soviet Union).

Today, however, it is not about a single magazine or newspaper. It is not about a single television or radio station that would be restricted in its freedom. It is about our media system as a whole. This media system is not being attacked by German institutions, but by a handful of digital giants. In the case of the *Spiegel* affair, democratic processes and structures were immediately put in place in 1962, and the offenders were quickly punished. But today, there is no visible sign of any serious resistance or concern by the responsible authorities or the public. Nobody really cares.

Why is that? How can we explain this bizarre inequality of treatment? First of all, the imminent takeover of our media system by the tech giants is unprecedented in history. That is why we have no mental frameworks, structures or archetypes to guide us. What lies ahead of us is literally unimaginable and inexplicable for us.

In contrast, the entire history of the mass media in general and the press in particular is characterized by one and the same theme, which appears in ever new variations and degrees of severity: *The continuous threat to the freedom of the press and freedom of speech from the power of the State.* Since the publication of the early newspapers in the 17th century, the independence of the press has had to be freed from the control of the State in a fight that lasted for centuries.

This can also be seen in the multifaceted history of press law. For a long time, the subject of press law was not *freedom* of the press, but its exact opposite. Press law was an instrument of repression by the State, "a tool used by rulers to *prevent* printed publications" that "initially served a police function".[1] Even up until the time of the German Weimar Republic, freedom of the press was not constitutionally guaranteed. And we all know what happened afterwards: the subjugation of the media under National Socialism completely destroyed the independence of the press. Editorial offices became the extended arm of State propaganda. All media were controlled by the State. Both the press and radio were subject to Nazi censorship.

After centuries of oppression, intimidation and harassment of the press, in which many journalists were threatened with persecution, prison sentences and death, it is completely understandable that we have recognized as a society how much the media need effective protection from State power. This is why today, we have very differentiated democratic media laws and constitutional guarantees of media freedom in Germany.

> *Freedom of opinion and freedom of the press*
>
> **German Constitution (Grundgesetz), article 5, paragraph 1:**
> "Everyone has the right to freely express and disseminate their opinions in speech, writing and pictures and to inform themselves without hindrance from generally accessible sources. Freedom of the press and freedom of reporting by radio and broadcasting are guaranteed. Censorship does not take place."

The media therefore serve a democratic purpose. In the first place, they create our democratic public sphere, a free market of information and opinions. The process of political decision-making, which in turn enables our democratic representation in elections, can only work if citizens are able to obtain information from a variety of independent sources. The independence of the media is a so-called 'serving freedom' because it fulfills the democratic function of enabling the forming of opinions. This is precisely why the principle of independence from the State is mandatory. Only free media can the perform their democratic function as a 'watchdog' of power, politics and the State.

The media sphere must therefore be protected in all circumstances from any conceivable inference by the State. It must never be controlled by politicians as a means to maintain power. Our media law fulfils the function of a protective wall, defending the territory of the media against any instrumentalization by politics and power. Within this protected zone, the media can develop freely and independently.

Our free media are threatened—but this time not by the State

We have seen that, for centuries, media were suppressed, harassed and censored by the state. In addition, in Germany we have experienced the full control of media during the Nazi regime and its catastrophic consequences for the world. Against this backdrop, it is both reasonable and necessary that we understand the vulnerability of the media to State intervention. In this sense, we have done an excellent job to protect the media in our democracy against control or access by political parties and State influence. Fortunately, another *Spiegel* scandal would be unthinkable in Germany today. Unfortunately, history repeats itself again and again, but not always in the same way. The dangers are often not lurking where you would think they are. How else could it happen that the invasion of our media system by Big Tech is taking place in broad daylight, right before our eyes? How can we explain that the digital giants are systematically taking over the territory of the media without us noticing?

The problem is that we do not perceive the current danger because we lack mental templates to quickly grasp what is going on. Imagine a castle that is armed with strong means against a possible enemy attack. It has a huge moat, staggered ramparts and thick defensive walls. Heavily armed soldiers patrol the battlements and towers. Everything is attuned to a certain enemy concept: the attacker who comes storming out of the woods to besiege the castle and force it to surrender by force. But this concept of the enemy is outdated. While the castle's inhabitants are busy scanning the horizon for possible attackers on the battlements, the completely new enemy has long since streamed through the wide-open castle gates in their hundreds, undetected, in the middle of the day quietly moving into the rooms inside the castle.

Metaphorically speaking, this is exactly what is happening to us right now. The digital giants taking over our media system no longer want to play the role that we have assigned to the media in a democracy. According to their own digital ideology, they see themselves as revolutionaries who want to replace an old, outdated analog world order with their new, supposedly 'better' digital order. Editorial offices, institutions, political bodies, state authorities—in their eyes, all of this belongs to the trash can of history anyway (☞ V.1–2). These new digital media do not see themselves as weak or subservient, especially not towards the State. They want to be the boss themselves. They do not want to be told anything by institutions, authorities, politics or society. They simply do not care. A figure like Elon Musk epitomizes the new paradigm.

At the same time, they cynically exploit our thought pattern of the weak and subservient media which have to be protected against evil interference. In fact, the tech giants have even extended this narrative in two dimensions. These two points are constantly repeated like mantras by the digital corporations in all political debates:

First, you could argue that the platforms themselves are even more free than the current media in one single aspect. Over the centuries, the media have increasingly emancipated themselves from the authorities. They became more diverse and more democratic. From the outset, the platforms have seen themselves as an organic extension of exactly the same process. They repeatedly emphasize that they have finally given all users an authentic voice for the first time. Any person, no matter how insignificant, is now able to communicate directly to a potential audience of millions (which is true on the one hand, but on the other hand this is now controlled by the digital giants). Consequently, the platforms have always seen themselves as facilitators of a new and more fundamental type of freedom of expression—also to counteract any form of possible content regulation.

The second mantra of the digital corporations is repeated as persistently: They are not actually media or media companies at all, but even less than that, namely 'only' platforms, so-called 'intermediaries' or, in the US, 'internet service providers'. We need to listen *very* carefully here. The digital corporations are not just saying that they are as vulnerable and weak as the other media. They go even further: *they are even less important than the weak media, they are 'just' a platform, 'just' an intermediary.* Why do they repeat this so often? Because, if we accept their argument, they can no longer be held legally responsible for the content. This is why they enjoy our protection in two dimensions. First, like the editorial media, they enjoy protection against state censorship and control. But *in addition* to this protection, they also enjoy the unique liability privilege that exempted platforms from any responsibility for content in Section 230 of the US Communications Decency Act since 1996. We will also come back to this (☞ IV.2).

The situation is indeed bizarre. In case of Big Tech, we are dealing with the largest media companies in the world, they have stock market valuations of many hundreds of billions of dollars. For two decades, these companies have been systematically squeezing the existing Western media companies out of the market. But the same media companies claim that they are not really media companies at all. Imagine if Volkswagen were to claim that it is not a car manufacturer or if Deutsche Bank were to say that it is not really a bank at all.

On the following pages we will perform an acid test relating to this assertion—and here is already the reveal: We will find that the exact opposite is the case.

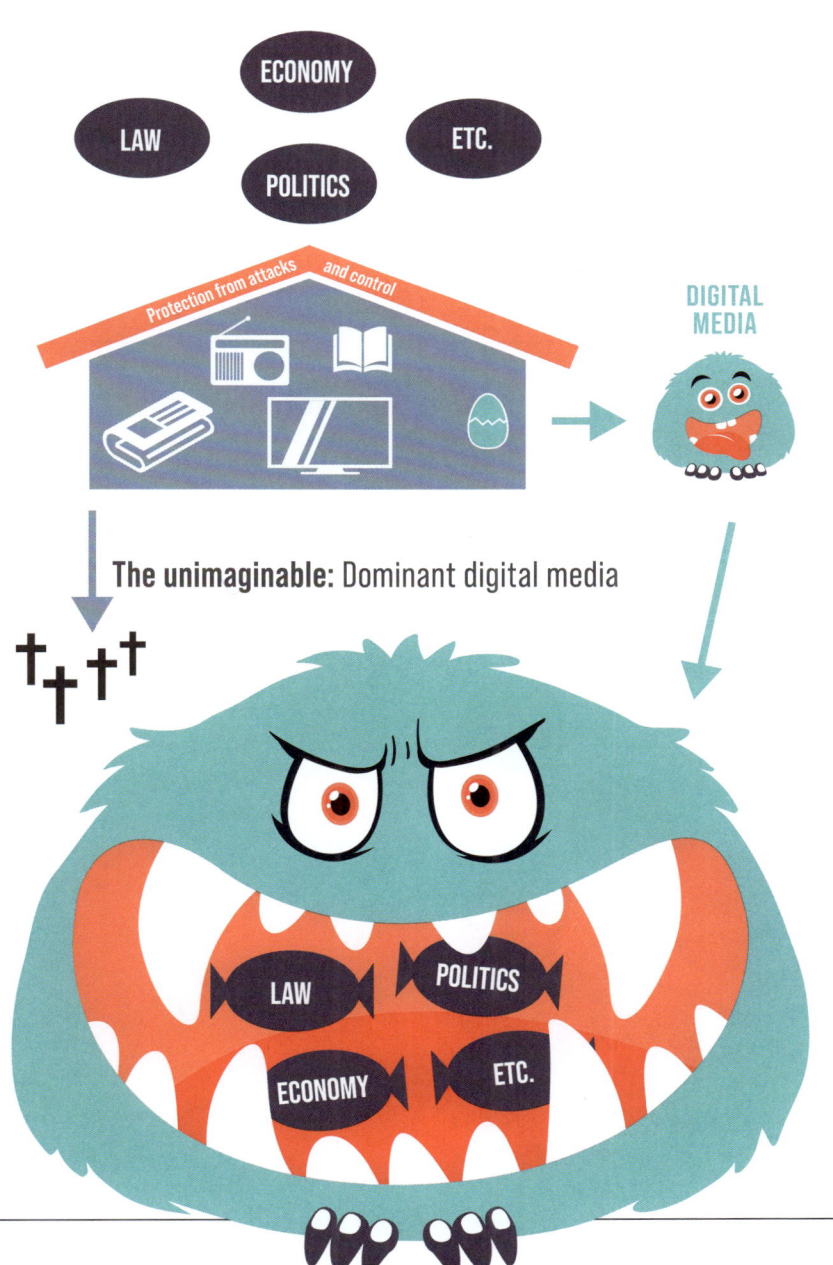

2. How Big Tech will take over the economy

While the digital corporations exploit the various protective mechanisms that ensure the independence of the media in the countries of the Western world, they simultaneously claim that they are not even media, but 'only' platforms. This is nonsense, even based on a very superficial assessment. First of all, it is obvious that social media, for example, are important media offerings for people today,

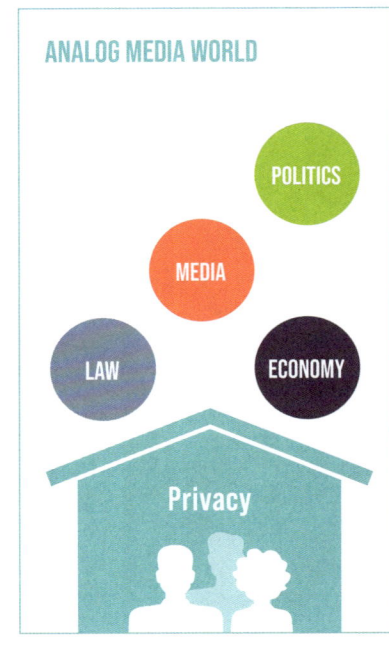
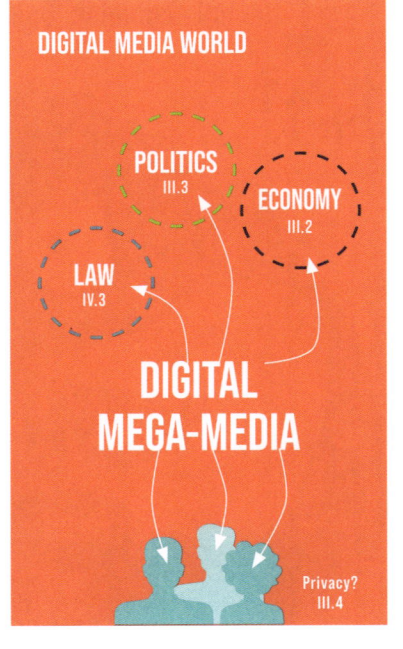

just as it was the case with radio or television in the 20th century. Ironically, as we will see in the following pages, these new mega-platforms are much *more* than just media. These new digital mega-media and their powers reach far beyond the sphere of analog media.

Let us compare the analog media with the new, digital media. It is immediately apparent that the analog media sphere used to be more clearly demarcated and separated from other areas of society. In analog times, this also created a balancing separation of powers, which implied important 'checks and balances'. We can use the term 'takeover' again here to show how the platforms' approach is changing our world. We will see that digital corporations have succeeded in sucking large parts of our social reality into the gravitational fields of their platforms. They are reaching into areas that the mass media previously had virtually no access to: the sphere of the economy, the sphere of politics and, in particular, into the private sphere of every individual (see the illustration on the previous page). On the following pages, we will take a closer look at how these relationships are now changing.

The intrusion of platforms into our privacy is certainly of greatest importance for our society. However, this book is primarily about the destruction of the free world by the tech giants. In this process, the intrusion of the platforms into the economic sphere is probably of even greater importance due to their incredible accumulation of economic power. This is why we are taking this as the starting point of our argumentation here.

Digital media as the basis for economic transactions

All tech giants generate most of their revenues in the media sector. If we compare this category with other economic fields, we have to realize that the size of the media market is not really outrageously big. If we look at Germany, the market value only amounts to 48 billion euros (2022). In contrast, the retail sector is much larger at about 589 billion euros (2021). The turnover in the automotive industry is 411 billion euros (2021).

Should we not be skeptical here? According to the key point made in this book, digital corporations are supposedly destroying democracy and economies. How is this possible if they are operating in a rather insignificant economic field? How would companies that are only active in such a small market sector supposed to be a threat to us? Even if you add the smartphone market to the equation, it does not change much (the market size for smartphones in Germany is expected to reach 11 billion euros in 2021).

In fact, we need to ask the question in a different way. If the tech giants are only present in a relatively small market, why on earth are they achieving astronomical valuations on the capital markets—valuations so high that they are now beyond human comprehension?

We can quickly resolve this apparent contradiction if we focus on the role of digital platforms in generating purchases and in all kinds of economic transactions. In the analog world of the 20th century, manufacturers who wanted to sell their products typically used mass media such as television or magazines to advertise their products. But that was already the end of the media's role. There was an unbridgeable gap between the media and the common forms of transactions. Consumers saw advertisements in the media sphere, but they made their purchases in completely different places, in the supermarket, for example, in the drugstore or in the shoe store.

Digital media have fundamentally changed this situation. Thanks to e-commerce, economic transactions (i.e. purchases) now take place *in the same digital media sphere* that also transmits traditional media content. What's more, the transition to economic transactions is seamless on the Internet. Wherever I am on the Internet, the possibility of a conversion, i.e. the transfer of my media usage into the *purchase* of any conceivable good, is always just a single click away.

It is now crystal clear why capital markets and investors who care mainly about the future of our economies believe that digital companies have this unimaginable potential. And it is also clear that we should no longer estimate the market in which the digital groups are active in Germany at a meager 50 billion euros, but that the entire retail volume of almost 600 billion euros is the potential prey of the digital groups.

The ongoing digital transformation will continue to massively shift the situation in favor of Big Tech. If we look at the sales development of the largest retail company in Germany, at the moment Edeka, and place Amazon next to it, we can assume that Amazon is likely to become the largest retail company in Germany in the next decade (i.e. online and offline combined). It is just a matter of time.

Digital media as Trojan horses to conquer other markets

The first, key insight is therefore that the media market merely serves as a Trojan horse for the tech giants. As a result of digitalization, the gap between media and transactions that existed in the analog world has been completely eliminated. This is why the digital 'touchpoints' have a completely different value for investors and capital markets than the analog ones. Thus, the media market is currently changing its nature in a fundamental way. In the future, it will no longer be limited to the currency of analog media ('attention'), *but will increasingly encompass the entire sphere of economic transactions.* As a result, this market is massively increasing its economic value. This happens automatically with every year of the ongoing digitalization process—without the dominating tech giants having to do anything. Which in turn also automatically increases the stock market value of Big Tech.

The implications of this transformation process are not only affecting the retail sector, which is why all brick-and-mortar retailers have been feverishly expanding their e-commerce presences for years. Digital disruption is equally affecting all companies that produce goods that are currently sold in the various retail channels.

Simply put yourself in the shoes of the producers. Whether it is household appliances, clothing, furniture, shoes, chocolate or shampoo—they all see their offline sales melting away faster than the ice in the Arctic. More and more transactions are taking place online. They all know that, in the future, digital channels will be key. The top-selling categories in German online retail are currently clothing, electrical goods and telecommunications, hardware and software, household goods and appliances, furniture, shoes and books.³

The producers have no choice: They also have to succeed in the digital sphere. There are two possible strategic alternatives available to them: Either they go where the traffic already is. Then they automatically end up on the leading platform, which is Amazon. Or they can try to set up their own webshop. But this is risky in two dimension. First, they are creating a huge channel conflict with their traditional retail partners, as they would directly compete against them with their direct online sales. Second, they are exposed to the same 'winner-takes-all' dynamic due to which nearly all independent offers end in the huge digital graveyard as we have shown (☞ I).

Do you realize what is happening here? Strategically, these huge corporations are faced with exactly the same choice between plague and cholera as the bloggers in our first chapter: either they try to succeed independently online, which is extremely costly and difficult given the concentration of traffic. Naturally, almost all such attempts result in failure. Or they give up and go exactly where the traffic already is. For bloggers, for example, that could be YouTube, for corporations, it is Amazon. But on Amazon, the brand manufacturers are again fully dependent on the platform, which can unilaterally dictate all terms and conditions. The more successful they are here, the greater their total dependence on Amazon. Anyone who has painstakingly built up traffic, followers and transactions on a mega-platform over many years is effectively locked in and must not mess with such a platform under any circumstances. The risk of losing everything and having to start from scratch is far too great.

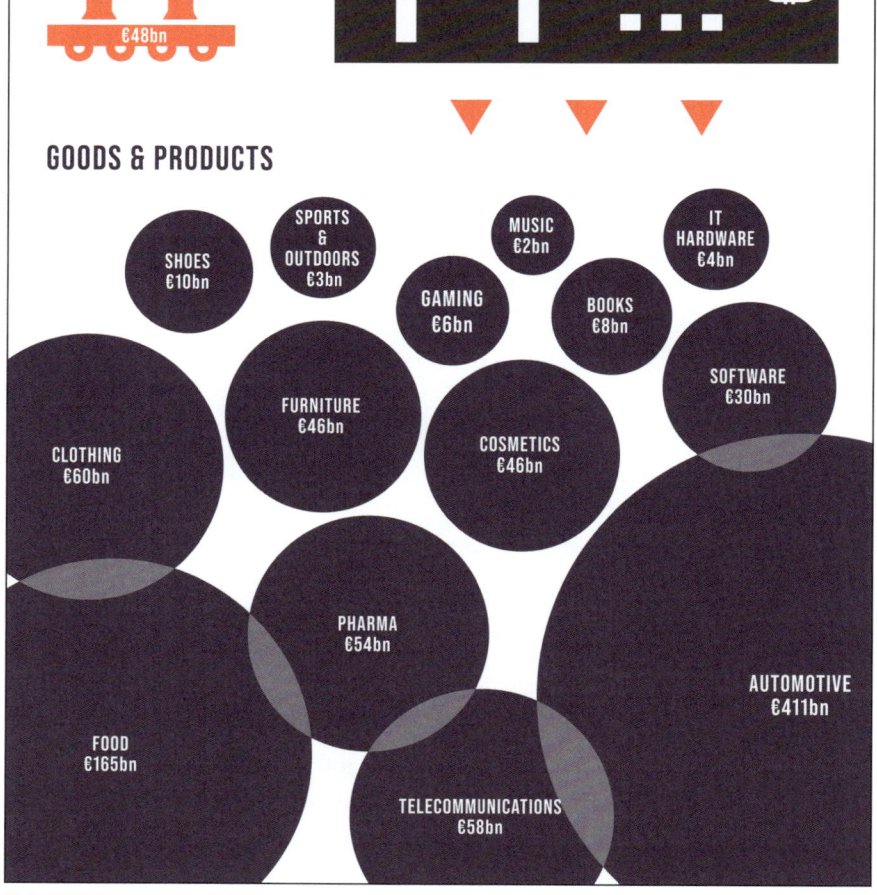

If you think that this form of dependency is already asymmetrical enough, wait a few minutes as there is more to come. First of all, manufacturers are faced with an additional disadvantage concerning data access. Once again, the mechanics of plague and cholera are in full effect. If manufacturers take the easy way out and offer their goods where the traffic already is (on Amazon), they will not be able to access any consumer data. Indeed, all transactions for their products generate a huge amount of useful data, but this remains with—well, guess who? Exactly, with Amazon. All manufacturers who sell their products there are only increasing Amazon's treasure trove of data with their own activities.

Once again, the only alternative is to have your own webshop, with all its disadvantages and the risk of ending up in the infinite graveyard of unused online offerings, just like the bloggers. Due to the dramatic threat to their business models, many global consumer goods companies have made astronomical investments in recent years to buy up smaller online companies that had managed to build successful business models with direct online sales (D2C, i.e. 'Direct-to-Consumer').

Despite the huge investments, to my knowledge hardly any manufacturer is satisfied with the development of these companies after the business integration.[4] Even the chosen route of not building up their own online presences themselves over the years, but buying them in via costly acquisitions, cannot overcome the

ACQUISITIONS OF DIGITAL INNOVATORS BY OFFLINE PLAYERS

	UNILEVER	PUIG	DR. OETKER	HENKEL	COTY
	US $ 1.0 bn	US $ 1.5 bn	€ 1.0 bn	€ 300 m	US $ 600 m
	Dollar Shave Club	**Charlotte Tilbury**	**Flaschenpost**	**Banana/HelloBody**	**Kylie Cosmetics**
Annual turnover:	US $ 150 m	US $ 140 m	€ 200 m	€ 100 m	US $ 125 m
Sales multiple	6.7	10.7	5.0	3.0	4.8

Source: AMP Digital Research, own research and estimates based on publicly published information

deadly pull of the digital monopolies. To emphasize this again and again: In a tragic way, the situation is the same for individual 'small' bloggers as it is for huge, globally active corporations.

Now that we recognize the extent of the problem, we can bring the various threads of our argument together and show how the digital groups will be able to exploit the huge potential that will simply fall into their laps in the coming years. As they operate unchallenged monopolies or oligopolies, these companies can just keep on booming simply as a result of the ongoing digital transformation—*without having to make any effort whatsoever*. They will only have to cash in all the revenues that the other market participants lose.

Thus, the dominance of tech giants in the media market is the Trojan horse that will help them to take over ever larger parts of our economy in the coming years. We will understand the extent of the problem once we have analyzed the sales funnel for the future digital economy.

The tech giants' monopolies dominate the sales funnel

Every potential buyer of a product goes through a kind of funnel, which we can explain here according to the common AIDA model (Attention—Interest—Desire—Action). At the top of this funnel, the consumer's attention is still diffuse and unspecific. Advertisers only try to communicate core messages such as the product name and rough performance features ('Attention'). Ideally, it is gradually possible to interest the user in the product. At this level, contact with further advertisements leads to a deeper and more intensive engagement with the product ('Interest'), which is then increasingly converted into a desire to buy ('Desire') and ideally leads to a conversion ('Action') at the lower end of this funnel.

The model is illustrated by the metaphor of the funnel, because every advertiser has to address a very large number of people 'at the top', at the level of superficial attention, simply because lots of potential consumers drop out on their way 'downwards' through the funnel towards the transaction. In many cases, advertisers have to generate tens of thousands of contact points with potential consumers at the top of the funnel in order to generate a single product order.

The more economic transactions take place on online channels, the greater is the *disproportionate shift of advertising to digital media channels*—again for a very simple reason. In contrast to analog channels, it is possible for advertisers to address highly specific potential buyers digitally (via targeting). They can also systematically pull them further and further down the funnel through precise tracking (e.g. using pixels or UTM parameters) until a purchase is finally made.

For example, manufacturers can select consumers in the upper funnel who have watched a video ad for a relatively long time (which is an indicator of interest). For this subgroup, they can use retargeting ads (in other words, the renewed display of precisely tailored ads that contain additional purchase arguments) to move them down towards a purchase, which can then be done with a click. This cycle is constantly reinforcing itself: the increasing trend towards online transactions is leading to a *disproportionate increase in the shift of advertising investments to digital channels*, which in turn leads to more online transactions.

Advertisers (as well as their media agencies) can only carry out this targeting or retargeting on the basis of anonymized and aggregated data from the platforms. On the other hand, the platforms themselves (Facebook, Instagram, YouTube or Google) have extensive data access to every single advertising contact with regard to all conceivable aspects of individual user behavior. Each individual campaign by the advertisers only increases the data accumulation of the digital corporations, naturally at the expense of the advertisers (i.e. manufacturers of goods), who even pay the tech giants additional money for this.

Each individual tech giant develops its respective 'galaxy' in this funnel. These digital ecosystems typically emerge out of the respective core competencies. Offerings such as streaming, video-on-demand and social media tend to be in the upper funnel. In contrast, the Google search engine is the key touchpoint in the lower funnel. For example, if a user enters "buy kettle" as a search query on Google, he is already close to making a transaction. It is also clear that the closer an ad can be correlated with a purchase, the higher the costs will be for the advertiser. The transaction itself is at the bottom of the funnel—for example, when an advertised product or service is ordered online from Amazon or a booking platform.

We can now quickly assign the offerings of the three largest tech giants to this funnel (see illustration): First of all, Alphabet has a leading offering in the upper funnel through its video-on-demand platform YouTube. It also occupies the most important gateway at the bottom of the funnel through the Google search engine and its various extensions (i.e. Google Maps). The key factor to note is that the data of individual users from both major platforms converge at one and the same tech giant. The strong pillar of Gmail provides an additional extension. Here too, Alphabet can read user-specific information from every single email sent and aggregate it with the data records from Google Search and YouTube.

Alphabet's business model therefore relies entirely on advertising. In this aspect, it is similar to its competitor Meta, which also generates its revenue almost exclusively from advertising. The difference is that Meta relies entirely on social media (Facebook, Instagram) and also has a quasi-monopoly in the field of instant messaging (WhatsApp). Meta is also similar to its competitor Alphabet

THE FUNNEL INVASION
Dominant market positions of Big Tech in the sales funnel

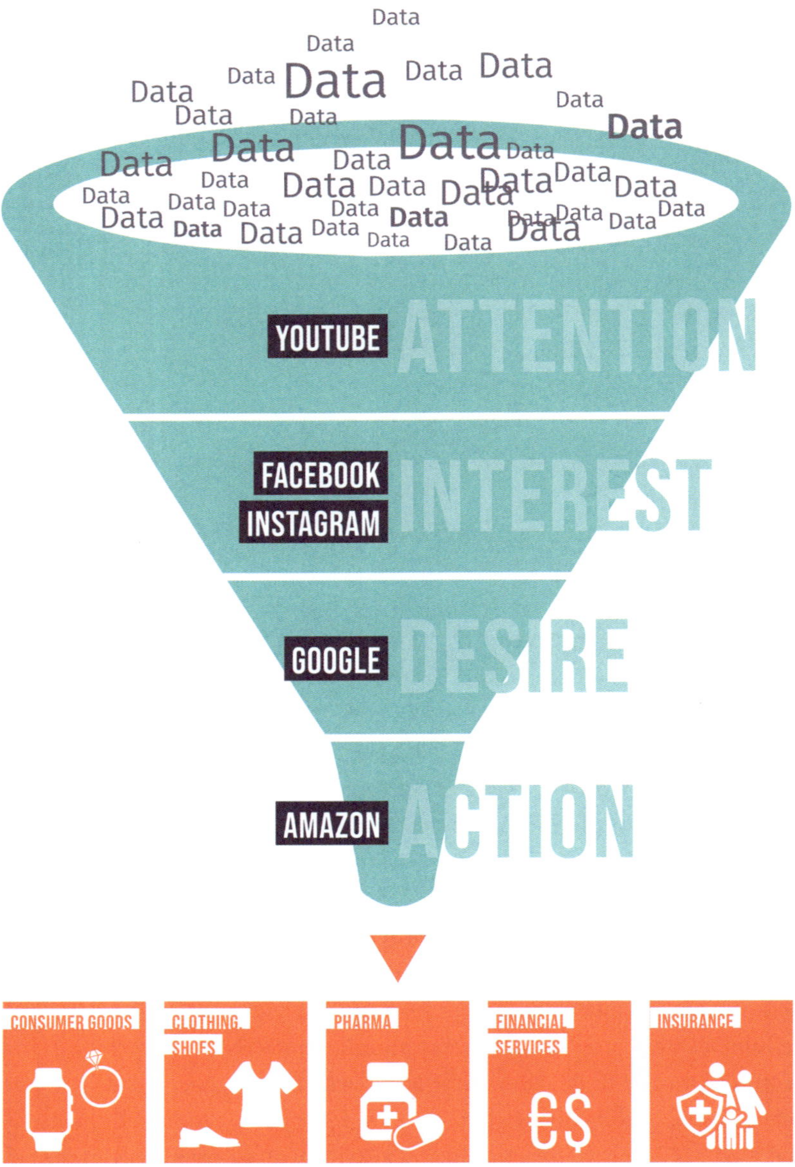

Data Data Data Data Data Data Data Data Data Data Data Data Data Data Data Data Data Data Data Data Data Data Data Data Data Data Data Data Data Data Data Data Data Data Data Data Data Data Data

YOUTUBE — ATTENTION

FACEBOOK / INSTAGRAM — INTEREST

GOOGLE — DESIRE

AMAZON — ACTION

 CONSUMER GOODS
 CLOTHING / SHOES
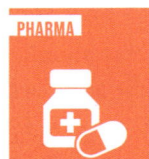 PHARMA
 FINANCIAL SERVICES
 INSURANCE

in its ability to aggregate large volumes of personal data across the three major platforms.

In this direct comparison, Amazon's third profile is particularly interesting because it is constructed in a completely different way. In the funnel, Amazon rolls up the field from the bottom. Its core business is online shopping, which is also where the company generates the majority of its sales. However, by creating the platform as an incredibly rich content universe for products, Amazon is also increasingly a search engine for products, surpassing Google in this field. At the same time, advertisers can book ads on the platform itself ('retail media'). Furthermore, Amazon is building a strong empire of its own in the upper funnel, both for fee-financed (Amazon Prime) and free video-on-demand (IMDb, twitch.tv). These platforms have a positive spillover effect on online shopping. In addition, they generate an increasing share of the Group's revenues.

Now that we have put all the pieces of the puzzle together, we can see a clear picture: The monopolies and dominant market positions of digital companies dominate the entire sales funnel from the very top to the lowest point, the purchase of the product. This finding is dramatic. *In the future, the majority of all economic transactions in our society will be processed through this digital sales funnel. The monopolies of the mega-platforms completely dominate the entire digital sales funnel.*

How the tech giants will bring other economic sectors under their control

We can now see clearly to what extent the strategic approaches of these companies are optimized down to the last detail. At the same time, it is clear how each individual tech giant uses the dominant positions of its respective core categories as leverage to capitalize on them as broadly as possible and extend them vertically, on the one hand through cross-platform network effects and on the other through the unfair abuse of existing dominant market positions. We have already shown how Alphabet has extended its original dominance of the search engine to around ten other adjacent business areas (☞ II.3). We can expect exactly the same dynamic from all tech giants in the future.

Of course, they try to achieve the strongest possible synergetic spillover effects between various sectors in order to generate additional positive, self-dynamic growth. It is difficult to imagine how competitors would have even the slightest chance of entering these markets without any of these leverage effects. The mega-platforms have systematically occupied the future digital sales funnel of our economy in a similar way as hundreds of years ago, a handful of colonial powers divided up the entire world among themselves. The territories are now taken, and anyone who steps onto the scene now is twenty years too late.

It is now also clear why the top 3 giants, Alphabet, Meta and Amazon, account for between 80 and 90 percent of all digital advertising investments globally (excluding China). As there are hardly any other relevant competitors existing in this funnel, this is only logical. In the future, they will be able to verticalize their dominant market positions at will—i.e. expand their dominance along the value chain. The most obvious and easiest step is to develop seamless interfaces from the platforms to e-commerce. This step has already been taken: Platforms from Facebook or Instagram to TikTok are extending their offerings into the area of online shopping with marketplaces, stores and their own payment options.[5]

The next logical step is for the mega-platforms to exploit their largely exclusive access to data in order to manufacture products themselves. Once again, the harvested data becomes an accelerator for the development of dominant market positions. This is because the platforms have billions of data points on every category from aquariums to sofas. They know all preferences, all demands, all desires. They know which features are most attractive, they can analyze all this data demographically—for example, they can recommend the right frying pan for a certain age group, a certain region, a certain household income and so on. They even know which advertising messages convert best. The more data the platforms accumulate, the less they will need products from brand manufacturers in the future. They akready know much more about any given category than most brand manufacturers, who have built up their expertise over decades. Big Tech can simply pick the bestselling brands, copy them, also utilizing their data, and have them produced by contract manufacturers themselves.

FUN FACT: Amazon already offers around 140 own brands.

Again, this is not a dystopian outlook concerning future scenarios. The transformation has already started. The e-commerce experts at Amalytix estimate that Amazon has a total of about 140 brands of its own, also demonstrating the dominant visibility of the 'Amazon Basics' product range on the platform.[6] Amazon is showing how tech giants will be able to increase the value of data vertically in ever new levels of value creation in the future.

The implications for the future of the economy are massive. First, the tech giants can easily nullify any possible advantage of traditional manufacturers in terms of know-how and expertise through their access to data. They have a huge ecosystem of low cost contract manufacturers out there in the market that they can use to produce their own goods. This in turn increases the price pressure on traditional producers. All of this is happening in a context of saturated markets that have barely been growing in Western countries for many years.

A massive substitution of value creation will therefore take place in the coming years. Sociologist Philipp Staab emphasizes the considerable price pressure, "which for manufacturers must feel like the unpleasant materialization of the total competition that classical liberal economics had always dreamed of". It is important to note that this transformation does not entail a greater quantity of goods that would be consumed. In fact, Western markets have hardly been growing since many years. It means that already existing consumption is being better organized—which reduces the value earned by manufacturers and increases the profit extraction of Big Tech. Our economy will increasingly be transformed into a pure procurement machine and supply chain for Big Tech. This is because the platforms are increasingly controlling access to the market and are therefore able to "set their own margins at will".[7]

Once again, the metaphor of the take*over* neatly describes what is happening: Big Tech has established its monopolies *on top of* the traditional economy and now fully controls the digital sales funnel. The platforms sit like gigantic parasites on the huge bodies of the Western economies, from which they can extract as much value as they like in the digital future. All of this is happening while the mega-platforms claim that they need to be 'protected' as they are as weak and vulnerable as media, and moreover: that they are 'only' platforms, intermediaries or service providers, which is supposed to be even less than 'only' media.

3. Why politicians will be dependent on platforms in the future

The consequences of digital media for politics have been described in many studies. Most critics agree that we are currently experiencing an alarming erosion of the political public sphere, leading to various manifestations such as fake news, hate speech, conspiracy theories and an increasing polarization of the various groups which form our society. As a result, what Habermas described early on as an inclusive and deliberative public sphere is increasingly breaking down. The basis for the formation of opinions in Western democracies is collapsing.[8] But how are the platforms managing to take control of areas of society that lie beyond their 'actual' field of the media—such as politics?

Let us approach this question from the perspective of politicians who rely on the media to convey their political content or programs to the public. It is quite fascinating to see that the platforms create a similar dilemma for politicians as the one we already described for media companies, bloggers or manufacturers. Most of today's leading politicians rose to prominence at a time when the analog media were still the leading media. According to this media logic, it is key that the press reports about you and your program, that you appear in talk shows and so on—these were the most important currencies of visibility. Under analog conditions, this visibility was largely dependent on the gatekeepers in the editorial media.

In analog times, the politicians and the media had to cooperate with each each other. Their symbiotic relationship has been described very well by academic research: Journalists give politicians visibility in the media system, and in return, politicians give journalists exclusive access to information that can be 'sold' in the media market as 'news'. This symbiosis has always been endangered by potential corruption. On the one hand, politicians have been trying to instrumentalize the media. On the other hand, dominant media moguls such as Rupert Murdoch have been able to abuse their power to influence politicians and governments in their favor.[9]

Here, too, digital media are bringing about a change that at first sight seems to be positive: They are enabling politicians to communicate directly with citizens, bypassing the editorial media.[10] But politicians face the same choice between plague and cholera as bloggers, influencers or manufacturers. Due to the media monopolies, it is hard for them to be successful on their own, free and independent domains. This approach would also be virtually hopeless, as the majority of traffic is in the closed silos of the platforms. It is therefore not surprising that they also avoid the gigantic graveyard of unused websites and are active mainly on the platforms—that is, on Facebook, Instagram and X—with the same dependence on Big Tech as the other players we already examined.

Political agenda setting on the platforms

The increasing presence of politicians on platforms has a very dangerous side effect. It automatically erodes editorial media, and not just in terms of usage time. Politicians now have the choice of broadcasting the 'news' that they create themselves, simply by posting them on their own channels on the platforms. This means that they are able to reap the rewards of their own prominence themselves, in the form of views, likes, followers and shares. They can grow their digital celebrity here without letting the editorial media participate. Or to put it another way: they can now exploit the 'media value' of their political prominence completely by themselves. However, the monetary reward for the bundled attention once again ends up with the platforms that earn good money with politicians' content. Why? Because they can monetize these valuable components of their 'program' wonderfully through advertising. Accordingly, we find a similarly symbiotic 'deal' as the one we described for the editorial media, but with three important differences. First, this deal leads to *direct* profits for the platforms. Second, the politicians are now dependent on the monopolies. Third, the more present politicians become on the platforms, the more this reduces the editorial media's claim to exclusivity, as many 'news' items initially appear directly on the platforms as direct messages from politicians.

This means that the editorial media are losing another advantage they enjoyed in the past. In analog times, the news media generated their social authority by being the first ones to introduce the public to new topics, a quality also known as 'agenda setting'. But agenda setting is becoming increasingly difficult because the news media now tend to be always too late compared to the real-time news users find on the platforms. As a result, they are in danger of offering less and less 'breaking news', increasingly slipping into the role of commentators. In the market of news (!) media, whose decisive currency is the novelty of the articles, they are inevitably losing significance. However, this transformation process is taking place gradually, such that we barely notice it. For most prominent politicians who have become known in the analog media system, a far-reaching break with the editorial media would still be counterproductive. Talk shows and television interviews are still important for them.

Several times in this book, we have simply 'switched off' the analog media in order to find out: What will the digital future look like? Here we can use an in-depth analysis of Donald Trump for a very simple reason: Trump has relied on digital media like no other politician before him. To a very large extent, he has abandoned the compromise with the gatekeepers of the editorial media described above. We see a rather dystopian real-life experiment that can show how platforms are encroaching on the political sphere.

Let us look at this in detail: What exactly happens when platforms become the leading political media? Trump's decision to rely primarily on Twitter and platforms such as Facebook was initially a highly controversial strategic gamble that perfectly matched his anti-establishment positioning: As an 'independent non-politician', he promised his supporters that he would drain the corrupt political swamp in Washington.

He could afford to break with many traditional gatekeepers in editorial media much more easily than any other politician in the Western world could before him (and after him) for two reasons. First, he appeared more independent in relation to the competing political elite. This gave his campaign additional credibility in the eyes of his supporters. He was now obviously anti-establishment also in the choice of his media channels. Second, he had already built up a huge celebrity following before his political candidacy. This foundation alone put him in a position to dispense with the compromises of the classic editorial media game of 'do ut des' (give and you shall receive).

No matter how repugnant we find Trump and his positions, we have to acknowledge that his strategic gamble was extremely risky at the time, because he broke with a large part of the 'mainstream media'. However, this set-up enabled Trump to fully exploit the real-time communication advantage of the platforms with ever new, ever more hair-raising, ever more spectacular claims. Over time, more and more of this content turned out to be sheer lies. For his followers, however, it did not matter. What counted for them was that Trump himself was true in a *different* way. Indeed, Trump was *genuine*, simply because a huge number of people received those messages *directly* from him. For the first time in human history, a politician really communicated with people 'at eye level'.

Trump's tremendous success as a communicator was based on this strategic gamble. He was the one who continuously set the media agenda from his Twitter profile. The traditional media only followed, they chased after him and then amplified his publicity with their secondary reporting. Trump mercilessly exploited the volatile, short attention spans on the net for his own benefit. He attracted incredible shockwaves of collective attention through the sheer digital entertainment of his tweets. At the same time, he pushed the editorial media into the role of pedantic, know-it-all party poopers. They were always outraged by his lies, thereby increasing the reach of his messages, and also engaged in diligent 'fact-checking'. Unfortunately, brazen lies are often much more entertaining than fact-checking, which is why Trump increasingly dominated the discourse.

> "Twitter is a wonderful thing for me, because I get the word out ...
> I might not be here talking to you right now as President
> if I didn't have an honest way of getting the word out."
>
> Donald Trump, March 15th, 2017 [11]

Trump thus turned the editorial media into hostages of his tweets. It is fascinating that the media logic he employed is similar to the one that terrorists use. Communicators like Trump, similar to terrorists, live from the fact that they literally *force* the media to report about them. When terrorists hijack an airplane or the US president tells an unbelievable lie, this *forces* the media to report about it, even if the media themselves know that this only increases the popularity of the perpetrators, that they are ultimately a pawn in a rigged game and that they operate according to rules that are not of their own making. The logic of the media leaves them no other choice, even if they clearly understand the diabolical PR strategy that is abusing them.

By January 6th 2021, it had become clear how catastrophic the effects of Trump's poker game with the media systems were. US democracy nearly crashed when his brainwashed supporters occupied the Capitol. It was precisely at this point that the platforms realized their crucial role in this game. The dramatic events apparently made even them a little doubtful for a second: Trump's profiles were blocked, first on Facebook and Instagram, then on Twitter.

No one is above the platforms

This leads us to several important insights for our topic. First, Trump's victorious advance would have been unthinkable without the support of the platforms: "I think that maybe I wouldn't be here if it wasn't for Twitter", Trump explained on Fox News.[12] Second, the actions of the platforms prove that they themselves interpreted it that way (otherwise they would not have touched Trump's profiles). Third, the platforms' actions show who is really in charge here. Yes, you can become president of the United States by your own dominant presence on digital platforms. But at the same time, you are then ultimately subject to the goodwill of the platforms. Or to put it another way: no one in this world is above the platforms. Ultimately, they can shut down any political figure as they please—even the President of the United States.

If we imagine a world in which the editorial media are 'switched off' and political discourse takes place primarily via the platforms, the platforms will completely control this discourse and, to put it in Habermas' words, destroy the inclusive, deliberative public sphere.

Trump seems to have come to a similar conclusion when he founded his own platform after being kicked off certain social media. In the context of his presidency, his first gamble had been to forgo the usual political symbiosis with the editorial media and communicate his policies directly to his followers via Twitter. In his second strategic bet, he raised the stakes again drastically by abandoning the symbiosis with existing platforms, replacing it with his own platform, Truth Social, which he could control completely himself. Now, no one can lock him out any more. Interestingly enough, Truth Social does not seem to be an economic success so far (which is understandable due to the dominance of the platform monopolies). However, Truth Social is more constructed as a device for the distribution of content onto the platforms, thus placing itself again above the platforms. By doing so, Trump has found a ways to immunize himself from a future potential ban by the platforms. But this also means: *No one* is above the platforms and their attention monopolies—not even Donald Trump.

At its core, the threat to our politics does not come from Donald Trump, but naturally arises from the attention economy of platforms which actively boost messages of hatred, anger and polarization. Politicians like Trump are only using the potential of these platforms as a propagandistic weapon. As a society, we are currently abandoning a media system that formed a strong, independent antithesis to the political sphere for decades. In the past, we had a pluralistic multitude of gatekeepers who created access and provided publicity in constant coordination with the political elites. At the same time, capable commentators interpreted the protagonists and their programs.

In the future era of platforms, politics will increasingly become a subordinate aspect of the platforms themselves, which they control to a very large extent. In recent years, it has often seemed as if the platforms themselves were surprised by the power that is suddenly in their hands. Sometimes they seemed caught off guard, as if they could no longer control the monsters they themselves had created. This is why at one point, they panicked and switched off Trump.

Will the platform owners continue to respect democratic values in the future, especially when radical, anti-democratic viewpoints serve their own interests? We can confidently doubt it. Every system that is based on total dominance tends to abuse its own power. This is exactly where the mega-platforms are heading. And Elon Musk seems to be the next chapter in the process of this natural 'Darth Vaderization' of the platforms. This development is also inevitable for a simple reason: the mega-platforms are still in competition with each other. The logic has been the same for decades: if we don't do it and take advantage, the others will do it. This already happened to data surveillance. It will most likely happen also to the field of politics.

To get an idea of what this future political world looks like, let us just imagine a right-wing media tycoon like Rupert Murdoch was owning these platforms, being able to use them as he pleases. Sooner or later, this scenario will come true, and malign owners will take over the political public sphere, exerting full control. God have mercy on us then—because at that point in time, we will no longer have a free media landscape that we would then need in order to raise objections or public appeals.

4. Mega-media are taking over our society

Since their inception, digital corporations have profited massively from the narrative of the weak, vulnerable media that we must protect against the power of the strong State. This is precisely why they love the concept of 'freedom'. They can always point to concepts such as freedom of speech and freedom of the media. By using these arguments, they have successfully fooled politicians and authorities for many years. With the same consistency, they claim that they are not even media, but 'only' platforms, 'only' intermediaries, even though they generate the majority of their revenues in the media sector. We have seen that the exact opposite is the case: these new digital media have superpowers that are unparalleled in the millennia-long history of the media.

We have shown the impact of Big Tech on politics and the economy. But these are not the only areas in which these mega media are eclipsing everything that was possible with analog media in earlier times. They also penetrate far into the privacy of users. The analog media of earlier times never had access to this sphere. In the 20th century, the territory of the private home largely eluded access by the public. The private zone of the family, personal friendships and gatherings, the exchange of intimacies was protected from media access. The same holds true for the sphere of personal education, work, private vacations, the neighborhood, school, university and so on. To a large extent, the mass media were excluded from here. Of course, even in earlier times, the mass media occasionally gained access to this sphere, but such 'exclusive' insights almost always involved public celebrities, and this access was the absolute exception and never the rule.

The revolution of the social media platforms consisted primarily of enabling every single person to publish personal details from their own lives in real time. The new digital mass media are therefore drastically expanding access. They invade our families, the sphere of childhood, they are present in our garden, they are present at every party, they provide insights into the most intimate details of our lives from pregnancy to deathbed. The private, protective fence around our lives is eradicated. This explains many of the phenomena we are currently dealing with, such as the loss of control over our privacy (*post privacy*), but also hate speech (personal attacks by strangers on private individuals), shitstorms and the like. Digital media are increasingly absorbing the private sphere into their media reality. In the case of business and politics, the hostile takeover of Big Tech primarily leads to massive accumulations of power. Beyond that, we see an invasion of privacy that is far beyond the reach of traditional mass media. Every individual in our society is far more dominated, influenced and manipulated by the platforms than was the case in the days of the more discreet analog media.

The attention economy of platforms is forcing people to be increasingly active on social media. They spend more and more time on the platforms, because this is the place where they encode their individuality in daily exchange with the community. Anyone who refuses to participate risks 'social death'. As the platforms' attention economy rewards personal, emotional or private insights, we have been experiencing a general competition to reveal the most intimate details of private life going on for almost twenty years now. Here, too, the dynamics described above mean that ever larger areas of our lives are penetrated by the mega-platforms, so that our free time increasingly consists of 'working' for them. Moreover, we have hardly any areas of retreat left which would be beyond the reach of the platforms. Thanks to their surveillance-capitalist spying on our privacy, the platforms also know a hundred times more intimate details about us than what we ourselves publish on the platforms.

But there are other areas besides business, politics and privacy that are increasingly being taken over by Big Tech. An example would be our *culture*. Thanks to their dominant market positions, digital companies own entire media genres (YouTube is the equivalent of digital television). This also applies to huge areas of culture that used to have their own ecosystems and industries. Let us take the *music industry* as an example. In the future, this will be replaced by the Spotify and Apple duopoly. Let us take the *book* market. In the future, Amazon will have such a dominant market position that it will be able to impose almost any conditions on authors and creatives. Many digital books bought from Amazon can only be read via Amazon—here, too, Amazon mercilessly exploits network effects that give competitors no chance. The situation is similar with audiobooks (Amazon Audible). Podcasts are largely in the hands of Spotify and Apple Music. The list could go on and on.[13]

Big Tech also owns the most important infrastructure for a future digitalized society—be it server farms, cloud computing or Musk's satellite internet.[14] They are expanding their dominant market positions into adjacent categories, their products are available internationally.[15] This gives them almost infinite potential for economic leverage. They can simply offer their products and services in almost any market without incurring major additional costs, giving them the possibility to scale their business models to the maximum. This naturally offers unbeatable cost advantages over any remaining competitors. In this sense, the ambitions of the tech giants are truly global—it is literally about 'world domination'.

Considering this dominance, a global digital currency would just be a logical extension. This would override one of the State's last areas of sovereignty. The tech giants regard nation states anyways as outdated structures that will be replaced by a new, international digital order in the future. The most ambitious initiative in this direction was Meta's plan to introduce its own cryptocurrency called Libra. After Facebook's announcement in June 2019, the regulatory authorities of the Western democracies apparently became a little uneasy. After they had completely failed to contain the economic dominance of tech monopolies, they did not want to repeat the same mistake and also hand over our monetary system to Big Tech without any resistance. For the first time since the advent of Big Tech, they took decisive action. After massive regulatory resistance as well as concerns about money laundering, consumer protection and fears of a possible destabilization of the global financial system, Meta had to abandon the project at the beginning of 2022. A statement by Sylvia Garcia, a US Democrat member of the House of Representatives, shows that politicians are gradually realizing the extent of the tech giants' ambitions "We need to get the message loud and clear to Mr. Zuckerberg that he's not a country on his own".[16]

We can also see how threatening the situation must have appeared to the authorities at the time. In parallel, even the European Union panicked and took immediate action: "The digital euro project can be seen as a counter-movement to Bitcoin or the failed Facebook initiative Libra, which was intended to put private money into circulation."[17] If the authorities in the USA and the EU had not woken up, Facebook could have encouraged its more than 2 billion users worldwide to use its own currency in order to introduce a global digital money through network effects.

Nevertheless, the situation remains scary. Even without Libra, digital companies are gaining ground in controlling electronic payments. A full 91 percent of people in Germany who use digital payment systems use PayPal, the undisputed market leader.[18] The tech giants are also ahead in the rapidly growing smartphone payment market, where Apple Pay and Google Pay are the market leaders.[19] Alphabet and Apple can once again transfer their existing dominant market positions to a new field and take advantage of network effects. For obvious reasons, the same network effects apply to currencies such as payment services as well as to media: the more participants use such a product, the more attractive the product becomes for all other users.

Our overview on the next page shows how the tech giants have succeeded in transferring the diverse use cases of digital media into ever new areas. They have expanded their digital media dominance to the maximum. They have managed to extend the access of their advertising into e-commerce transactions, they 'own' the entire digital value creation funnel. In the future they will increasingly produce and digitally monetize their own products. They control almost the entire digital public sphere and penetrate the most intimate secrets of our privacy. They continue to expand their supremacy worldwide. Against this backdrop, it is even more inconceivable that these mega-media have been able to get away with spurious claims for decades. Their claim to be 'weak' and pretence that they are 'mere' intermediaries was their justification for needing to be protected from the State and regulation.[20]

The best way to see how strong these mega-media really are is to compare what can be done with analog media on the one hand and digital platforms on the other from the perspective of the owners. For analog media, this is a simple exercise: essentially, they carry content that entertains and informs the audience, and they sell the audience's bundled attention as advertising.

Platforms also entertain, inform and sell advertising. But even here they have 'superpowers' compared to analog media, because, through the accumulation of data, they know all the interests, preferences and needs of users in detail, which is why they are able to target ads precisely. In contrast to editorial media, digital media can sell products online, which also means that they can place ads along the funnel (retargeting). Because they know the data on all views and conversions, they can also use this data to develop their own products, which they then sell online in their own funnel.

Beyond these economic 'superpowers', the owners can also use their platforms to destroy our democracy from within: On the one hand, they are able to control the political public through traffic manipulation for their own goals. On the other hand, they can carry out downright secret service operations on personal adversaries in order to impose sanctions or take advantage in other ways. In the following sections, we take a look at both aspects, examining specific examples.

WHAT CAN YOU DO WITH...

... ANALOG MASS MEDIA?

... DIGITAL PLATFORMS?

What the media always do

Economic exploitation

  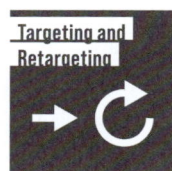

Endangering democracy

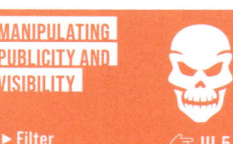
- Filter
- Blacklists
- Shadow Banning etc.

☞ III.5

- Blackmailing
- Control politicians
- Abuse of dependencies

☞ III.6

5. Tech giants manipulate traffic

When Elon Musk bought Twitter, his wild, erratic actions made clear to everyone how comprehensively the owners of the platforms can control content and user access. Let us recall several of Musk's actions during the first few weeks after the takeover: first, the accounts of various US journalists were blocked (they worked for the *New York Times,* the *Washington Post, CNN* and other media). Their posts displeased Musk—they had allegedly shared his whereabouts. However, Twitter did not provide any justification for its actions, nor did the people concerned receive a warning.

Musk then responded to pranksters who had posted critical or satirical claims about brand manufacturers (such as Nestlé: "We steal your water and sell it back to you"; the headline of a fake Pepsi profile read "Coke is better"; Tesla was not spared either: "the 53 percent drop in stock price doesn't phase us. If there's anyone who knows about crashing, it's us"). Musk introduced restrictions to stop the exodus of advertising customers.

During those days, more and more angry users emerged. They motivated the community to leave Twitter and join alternatives such as Mastodon. Musk responded with a ban on posting links to rival networks, digital referrals to such networks or drawing attention to the new profiles on alternative platforms. Musk also apparently changed the directives for dealing with hate speech. While the number of tweets deemed to be hate speech by Twitter doubled in the first few weeks after the takeover, a few weeks later, in November 2022, the proportion was a third below the average values before the takeover.[21]

Traffic was also manipulated to feed Elon Musk's ego—he apparently threatened his employees "with dismissal if they didn't make his tweets more successful than Joe Biden's. [...] Musk had made this 'request' after President Joe Biden received more attention for an Eagles tweet. […] Musk then had 80 engineers working on Sunday evening to ensure that his tweets would also get a great response—otherwise they would lose their jobs. [...] According to the report, Twitter engineers worked through the night on a system that allowed Musk to rate his tweets 'a factor of 1.000' higher than those of other users, according to 'Platformer'."[22]

The possibilities for platforms to actively influence the visibility of content are almost unlimited. The examples discussed show that the very idea of 'platforms' or 'intermediaries' as supposedly content-neutral 'surfaces', 'mediators' or 'containers' is fundamentally wrong. This neutrality does not exist anywhere, not on Twitter/X or any other platform.

People who think that these systematic traffic manipulations are only controlled by algorithms[23] fail to recognize the gravity of the situation. In the case of Twitter, the publication of previously secret documents and information from the former Twitter universe by journalist Matt Taibbi in the so-called 'Twitter Files' scandal was particularly instructive. The evidence indicates that Twitter had cooperated very closely with US government agencies such as the FBI, the CIA and the Treasury Department on critical topics before Musk's takeover in order to manipulate the flow of information within the platform. In the context of the COVID-19 pandemic, these measures are said to have led to the blocking of profiles of controversial individuals. Twitter was even paid for its cooperation and received 3.4 million US dollars from the FBI until 2019.

The means of traffic manipulation include visibility filters and various blacklists, such as a 'Search Blacklist' or 'Trends Blacklist'. A command called 'Do Not Amplify' is particularly interesting. The very instruction to "not amplify" specific content only makes sense if, in return, other content that is considered desirable for Twitter was amplified to be made more visible to users. Taibbi and his colleagues have collected evidence suggesting that such practices were also common on Facebook and Google.[24] There have also been repeated reports of manipulation on TikTok, for example through word filters. Posts with terms such as 'homo', 'gay', 'LGBTQ', 'Nazi', 'porn' or 'Sex' were blocked. These manipulations were not recognizable to the authors of the content, a practice which is called 'shadow banning'.[25]

When platforms claim that they are just neutral public forums that provide pure user interfaces for people to interact, they are lying. They manipulate traffic to their own liking: "'We control visibility quite a bit. And we control the amplification of your content quite a bit. And normal people don not know how much we do', one Twitter engineer told us. Two additional Twitter employees confirmed."[26]

Such suspicions have often been voiced in public. They are regularly rejected by the tech giants. They have often denied facts that they later had to admit. This was also the case here: In July 2018, Vijaya Gadde, then Twitter's Head of Legal Policy and Trust, and Kayvon Beykpour, then the company's Head of Product, had stated on the Twitter blog that they "do not shadow ban. And we certainly don't shadow ban based on political viewpoints or ideology."[27] What is particularly problematic is that such manipulations take place in the black boxes of the platforms without us having any chance to check or control them. Scientific analyses cannot gain clarity on this topic, as researchers cannot access the black boxes of the platforms. We only know one thing with absolute certainty: we cannot believe a single statement the tech giants make, we cannot trust them on anything.

Also the above mentioned manipulations only came to light on Twitter due to the chaos after Musk's takeover. On the one hand, we recognize the manipulations of Musk himself. On the other hand, the publication of the Twitter Files is also a form of propaganda by which Musk is telling us: Look how bad things were on Twitter already before my time. Additionally, there is a certain danger in making judgments based on one's own political preferences—according to which it is 'good' if Trump is locked out of the platform, for example, and 'bad' if the people locked out are journalists.

The key insight is more fundamental. We realize just how extensive the platforms' interference in traffic really is. "In early May, Colombian Instagram users noticed that content they posted in relation to ongoing protests in the country tended to disappear. The same happened in Palestine and Israel where findings hint at systematic efforts to remove certain types of Palestinian content. Instagram said the 'issue' had been fixed a few days later and that they have never intended to silence protesters. However, subsequent reporting by *BuzzFeed News* showed that more was at play and that moderation teams could arbitrarily silence communities (in this case, Facebook considered the Al-Aqsa mosque to be a terrorist organization)."[28]

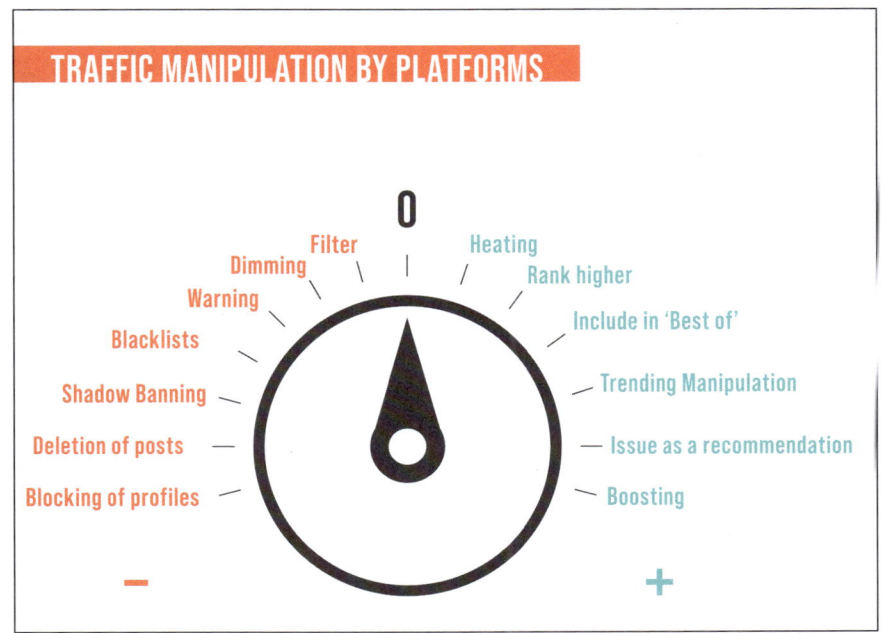

It is clear that such manipulations are commonly used for commercial purposes. For TikTok, for example, it has been proven that certain influencers with major brand partners are actively pushed in terms of visibility and reach by a so-called 'heating' of their posts.[29] These sorts of incidents remind us of reports we hear time and again from YouTubers: everything is going well up to a certain point, but then out of the blue the clicks collapse, probably because Alphabet has changed the algorithms.

Here is another story from my personal environment that was told to me confidentially. A friend of mine worked for a digital agency that had developed a new online presence for a ministry of the German government. Unfortunately, the traffic was pretty poor after the launch. But luckily, one of the tech giants learned about the problem when the issue was discussed in an agency meeting. And who would not love to help when it comes to the German government? The tech giant pushed a little from behind. All of a sudden, the traffic went up. Nice side effect: the ministry even won a prize for the great digital execution.

We can now conduct our experiment again, switch off the analog media and ask ourselves: Who will control the platforms in the future? The central insight from cases such as the Twitter Files leads us back to the core of the ideology we have described above: the supposedly weak media, which must be protected from strong external forces (typically the State), particularly against censorship and other forms of instrumentalization. Nowadays, this danger does not threaten digital platforms primarily from the outside, but above all from within. After all, it is these mega-media themselves that censor, manipulate and instrumentalize.

None other than Jack Dorsey, the founder of Twitter, expressed this exact insight in the context of the Twitter Files. His remarkable reflection describes exactly what is happening right now: How the threat of centralized control, which once emanated from governments, will emanate from platforms in the future. In the end, it will be individuals who decide what content is played out to users in digital media. According to Dorsey, the platforms have "become far too powerful".

Jack Dorsey's statement of 12/13/2022 on the 'Twitter Files'[30]

"Companies [like Twitter, today X, M. A.] have become far too powerful, and that became completely clear to me with our suspension of Trump's account. [...]

Of course governments want to shape and control the public conversation, and will use every method at their disposal to do so, including the media. And the power a corporation wields to do the same is only growing. It's critical that the people have tools to resist this, and that those tools are ultimately owned by the people. Allowing a government or a few corporations to own the public conversation is a path towards centralized control. [...]

The problem today is that we have companies who own both the protocol and discovery of content. Which ultimately puts one person in charge of what's available and seen, or not."

6. Spying and policing activities by Big Tech

The fact that digital corporations are spying on our personal privacy and accumulating ever greater amounts of data in order to make ever better predictions about our behavior and earn lots of money has been well known since Shoshana Zuboff's reference work on digital 'surveillance capitalism'. We have already described the pattern of 'Darth Vaderization', which is constantly being repeated in new variations: Companies or managers who originally pursued useful goals out of idealistic motives end up on the 'Dark side of the Force'. Zuboff has described this process in great detail using Google as an example: Two young students, Larry Page and Sergey Brin, founded the company in 1998, which initially struggled to stay afloat, generating disparate revenues from different, seemingly uncoordinated areas. When the dotcom bubble burst in 2000, many people doubted the company's ability to survive. It was around this time that Google discovered the potential of the data it was using to improve the efficiency of online advertising.

Although the idealistic founders initially had no interest in advertising, they now dropped all scruples and developed their new business model: "they took things from users without asking".[31] This move explains the extreme secrecy regarding internal information: under no circumstances should the public find out that Google earns money by spying on its customers, especially as Google had always emphasized its close and trusting relationship with the user community. Google's systematic betrayal of its own customers by secretly spying on them began in the early 2000s. The business model of data extraction was then adopted by Facebook, which underwent a similar 'Darth Vaderization' as Google—and so on.

Zuboff has also described the general consequences of the tech giants' surveillance activities on our society: We are losing our freedom through the countless behavioral nudges we receive every day based on this data—because we cannot even grasp these millions of tiny micro-manipulations that we are exposed to. We don't notice how our behavior is increasingly remote-controlled by tech companies. We are increasingly losing our individual autonomy. The digital corporations are like puppeteers who intervene ever more deeply into our private lives without us noticing it. Like puppets, we dance to their algorithms. The asymmetry of knowledge is disturbing, leading us to the question: What will the world look like when the analog media have largely disappeared and the digital corporations will own our media system in a few years?

To answer this question, we first need to find out: What exactly do the digital companies know about us? More precisely: What is the *maximum* they can find out about a single person if they are really determined to exert their full powers? Thanks to a masterpiece of US investigative journalism at TikTok, we can now better assess this question. Similar to Musk's Twitter takeover, thanks to a glitch, we can see just how extensively the tech giants can already conduct intelligence-like operations on individuals. The story of this revelation reads like a thriller. Back in October 2022, *Forbes* magazine reported that TikTok was able to spy on the data of individual users. Just as Twitter had denied traffic manipulation, TikTok also immediately denied it, according to the usual PR rituals of the digital industry. Among other things, the company said in an official public statement it does not collect precise GPS location information from US users, and that it "could not monitor US users in the way the article suggested".[32]

Internally, however, TikTok acted in exactly the opposite way (we will come back to the cynicism of this pattern of behavior in our 'flywheel of bullshitting', which is widespread among tech giants). The executives at TikTok were obviously fed up with the constant critical reporting by *Forbes* and *BuzzFeed*, which also repeatedly drew on insider information from within their own company. TikTok knew that there was a leak somewhere in their own organization. But who were the TikTok employees who had secretly transmitted information to the journalists?

TikTok used genuine secret service methods to find out. Of course, TikTok knew the identities of the US journalists from the author details of their articles. Their location and movement data were also known via their TikTok accounts—despite all assurances that they could not and did not know exactly that. The TikTok spies wanted to identify the 'mole' by comparing the movement data of the journalists with that of their own employees: Were there any overlaps at any point? Was a TikTok employee once at the same place as one of the journalists at any time? Who met with whom and possibly leaked information? Such spying methods can be used to provide data-based evidence of a meeting and at the same time prove who is responsible in one's own organization. Then you can act accordingly, in plain language: fire the 'wrongdoers'.

The fact that TikTok had to officially admit they were spying on US journalists[33] is a similar lucky strike as the discoveries we discussed for Elon Musk and Twitter. Although all industry insiders are aware of the enormous possibilities of personal data tracking available to digital companies, it is often difficult even for experts to assess: What exactly do they know about us? And the digital companies naturally keep their practices strictly secret.

After all, it is known from investigative practices that whistleblowers from digital companies often take major precautions when meeting with journalists. The US magazine *Wired*, for example, reported about a meeting with an anonymous Facebook employee. The employee insisted that all smartphones had to be switched off during the meeting[34]—for fear of the very case that has now been made public at TikTok: That Facebook could find out who was talking to a journalist by analyzing location data. Everyone in the industry also knows that digital companies are not squeamish in such cases. Allegedly, for example, Facebook had a 'rat catching team', an internal secret police that was responsible for monitoring employees and punishing any misconduct with sanctions.[35]

What can digital companies find out about individuals?

Importantly, the public can now at least see the tip of the iceberg of what options are available to digital companies to spy on single individuals. We now know for sure that TikTok is able to analyze location-based data over time. We know that platforms can use cookies to collect data not only about the time periods the platform itself is visited by a user, but also during the time intervals in which the platform is not used at all. Each time the platform is accessed, the tech giant receives feedback on what a user has done since then.

Digital experts from *TheWrap* were able to gain access to two so-called whitehat studies by cybersecurity hackers and, after reviewing the results, concluded that TikTok is able to "circumvent security protections on Apple and Google app stores" in order to gain "full access to user data". "The TikTok browser not only has access to convert from web to device, but it also has the ability to query things on the device itself. Third parties and advertisers can end up tracking TikTok users over time across devices and installs." This would certainly explain the intelligence-like use in the case of the US journalists. *TheWrap* also noted, "experts note that TikTok's data mining may be no worse than that of major social networks like Facebook".[36]

There is now additional evidence that the data flows resulting from the use of TikTok are very far-reaching. TikTok is able to read users' private text messages, identify objects and scenes that appear, create faceprints and voiceprints, access location data and even identify the text of spoken words.[37] A study by Brian Klais examined a wide range of apps in early 2022 and found that they are all in contact with an average of 15 other domains, 12 of which are third-party domains. Comparing various social media apps, they found that TikTok and YouTube used the highest amount of such contacts. TikTok was in contact with 14 domains,

13 of which were third-party domains. The problem is that it is difficult for users to find out what the third-party domains they are connected to are doing with their data, particularly as they also access their usage data beyond the app's usage time. As a last resort, users have only two options: they can either use the app or not.³⁸

TikTok's confession proves that digital companies can apparently use the data available to them for their own surveillance projects. Furthermore, the case proves that they run espionage activities. At the same time, the management's apology raises a lot of additional questions rather than providing trustworthy answers. We can assume that such specific surveillance of individuals only comes to light in extremely rare cases. It is likely that a lot more people have been monitored in recent years, and that such practices are also common in other digital companies.

Denial, lies, PR blah-blah

When caught in the act, Big Tech always acts by adopting the same pattern of behavior as in the TikTok case: first a consistent denial, then a brazen lie to the public, followed by a theatrical management performance with the usual PR blah-blah: We are so shocked and outraged by the evil wrongdoings of alleged individual perpetrators who had acted in contradiction to our company's noble values, and so on. This is typically accompanied by a series of dismissals of some scapegoats. If employees of the tech giants are afraid to speak to members of the press in front of switched-on smartphones, it can be assumed that the top managers of the responsible companies are also well aware of what is going on—one of the fired scapegoats, Song Ye, reported directly to TikTok CEO Rubo Liang.

We should feel a little uneasy when thinking about the photo of Mark Zuckerberg from 2016, on whose laptop the camera and possibly also the microphone input were taped. We know that Uber has tracked journalists who have reported on the company.³⁹ Microsoft read the Hotmail account of a French blogger in a similar case in 2012.⁴⁰ In the case of TikTok, we have clear proof of how easily the most intimate information about individuals can be analyzed for specific purposes. We cannot attach enough importance to this evidence. And it would be negligent to limit this to TikTok. We can all imagine what the future holds for us if platforms are able to spy on our entire private lives as they wish. When it comes to pursuing their own interests, they could, for example, take a closer look at politicians—and find out if someone can no longer service a bank loan, is having an affair, is consuming porn, has changed his or her sexual orientation, and so on. They could easily use all this information for their own interest: "It would be a shame if the public found out that you are having an extramarital, homosexual relationship for more than 17 months now." We would all be vulnerable to being blackmailed.

It is high time to take a closer look: What is the maximum the platforms can actually find out about us? And above all, do we really want to allow them to do this?

7. The principle of maximum takeover

The argument in the last sections (III.1-6) has gone through several stages: Our starting point was the mainstream thinking of the media being weak and vulnerable, which protects editorial media from the encroachments of governments and power. It originates from centuries of State control and censorship of the media. This explains why this view is so deeply rooted in our democratic mindset.

The digital corporations have taken advantage of these far reaching protection mechanisms for their mega-platforms. This is why they are constantly preaching the protection of freedom of speech and media freedom, while at the same time claiming that they are not even media, but 'only' platforms, 'only' intermediaries, claiming no responsibility for the content that is carried on their platforms.

Our extensive acid test has proven that the opposite is true. The platforms are indeed mega-media that in many respects exceed the powers of analog mass media: They additionally penetrate into our private and intimate sphere, you can conduct economic transactions with them, they enable political communication to be played out directly. In this way, the platforms are taking over ever larger areas of politics, the economy and also individual privacy, fields to which the analog mass media never had access in this form. We need to note that the media market is anyways just a Trojan horse for the tech giants, through which they will continue to penetrate the rest of the economy in the future—initially through taking a stranglehold over online commerce and then over the production and distribution of their own products.

They are mega-media with enormous power and possibilities. And yet they have managed to get away with being treated as intermediaries. Imagine if the possession of firearms was banned in a country, and this ban applied to pistols, revolvers, shotguns, rifles and so on, but not to machine guns. Yes, you read that correct. The carrying of firearms would be strictly prohibited, with severe penalties. But machine guns: no problem. Because, as the manufacturers of machine guns explain to us, machine guns are not firearms at all, but only inter-ammunition devices that merely transfer the ammunition in a neutral manner. The bullets are not ejected individually by the user, but automatically by a tool which is only a service provider. That is why machine gun manufacturers do not count as arms companies and do not need to worry about pesky legal regulations that could only disturb their booming business. Whenever someone tried to reasonably explain that machine guns are also used for shooting, that they are even much more dangerous than the other prohibited firearms, that the death statistics clearly prove that machine guns are responsible for most murders and accidents in our country, the machine gun companies would furrow their brows thoughtfully and then point out to the person in a friendly and firm manner that for many years, this has been clearly laid down in the law: machine guns are not firearms. They are just inter-ammunition devices and therefore no rules are needed. That's it.

By the way, the term 'intermediary' itself is only a kind of paraphrase of the term 'medium'. Media scientists essentially define a medium as an 'intermediary' or 'mediator'.[41] The 'medium' is imagined as a kind of tool that stands in between ('inter') two poles of mediation. This makes the utter nonsense of this position completely clear: "Social media are not media, but something completely different." Namely what? 'Intermediaries'. Ok. And 'Intermediary' is a euphemism for what? Exactly, for media.

For years, digital companies have been telling us that they are not media. The politicians and authorities have faithfully accepted this. What idiots we are, the tech giants think, that we accept this nonsense. Or, as nineteen-year-old Mark Zuckerberg said: "Dumb Fucks".

The flywheel of bullshitting

We have seen that digital media have powers that the analog media can only ever dream of. Platform owners can manipulate traffic for their own purposes and are even able to spy on individuals to gain an advantage. Because it is generally extremely difficult to peer into the black boxes of the tech giants (especially as their internal guidelines punish any disclosure of information with brutal penalties), we can assume that the number of unreported cases of similar offenses is hundreds of times higher than the number of cases that have become public knowledge.

Using Google as an example, Shoshana Zuboff has developed a model that she calls the "Dispossession cycle". It shows how tech giants systematically take over digital territories. First, they invade an unprotected area and claim it as their property. Here they often knowingly break laws: "There are hundreds of cases launched against Google by countries, states, groups, and individuals, and there are many more cases that never become public. […] The legal challenges are varied, but they nearly always come back to the same thing: unilateral incursion met by resistance." [42]

Zuboff's list of examples for Google alone is dizzying:

- "digitalization of books [without the authors' permission]
- the collection of personal information through Street View's Wi-Fi and camera capabilities,
- the capture of voice communications,
- the bypassing of privacy settings,
- the manipulation of search results,
- the extensive retention of search data,
- the tracking of smartphone location data,
- the secret collection of student data for commercial purposes,
- the consolidation of user profiles across all Google's services and devices"

In the first phase of the expropriation cycle, a digital company seizes a specific territory and takes possession of it. This is noticed by the public at some point and the second phase begins. Typically, outraged victims contest the appropriation in court. Due to the slow proceedings, the various appeals and court instances, these lawsuits take so long that the tech giants gain a lot of time during which their product asserts itself and the desired network effects kick in. What began as a hostile, often unlawful takeover is gradually turning into a practice that society is getting used to. At some point, people find it 'normal' to be spied on 24 hours a day by a social media platform. This is followed by the final phase, in which the tech giants typically make minor adjustments as well as adjustments to their communications. In most cases, they explain to people that the takeover that has already taken place is actually a great thing for them because it makes their lives better, improves the world and so on.

We have taken Zuboff's model and developed it further into our 'Flywheel of Bullshitting'. The wheel is supposed to symbolize that this process is never complete. Due to the intentional and repeated violations of the law, the lies and denials never come to an end. In fact, there are usually several flywheels running in parallel: on one field, tech giants are actively covering up and deceiving the public, while at the same time apologies are being made on other fields, stating that they have messed up badly, that something like this will never happen again, and so on.

The only question is how far digital companies will go in the future, especially in a world in which analog media has largely disappeared and the political public sphere virtually 'belongs' to them. There will be hardly any mechanisms of media control. If you were to ask the bosses of the tech giants about this today, they would of course be "shocked" that you think they would even be capable of such terrible misdeeds as traffic manipulation, espionage and blackmailing innocent people. They would call out their company's supposed 'values' (fairness, transparency, trustworthiness, sustainability, diversity and so on, take your pick) with the usual PR talk.

We can completely reject such assurances. In fact, the tech giants have no choice but to continue on their path of accumulating power. Their key problem is that they currently operate monopolies in their respective categories and competition has already been done away with. But if we go one level higher, GAFAM are still in competition *with each other*. They are therefore always driven by the threat of losing ground to their peers.

This inevitably leads to the principle of maximum takeover: the individual digital groups are under considerable pressure to use all possible (and even illegal) means to maximize their growth. That means: if you are in a position to gain economic advantages by systematically manipulating your own traffic, you will do it. No one will notice, it will never be exposed anywhere in public. And within the digital companies, it will be assumed that competitors are doing the same anyway.

This also applies to influencing or even blackmailing politicians or decision-makers. They will secretly boost preferred political candidates—to push their content visibility, to strengthen visibility of their posts. It will also be easy to convince politicians to make this decision and not that one. "How many impressions do you achieve on average per post—1.8 million? That's an impressive figure! Maybe you'll reconsider your decision on data protection next week. It would be a shame if your performance went down in the future."

In a way, a conversation like this will not even be necessary. After all, if you are a politician, you will probably be able to see directly from your digital results after important decisions whether the tech giants were happy about your position or whether you annoyed them. So who do you actually turn to when your visibility as a politician plummets? Do you call Facebook's headquarters?

It is therefore utter nonsense to listen to ethical assurances and positive intentions when it comes to platforms. We should rather focus on one of their mantras: if it is possible to develop a technology, someone will do it. Resistance to it would be virtually futile. This ideology is also known as 'inevitabilism'. However, the same also applies to the abuse of the infinite power that is already available to digital corporations. This power is already beyond our control. The scenarios outlined above as to how they can take advantage of situations are already possible. And simply because they are possible, the tech giants will use them. It follows from the principle of maximum takeover: they will do it to further maximize their own power. And because they assume: If we don't do it, the others will. It should be clear by now that these platforms are not 'weak' media.

In a hundred years from now, people who study our times will wonder how on earth this could have happened: A handful of mega-platforms were able to grow into monsters behind a protective wall for supposedly 'weak' media. For decades, without us noticing. On the contrary: Throughout these years, we have tended, looked after, privileged, cared for and protected the cute digital companies. We have carefully nurtured them and fed them daily. The tech giants secretly laughed at us and thought to themselves: "Why don't they notice? Dumb fucks."

By the time we realized the error in our thinking, it was too late.

CHAPTER IV

MONOPOLIES, FAKE NEWS, HATE SPEECH:

Is this actually legal?

1. Insufficient laws against monopolies

Monopolies stand in stark contradiction to our democratic, free and pluralistic fundamental values. This is because, historically speaking, every form of power has a tendency to develop an ethically questionable life of its own, i.e. to spill over into elections, party programs, politicians and jurisdiction. This is why the 'checks and balances' of fair competition, in which different companies, groups and parties compete on a level playing field, always have a balancing and stabilizing effect on democracies and discourses. We must ensure "that we control the economic structures—before they control us", according to the US legal scholar Tim Wu.[1] Monopolies must be a taboo, especially in the field of media.

I will base the following set of arguments on a review of the legal situation in Germany and Europe—also assuming that the outcome would be similar for most other Western countries. This is the case as the following underlying principles of free, independent media are generally similar in most Western countries:

- ▶ The media or media genres should not be controlled or owned by the State or other agents of power, such as religious groups or private companies.

- ▶ No constraints (such as censorship) should be imposed on the media by the State or other powers. In addition, dependencies or conflicts of interest between the media and the State should be avoided.

- ▶ The media sphere should be pluralistic, meaning that neither an individual monopolist nor a few oligopolistic providers should be allowed to have control of major media genres that are perceived to be essential for the formation of political opinions in democracy (i.e. television).

- ▶ Journalism and professional editorial media are regarded as an essential part of the democratic public sphere.

In the following analysis of German and European legislation protecting media freedom, we will see that the status quo dominated by digital monopolies violates all these basic principles. Even more disturbing is the fact that current legislation does not provide frameworks or provisions that would allow us to restore media freedom. I would assume that, even if the specific rules and regulations differ from one country to another, the outcome would be similar. Thus, the following analysis can also be used as a blueprint to carry out the same assessment for other Western democracies.

Since Germany has a free economic system based on competition, common sense would suggest that monopolies should be illegal in Germany, the EU and actually also in the USA, simply because they are fundamentally at odds with our free, pluralistic value system. And indeed—if we go back in time, there was a clear legal position against monopolies, at least in the USA, clear not just in terms of words, but also in terms of action. In 1890, senator John Sherman expressed this attitude in the famous 'Sherman Act': "every person who shall monopolize, or attempt to monopolize ... any part of the trade or commerce among the several States, or with foreign nations, shall be deemed guilty of a felony."[2]

This legal philosophy of breaking up monopolies to restore competition was applied in the USA for many decades. The tough proceedings against Standard Oil (John D. Rockefeller) and American Tobacco (James Buchanan Duke) in 1911 are well known. The experience of German National Socialism further encouraged the US government in its approach. The close links between extreme concentrations of economic power (Krupp, Siemens, I.G. Farben) and the National Socialist regime were a frightening example of the massive social dangers of uncontrollable accumulation of power. Famous cases from the decades after the Second World War include the break-up of the Hollywood studio system in 1948 (I will come back to this) and the break-up of AT&T in 1982. But then the tide turned. Strictly speaking, it would still be legally possible to break up monopolies in the USA. However, the legal practice was largely scaled back there and stopped until around the turn of the millennium.

In Germany and the EU, on the other hand, there are not even any effective legal options for breaking up monopolies. This means that, in the Western world, there is currently no common practice visible that would eliminate monopolies that damage societies in order to safeguard free, open markets and media. And even the new 'Digital Markets Act' of the EU is nothing more than a toothless tiger in the face of the power of the tech giants. The EU can only impose rules of conduct on monopolists—which, given the hopeless inferiority of the European authorities in terms of digital expertise, are unlikely to change the status quo.

Monopolies are therefore currently completely legal in the Western world. Interestingly enough, the topic itself is not called 'monopoly law', but 'antitrust law', a term that perfectly encapsulates the core problem of the existing legislation. In a trust, several companies attempt to control a certain market through collusion, i.e. to undermine fair competition or gain a dominant market position. On the basis of antitrust law, the State has numerous possibilities to prohibit company mergers, trusts, cartels or agreements between competitors and to prevent a monopoly from being created. Even pure price agreements between competitors are sanctioned by draconian penalties. However, the State can do frighteningly little against *existing* monopolies.

Google's search engine is a perfect example of a monopoly that has arisen naturally. In such cases, we can hardly challenge monopolies or near-monopolies on the basis of current legislation.[3] Sanctions are possible in the case of abusive behavior, but this is often difficult to prove.

> **FUN FACT:** If a company wants to create a monopoly by taking over a competitor, the authorities will intervene. However, if the monopoly emerges naturally (the Google search engine, for example), there are no sanctions.

Common sense tells us that this distinction is completely irrational. If we agree that the complete eradication of competition through monopolies is unacceptable not only for economic, but also for social and political reasons, then it should make no difference at all how a monopoly has come about and at what point in time the intervention of the State takes place—that is, before or after a monopoly has been established.

The strange logic of legislation can fully explain the strategic approach of digital companies. As a tech company, you have to try to achieve a dominant market position by any means necessary. As soon as you have achieved this and there is no more competition, you are safe and nobody can mess with you any more. This is because there is no provision for a break-up and, at best, behavioral guidelines are conceivable. This is precisely what explains the aggressive approach of digital groups when it comes to killer acquisitions, namely when they simply buy up innovators or competitors (☞ II.4).

Worse still, when authorities make serious errors of judgment, as in the case of Facebook's takeover of Instagram and then WhatsApp, the result is irreversible.[4] Due to this irrational jurisdiction, a company like Meta has a good laugh as soon as the acquisition is completed. Once the deal is done, we can no longer intervene.

Are the digital companies so evil or are we so stupid?

The spirit of this legislation is bizarre, because it ignores basic norms that normally apply to situations that are regulated by law. Theft is a theft, regardless of whether it is committed by one person or by several people who come together for this purpose. In the case of theft, it is also not necessary for authorities to be prevent it before it is carried out. Imagine if a thief would be equally safe after a robbery: well guys, the bank has already been robbed, now it's too late.

In addition, this legal practice allows digital companies to leverage their superior digital expertise against weak authorities, which in most cases are not qualified to recognize the future economic potential behind an acquisition. In addition, the antitrust authorities usually take a normative approach within their regulatory bubble. This means that they are not at all interested in the question of how bad a dominant market position is for society. They proceed according to principles, but not according to relevance or on the basis of empirical findings. This is the only way to explain why the German Federal Antitrust Office often takes action in completely insignificant cases, while almost nothing is done against the digital giants that are in the process of taking over our digital media system.

Anyone who thinks this is an exaggeration should take a look at their official press release from September 28, 2021: "The German Federal Antitrust Office has prohibited the acquisition of sole control of the publishing companies of the *East-Thuringia Daily* by a company belonging to the Funke media group. Funke is the publisher of the *Thuringia Daily*, whose circulation area partially overlaps with that of the *East-Thuringia Daily*. The now prohibited merger would have brought *East-Thuringia Daily* and *Thuringia Daily* under the sole control of the Funke media group."[5]

This passage is neither satire nor quoted from Monty Python, it is all meant seriously. Such examples show the whole folly of the existing law that the authorities are executing. Mergers can be stopped in advance (as is the case with the *East-Thuringia Daily*), but we can't do anything about monopolies like Google's search engine. We shrug our shoulders. That's just the way it is. It makes you wonder: are the digital companies really so evil or are we so stupid? We have rules like "keep dogs on a lead", but we let the wolves roam around free and are then surprised when wolves do what they usually do.

The digital companies are actually just creatively exploiting the loopholes in our law which are actually wide open gates. We have been passively watching now for two decades. If we only stop the formation of monopolies by preventing mergers, but not the monopolies themselves, it is completely logical that the digital corporations will do all they can to set up monopolies. They can exploit these monopolies undisturbed for all eternity to the detriment of society and we can do nothing about it.

"Competition is for losers"

Within the Big Tech ecosystem, the approach to deliberately create monopolies is openly proclaimed as a core element of successful entrepreneurial strategy. None other than Peter Thiel, founder of PayPal and Palantir as well as one of the first investors in Facebook, explained this at Stanford back in 2014: "Competition is for losers".[6] And we should directly add what that implies: Diversity, equal opportunities and democracy are also for losers.

In his book *Zero to One*, he explains to all readers who are not lucky enough to spend their working life with a monopolist how wonderful the world is when you no longer have to deal with annoying competitors: "Whereas a competitive firm must sell at the market price, a monopoly owns its market, so it can set its own prices. Since it has no competition, it produces at the quantity and price combination that maximizes its profits."[7]

Thiel reveals how the digital giants have established their monopolies and eliminated the competition, namely (surprise!) through network effects and economies of scale (☞ II). He also explains to the stunned audience why the tech giants are so reluctant to talk about this topic: "Monopolists lie to protect themselves. They know that bragging about their great monopoly invites being audited, scrutinized, and attacked. Since they very much want their monopoly profits to continue unmolested, they tend to do whatever they can to conceal their monopoly—usually by exaggerating the power of their (nonexistent) competition"[8]

We could fill a second book with the various strategies used by the tech giants to disguise their monopolies. One method is to simply increase the size of the market to such an extent that the monopoly's share of it becomes smaller and smaller. Thiel himself quotes former Google CEO Eric Schmidt: "We face an extremely competitive landscape in which consumers have a multitude of options to access information."[9]

Equally popular is the claim that strong market positions could be wiped out by new digital disruptors at any time. US scientist Matthew Hindman has been researching the systematic destruction of the free market economy by tech giants since 2010 and knows this smokescreen only too well: "Google has repeatedly told regulators that there is no need to regulate Google on the grounds that 'competition is just a single click away'".[10]

At Amazon, Jeff Bezos' 'Day One' mantra is preached: you should approach every day as you did the first day after the company was founded, otherwise you are threatened with decline and downfall. Bezos also said: "Amazon will also go bankrupt. If you look at the big companies, their lifespan is 30 years plus, not 100 years plus."[11]

These narratives are deceptive maneuvers to distract from the fact that Big Tech has established market monopolies that are generally irreversible. Huge territories are seized and then secured with insurmountable walls, for the simple purpose of dominating these areas forever and exploiting the inhabitants living in them at will. Anyone looking at charts displaying the annual revenue progression of the tech giants can only see one direction for decades: upwards. You might like to ask yourself where the competition is that has supposedly been "just a click away" for all those years. Or how soon Amazon will go bankrupt, as Bezos has predicted—tomorrow, for example?[12]

Digital monopolies cover content and transmission channels at the same time—and nothing happens

Let's take another look at a famous antitrust case from the past, which shows very well how far Western societies have since abandoned the original democratic ideal of a free and fair market economy with pluralistic competition. In 1948, when the philosophy of the Sherman Act was still the guiding principle of competition law in the USA, the Hollywood studio system was shattered by the case 'United States vs. Paramount Pictures, Inc.'.

The case is particularly interesting, also because it is a good example of what economists call 'vertical integration'. Vertical integration always occurs when companies occupy more and more markets along the value chain. A successful product manufacturer could, for example, expand its activities to include sales by operating more and more retail outlets in order to capture the profits from these outlets—and so on. In the Hollywood studio system, the powerful studios achieved vertical integration as they owned a large number of movie theaters. This allowed them to influence which films were shown in those movie theaters, maximizing prices and profits, forcing movie theaters to show their films through 'block booking' and putting smaller and independent movie theaters at a disadvantage. The decision in 1948 marked the end of the golden years of the studio system.

As with today's digital corporations, this legal case was also about media companies. Certainly, the scale of the threat at the time was ridiculously small compared to the catastrophic conditions of today, because it was only about a single type of media (films for movie theaters). Furthermore, the 'Big 5' (Paramount, Metro-Goldwyn-Mayer, Warner Bros., 20th Century Fox, RKO) were competing against each other and against three other challengers, the "Little 3", who did not own any movie theaters (Universal, Columbia, United Artists).[13] The extent of vertical integration was also minuscule from today's perspective: in 1945, only

17 percent of all movie theaters belonged to the studios concerned, many of them only in shares. At the time, these 17 percent of cinemas generated 45 percent of revenues.[14] Compared to the situation of today, where most digital markets are fully covered by monopolies or oligopolies, the constraints on fair competition were ridiculously small.

The key problem criticized at the time was that the studios held dominant positions on two levels. They had control over the *media content* they produced (films) and at the same time over the *transmission channels* (movie theaters). This dual dominance was the only reason why they were able to determine the conditions of film distribution at will and also force distribution via packages.

The case therefore illustrates *the worst conceivable situation for dominant positions in the media market*. Dominant positions are bad enough when they exist in a single market. But imagine what would happen if individual players were to create monopolies in the media market, covering both *media content* and *transmission channels*. A single company could own television, not just all the content, but also the transmission channels.

Do you notice anything? *This worst imaginable situation is the case with almost all digital monopolies!* This is because most of GAFAM's digital monopolies cover both the transmission channels and the program content. Although they are not operators of telecommunications infrastructure, they are nevertheless monopolists in two different aspects, because they own the structure and visibility of content and at the same time control the communication channels distributing them, as is the case with YouTube, Facebook/Instagram, WhatsApp and so on. This further increases their dominant market position in terms of their ability to grant access to content. We notice our double dependence on these platforms precisely when, for example, a Meta server goes down for a few hours and WhatsApp is no longer available—we then have no access to the channel and no access to the content at the same time. In 1948, the US government abolished the Hollywood studio system for good reasons. Against the current digital monopolies, we do—nothing.

We do nothing despite the fact that media genres such as video-on-demand (YouTube), search (Google) and social media (Facebook/Instagram) are far more important for shaping political opinion and for democracy than the movie theaters of the past.

We do nothing despite the fact that only one media genre was affected at the time, whereas today the entire spectrum of digital media genres is controlled by such monopolies.

We do nothing despite the fact that there was intense competition among the studios at the time in relation to the monopolized digital media genres.

We do nothing despite the fact that the degree of vertical integration at the time was ridiculously low compared to the huge reach of the tech giants, which often encompasses not just two, but half a dozen or more levels (☞ II.3).

Meanwhile, the booming tech giants continue with their hostile takeover of markets in broad daylight. They openly tell us that competition is for losers and laugh hysterically that we are so stupid and don't understand what is happening. We all watch their hostile takeover: academics, the media, politicians, authorities, publicists, lawyers. Nothing happens. But at least the German Federal Antitrust Office has ensured that economic competition between the *East Thuringia Daily* and the *Thuringia Daily* will be kept alive in the future.

Digression: Why is the German Federal Antitrust Office not intervening?

If we want to break the dominance of the digital corporations as a society, there is almost only one hope for us—and that is the antitrust authorities (i.e. the German Federal Antitrust Office and EU Commission). In Germany, the Federal Antitrust Office is supposed to ensure that fair and free competition prevails in our economy. The authority can impose fines amounting to 10 percent of annual turnover as a penalty under antitrust law. Such sanctions can amount to several billion euros.

We have seen that digital companies intentionally break the laws in many areas. We can therefore assume that they are proactively planning enough financial resources to easily fight dozens or even hundreds of lawsuits in parallel and also pay possible penalties without facing any issues. In this game, it is only the antitrust penalties that are taking on dimensions for the tech giants that are more than just annoying flies they wipe off their faces while quietly establishing their monopolies and exploiting Western societies. So if there is one institution that could stop the destruction of our democracy and our economy by the tech giants, it is the Federal Antitrust Office.

When the German Federal Antitrust Office presented a 232-page "sector investigation" into online advertising at the beginning of September 2022, it was a minor sensation that could have given us some hope for future change. As we already know (☞ I), free competition in this field has been completely done away with. And the Federal Antitrust Office is the central German authority when it comes to competition. On the occasion of this investigation, the independent authority could have presented the catastrophic situation openly to the German public. This could have been formulated in a rousing appeal. It should have sounded like this:

"As the Federal Antitrust Office, we are responsible for fair competition and equal opportunities in Germany. Unfortunately, we have to point out to the people of this country that fair competition and open markets in the field of digital media have been completely done away with. No one in Germany is more frustrated by this than us competition authorities. Why? Because we know that the status quo poses a huge threat to society beyond the economic damage. After all, digital media do not only represent an economic competitive factor. They are a major cornerstone of our democratic public. As a federal authority, however, our hands are tied because we lack the legal instruments to take action here. This is the case because we cannot break up established monopolies. We therefore recommend that politicians very quickly create an appropriate legal framework that would enable us to re-establish competition in this important market—before it is too late and our free democratic order is irretrievably destroyed by digital monopolies."

The institution's assessment should have sounded something like this. However, the paper did not use that opportunity and was a full disappointment. Why? Because the sector investigation into online advertising is not about online advertising at all. It is only about 'AdTech'—i.e. various services related to online advertising that are typically offered as digital tools. The report then loses itself in the ramifications of these "intermediary services" for digital advertisements, such as Ad Servers, SSPs (Supply Side Platforms), DSPs (Demand Side Platforms), AdExchange, user tracking, DMPs (Data Management Platforms), targeting, brand safety measures, AdFraud prevention, viewability measurement, anti-adblocking measures and so on. The authority examines in detail whether specific markets exist and to what extent competition is dominated by Google's services in particular.

Google does indeed hold dominant positions in many of these services. We have already presented Google's various products in these markets (☞ II.3). It is obvious that Google can exploit massive asymmetries and leverage effects in the entire online advertising market, above all by its privileged access to data and many opportunities for self-preferencing. But in its alleged 'sector investigation', the Federal Antitrust Office is simply picking out a minuscule section of this sector and is obviously overlooking the nuclear damage in the sector as a whole. What has gone wrong? Are the officials at the Federal Antitrust Office unaware that, according to industry insiders, the top 4 digital advertising groups account for 80 percent of advertising investments in Germany and are growing at a disproportionately high rate?[15] Did they not notice in their "sector investigation on online advertising" (the title they chose themselves!) that they forgot online advertising itself? Do they not know that this online advertising represents the financial basis for digital editorial media?

This selective perception may result from the fact that the authority is mainly concerned with aspects it can tackle as part of its supervision on abuse of market power. A great trick, so to speak. The rest is eliminated and accordingly no longer exists. It is certainly to be welcomed that the Federal Antitrust Office illuminates the vertical integration of various AdTech services with outstanding precision: Right on. But the core problem is a different, much bigger one.

The antitrust officers state themselves in their own investigation that "in the mid term, most, if not all, media channels will merge via the internet and all (media) advertising will become a form of online advertising".[16] Which in turn means that our media system will inevitably fall into the laps of the tech giants in the coming years as a result of the digital transformation. It is precisely at this point that the institution ducks away from its own findings and sets the narrowest imaginable framework of its own competence. The authority could have shown that it recognizes its democratic political responsibility in the field of media, even if some aspects are beyond its direct area of responsibility. Here, the institution could have been courageous by suggesting a fair structuring of the advertising-financed publishing market. Unfortunately, with the narrow scope of the investigation, the authority has clearly documented that it does not consider itself responsible for all these important social and political issues, and even more: that it is not even interested in these implications.

But even if we accept such an attitude of technocratic despondency refusing to take any democratic responsibility: It is still unacceptable not to present a transparent "sector investigation" that would fully expose all aspects of the total damage in digital media competition, including those aspects that the institution cannot cure by itself on the basis of current legal frameworks. After all, nobody understands this topic better than the authors of this report. However, this creates the deceptive illusion among the public that if the Federal Antitrust Office takes action against ad servers or demand-side platforms, this could change the desolate situation.

And even if we accept the restriction to AdTech: Google's self-service system described above has been on the market for many years, the analyses of the sector inquiry will have consumed a lot of processing time, the authority's verdict here is clear, and a lot of time has passed again since then. A layman would ask: "Why have they not stopped Google entirely at least in this tiny field?" Well, because this sector investigation is just the "discussion report". So they've been discussing it in Bonn now for another eight months. Then there will be a final report. And then? We'll see...

The inaction of authorities is in fact so frustrating that, as a democrat, you want to bang your head against the wall. An institution like the German Federal Antitrust Office has the power, the expertise, the financial resources and, above all, the reputation and authority to make substantial changes to the abolition of competition by the tech giants. One can expect a federal authority to be able to think outside the box and understand the democratic implications of its actions. However, if the authority continues to proceed with this attitude, we cannot expect any help from the competition authorities in Bonn in the future either. The tech giants should be laughing their heads off.

Our media law has no weapons to use against the tech monopolies

Our analysis has shown so far that we can hardly attack the existing digital monopolies on the basis of existing antitrust law. In Germany, this field is regulated by the 'Act against Restraints of Competition' (GWB). It is part of competition law and applies to all kinds of markets, whether media, cars, soft drinks or cookies. That's why an authority like the Federal Antitrust Office doesn't just deal with the media market, but with all markets in Germany, and it always acts on the basis of the GWB.

Common sense would tells us that the media markets need very special precautions against monopolies. After all, the free, democratic forming of opinions is supposed to take place in this media market. The social damage caused by monopolies is therefore many times greater. It would be regrettable if, for example, a food manufacturer in Germany were to succeed in establishing a monopoly for cookies by killing off all its competitors—but the damage would be acceptable. Consumers can simply switch to neighboring categories, such as snack bars or chocolate. In contrast, the media market forms the basis of our democracy and therefore requires very special protection.

In fact, comprehensive legal regulations are in place to ensure that a takeover of the media system by dominant competitors is prevented. This could actually be good news. But as we will see, even these laws can hardly do anything against the dominant market positions of the tech giants.

German media law is complex. For laypersons, it is initially surprising that there are even two different perspectives of legislation that apply in parallel: The view of the media as infrastructure for the transmission of information is regulated in the area of individual communication by the 'Telecommunications Act' (TKG), while the aspects of mass distribution and the content of the media is primarily regulated by the 'Interstate Media Treaty' (MStV), which has replaced the former 'Interstate Broadcasting Treaty' (RStV).

It is also confusing for non-experts that the competencies for both aspects are divided between different authorities: The federal government is responsible for the transmission channels, while the federal states are responsible for the content of the media. In addition, we have the antitrust and copyright regulations already described—these are in turn the responsibility of the federal government (or parts of the European legal framework), as the illustration on the next double page shows.

There are simple reasons for these different responsibilities. They arise from the intention to protect the media from possible encroachments by state or political power. It is therefore a kind of separation of powers: By allocating different aspects of responsibility to different bodies, the legislator deliberately creates a complex system of checks and balances, which forces the various fields and parties to engage in elaborate coordination and harmonization of different interests.

Thus, the legislator creates a legal protective wall that safeguards the independence of the media that has always been endangered by State power (we recall the conceptual paradigm of the media in need of protection from Chapter III.1—and these are the legal implications). "The division of powers between the Federal Government and the states [...] serves—in the sense of a vertical division of powers—the purpose to balance power and secure freedom".[17] With regard to our basic question of the legitimacy of monopolies in the field of media, both legal standards (TKG/MStV) are characterized by strongly anti-monopolistic views.

Let us first look at the dimension of the medium as a channel. Here, we are ony concerned with the transmission of information and data through infrastructure, whereas we completely disregard the aspect of content. The Telecommunications Act (TKG) aims to promote competition and prevent individual companies from having "significant market power" (§ 11)—according to a common rule of thumb, a market share of over 40 percent is considered critical.[18]

The Interstate Media Treaty (MStV) pursues the legislative purpose of ensuring provider and media diversity so that pluralistic opinion-forming processes remain possible and stimulated in our participatory party democracy. For mass communication, the MStV contains regulations that govern access to central content (e.g. 'must-carry' regulations for platform operators and broadcasters). §§ 59, 60, 64 MStV stipulate that a diversity of opinions have to be safeguarded in broadcasting. Platform operators are not mentioned here.

But how can one ensure that no dominant market position is created? For telecommunications, the Federal Network Agency is responsible. The Federal Network Agency can take regulatory action at various levels if dominant market positions are identified. It can oblige companies to create interoperability or to grant other competitors access to their own infrastructure in order to create interoperability. However, there is no legislation that can be used to break up established monopolies.

Let us now switch to the content side of the media. This aspect is regulated by the Interstate Media Treaty (MStV). It stipulates (§ 60 MStV, formerly § 26 RStV) that no competitor should have more than a 30 percent audience share in a media channel. If specific thresholds are exceeded, the responsible state media authority can withdraw licenses for individual channels or even revoke the license of the company itself. Here, too, we find specified and transparent methods for determining audience shares plus an independent authority to review and assess the respective market power (the Commission on Concentration in the Media, KEK).

The KEK can express concerns about mergers of media broadcasters and propose measures to reduce media dominance, but only in the field of content providers. If no agreement can be reached with the media company, measures are initiated to reduce the dominance of the company in question. In this case, "the competent state media authority shall follow the KEK's directions and revoke the licenses of as many channels attributable to the company until the company no longer has a dominant influence on public opinion." (§ 60.4 MStV) Once again, however, these regulations do not allow for the regulation of digital platforms.

Thus, dominant broadcasters would not be granted a license for new channels, or the license for existing channels could be revoked. However, none of this applies to platforms. Platforms are not in the field of broadcasting, accordingly they also do not have to be licensed. Again, we do not find a legal basis here that would enable authorities to break up digital monopolies.

We have explained these regulations in detail here, because they lead to key findings. As we have already recognized before, the provisions of antitrust law offer hardly any instruments to break up existing monopolies. We then examined the most important pieces of German media law and found a completely different situation. We recognize a clear and detailed awareness of the danger of market dominance, including concrete aspects such as the dangers of access restrictions by the dominant incumbent or the verticalization of market power. Moreover, we find specific regulations for transmission channels and content. We have clearly defined upper limits for dominant market positions as well as accountable authorities. We even find specific guidelines for the scientific measurement of this market power as well as clear and tough sanctions that the authorities can apply to limit dominant positions. However, although the anti-competitive dynamics of monopoly formation represents the most serious social problem posed by digital media (especially as this dominance only reinforces all other publicly discussed issues such as hate speech, fake news, data surveillance, etc.), there is a lack of corresponding regulations in the legislation on digital media. For example, the Telemedia Act and the Network Enforcement Act primarily deal with information obligations and liability issues. There are neither established authorities nor common measurements for determining market power.

The existing legislation and regulatory tools are therefore not sufficient in the field of digital monopolies. This is also the conclusion currently reached by the KEK, which acknowledges a "significant change in media use": "The specific platform economy and the associated 'platform revolution' already described in the KEK's previous concentration report are generating a longterm impact on developments in the media sector. The current media concentration law has practically no answers to this".[19] The same authority's diversity report also clearly

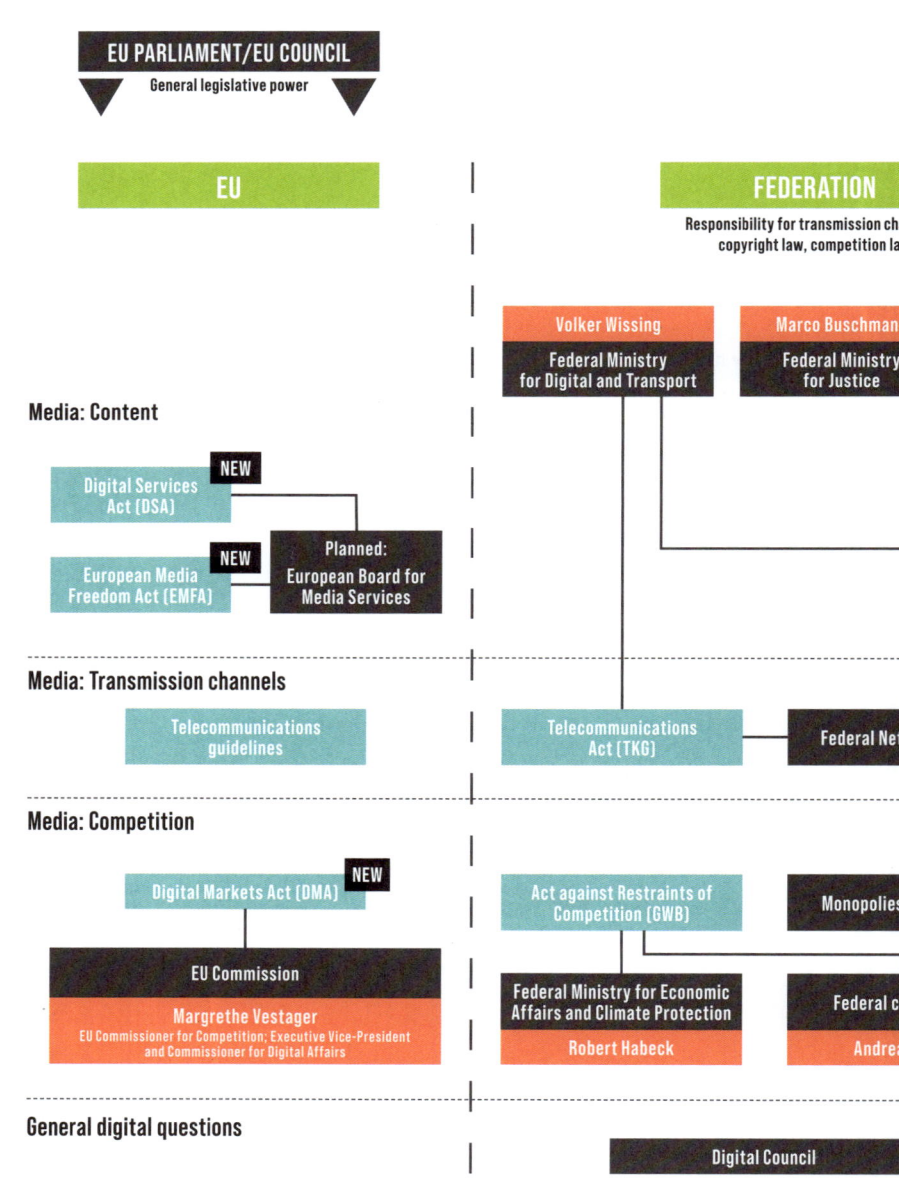

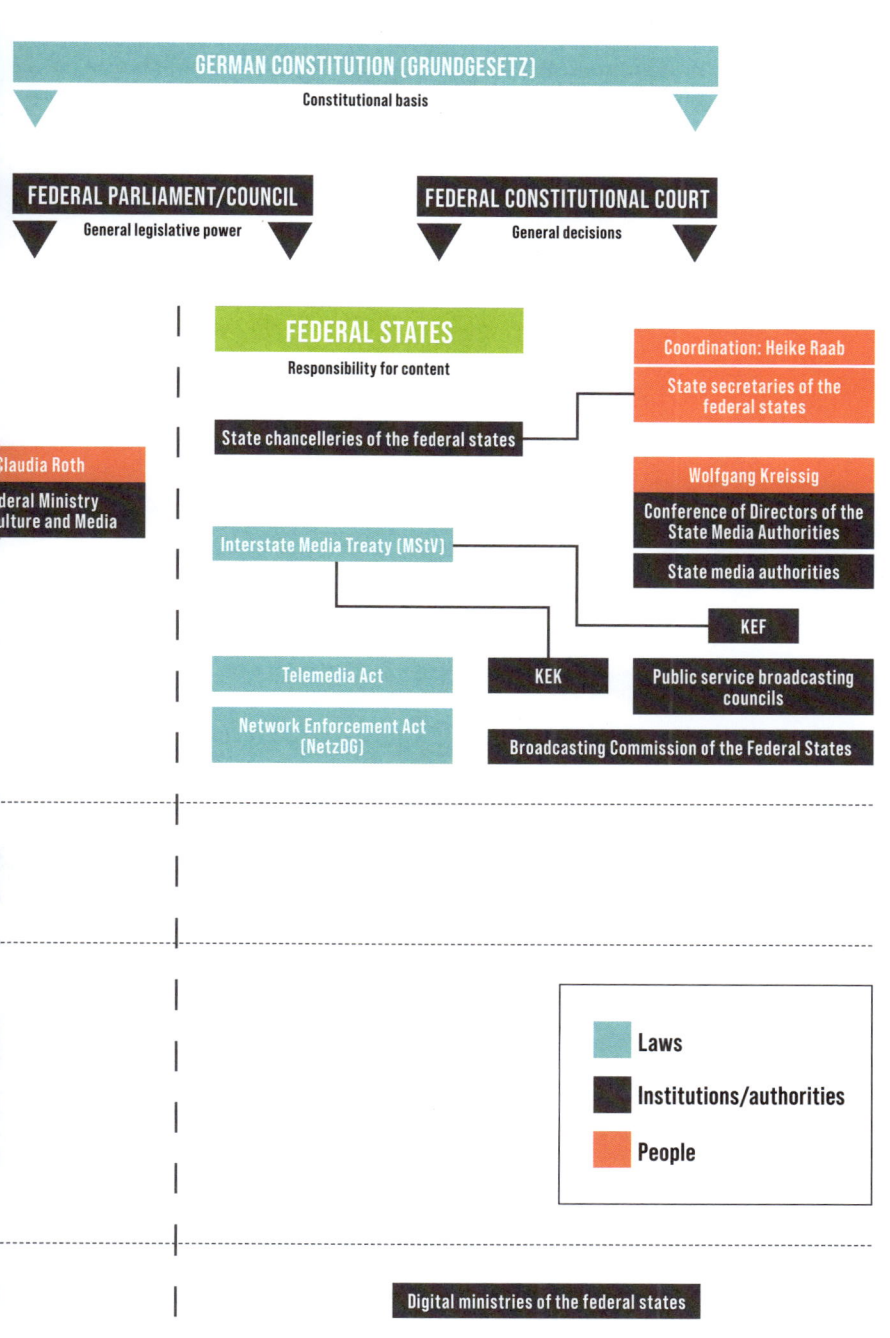

identifies the unresolved problem of digital monopolies, with the authors continuing: "If user profiles are now also created on the basis of access to usage data and individual targeting becomes possible as a result, this further increases the potential influence on opinion-forming considerably. The traditional regulatory tools—in particular the current media concentration law—are not sufficient to counter this problem."[20]

Interim conclusion: The whole misery at a glance

If we now summarize the previous aspects of our argumentation, the current situation can only be described as dramatic:

▶ Digital media have overtaken analog media and are already the leading media, and this transformation will continue and accelerate in the future (☞ I.2)

▶ The use of digital media is extremely concentrated (☞ I) and under the control of a handful of tech giants (☞ I.3)

▶ The power of these digital media massively exceeds that of analog media. They invade our privacy more deeply, they cover ever larger areas of politics and, above all, the owners of the platforms have enormous economic power thanks to their access to financial transactions (☞ III)

▶ Thanks to their rights to define terms and conditions, the owners can use their platforms more or less freely for their own interests. They can manipulate traffic flows (☞ III.5) and even spy on individuals in secret service-like operations (☞ III.6)

▶ Many aspects of the platform monopolies are unconstitutional (☞ IV.4)

Despite this situation, we currently have no way of controlling the power of digital media monopolies:

▶ Antitrust law does not permit effective action against existing monopolies.

▶ Although we have a consistently anti-monopolistic media law, the existing legal regulations mainly apply to analog media such as broadcasting or the press, but not to platforms.

2. Maximum profits for tech giants without liability

Do you remember how Neil Young quit Spotify in January 2022? He boycotted the platform because it offered Joe Rogan's controversial podcasts. The boycott went through the usual attention spikes of media outrage. There was digital attention for around two weeks, after which the case was all forgotten, and (of course) Spotify suffered no damage. After all, Neil Young may be a great artist, but his absence from the platform will not cause millions of users to leave Spotify because of him. Of course, the power of his celebrity does not extend that far. Even in the music market, the few providers (mainly Spotify and Apple) are protected by strong network effects. Resistance is futile here.

At the heart of the case is the question as to whether the platforms are responsible for their content. The case leads to a fundamental dilemma. At a superficial glance, you would think: What does Spotify have to do with this? After all the discussions about Facebook or YouTube, we have already come to terms with the fact that platforms do not have to take responsibility for the content they carry, and Spotify has argued the same way in the past.

FUN FACT: What would be punishable on television is legal on platforms

In fact, there is a legal liability privilege for platforms. In contrast to editorial content providers (e.g. television, radio or newspapers), they do not have to assume any liability for critical content.[21] Let us remember the accusations that were made against Joe Rogan. Among other things, he recommended Ivermectin (a drug against parasites) against COVID-19 in the context of his general criticism of vaccinations. He also repeatedly uttered racist insults. German as well as international legislation stipulates that platforms such as Spotify are not liable as long as they do not 'appropriate' the content concerned.

But there is a deeper problem lurking here, linked to the aspect of monetization. This is quite obvious in a case like Joe Rogan. Spotify paid Joe Rogan 100 million US dollars for the exclusive usage rights for his podcasts in order to generate profits. The supposedly clear line that separates platforms and editorial offices is in reality not a clear line at all.

Let's spell that out: If Joe Rogan's abominable content is consumed via Spotify, the platform is not responsible (even though it paid 100 million US dollars for this content). If Joe Rogan were to appear on television with exactly the same content, the broadcaster would have to assume comprehensive liability. This unequal treatment and distortion of competition cannot be objectively justified, as the economic model of monetization is identical. Both a television channel and Spotify generate revenue by monetizing the consumption of their media content, for example through fees or advertising.

The liability mechanics work quite well with editorial content. Let's imagine what the situation would have been like if Joe Rogan had hosted a show on television. It is certainly questionable which parts of Joe Rogan's content would be legally contestable here. I'm not a lawyer, but I would assume that he might have gotten away in court with his claims about Ivermectin against COVID-19. Not likely with his racist insults, which would then have resulted in penalties.

However, another point is much more important: liability generally has a civilizing effect on discourse. In Germany, we still remember, for example, the (voluntary!) withdrawal of questionable content by the television cabaret artist Lisa Fitz because of false factual claims—even though these statements were rather trivial compared to the content of Joe Rogan.

Spotify and the platforms can earn money even from illegal and criminal content. However, the aspect of monetization is not sufficiently considered in the ongoing debate about how to control the growing flood of illegal content on the internet (i.e. false factual claims, defamation, incitement to crime, slander, defamation, Holocaust denial, etc.).

Platforms are exempt from liability

The public debate on this important issue is currently reduced to a trade-off between two goods—*control* (e.g. deletion) of criminal content versus *freedom of expression*. Any initiative that considers control or liability, however, generates warnings that freedom of speech is at risk and the networks would be 'censored'. This anti-regulatory attitude dates back to the early days of net culture. Back then, the new digital media actually did create a new dimension of freedom of expression. For the first time, the new forums, communities and platforms enabled everyone in society to communicate opinions on any topic directly to the public. Previously, the gatekeepers of traditional media had effectively blocked this access to most of the general public. To this day, this 'access' must be positively recognized as the central democratic and political achievement of digital platforms. However, these digital channels were still insignificant at the time. The still emerging multi-sided business models were not yet understood, and the insignificant startups enjoyed puppy protection. Regulators were not concerned about the potential downsides of those laws.

The legislation was fixed in the famous Section 230 of the US 'Communications Decency Act' (CDA) from 1996. At that time, it was unclear whether the operators of online discussion forums and similar communities should be held liable for the content published there. The law explicitly regards itself as an impulse to promote new, modern and innovative technologies. It proclaims the objective "to promote the continued development of the Internet and other interactive computer services and other interactive media". As a central provision, it states: "No provider or user of an interactive computer service shall be treated as the publisher or speaker of any information provided by another information content provider."[23] This marked the starting point of the legally different treatment of editorial media versus platforms (also called 'service providers' or 'intermediaries'). We should take into consideration that this happened eight years before Facebook was founded. Of course, it is immediately understandable why Facebook and other platforms protect this law as if it was sacrosanct: it frees them from any responsibility for the content, they are completely immunized from having any liability.

Thus, any critical discussion of liability for intermediaries immediately leads to a minefield of vehement accusations that people want to 'censor' the internet and abolish 'freedom'. We recognize the underlying, strongly anchored conceptual paradigm of weak, vulnerable media (☞ III.1), which in the case of editorial media had been facing repression from State authorities for centuries. Nevertheless, we should also take into consideration that the situation today is very different from the one in 1996.

First, it is questionable whether the problem of extensive 'control' of access to the public sphere still exists today. Digital media have certainly created a paradigm shift here. Is the lack of 'access' to the digital public sphere really still the main problem for people today? Especially at a time when there are so many different channels and opportunities available to them? This was indeed a problem in 1996, but the situation today is hardly comparable.

And isn't the greatest danger of 'censorship' the interest-driven manipulation of traffic by Big Tech (☞ III.5)? In the history of media, any type of intervention by

NO LIABILITY AND MAXIMUM MONETIZATION FOR PLATFORMS

PLATFORMS

USER	INFLUENCER	YOUTUBER	PODCASTER
Instagram Facebook Pinterest	Instagram Facebook Pinterest	YouTube	Spotify Apple Podcast Deezer

EDITORIAL MEDIA

INDEPENDENT WEBSITES

News websites (e.g. spiegel.de, faz.net, sueddeutsche.de)
Blogs on own domains

MONETIZATION

CONTENT / ADVERTISING / CONTENT

Content = 'program' for advertising or fees

REWARD FOR THE AUTHOR

USER GENERATED CONTENT:	VIDEO CREATOR:	VIP PODCAST:	JOURNALISTS
0 € Platform pays nothing (Facebook, Instagram, TikTok etc.)	**55 %** of advertising revenue* (YouTube)	**?** A matter for negotiation** (Joe Rogan Case)	Salaries, author royalties/fees

NO LIABILITY FOR CONTENT

FULL LIABILITY FOR CONTENT

* Percentage share of advertising revenue goes to Creator; last published number: 55 %[22]
** Payment of license fees for well known authors (e.g. Joe Rogan, US $ 100 million)

the State was at least visible to the authors. Today, these processes take place inside the black boxes of the platforms that we no longer have access to. Thus, by keeping platforms exempt from liability, we do not save digital media 'freedom' at all. In fact, we hand media freedom over to the digital corporations—and completely lose our access to this freedom as a result.

The second crucial aspect we need to examine is the role of fake news and false factual claims spread via platforms. Since an armed mob stormed the Capitol in Washington on 6th January 2021, we understand to what extent false information can endanger our democracies. The US Supreme Court is currently hearing a case brought forward by the family of a victim of the 'Islamic State' (IS). Student Nohemi Gonzales was killed in the terrorist attacks in Paris in 2015. The allegation is that YouTube actively recommended the terrorist group's videos to certain users. As always, Alphabet and Google are playing the role of philanthropic freedom fighters and warn: "An expected ruling in a case before the US Supreme Court on immunity from liability for social networks such as YouTube, Facebook, Instagram, TikTok and Twitter could 'upend the Internet' and lead to widespread censorship. If the judges restrict the privileges, large service providers would be forced to block more potentially offensive or harmful content."[24]

The case proves from yet another new perspective that one of the central basic assumptions about the platforms is fundamentally wrong—namely the idea that they are 'neutral' digital transmitters or interfaces. The entire business model of algorithm-driven content recommendation is the exact opposite of this supposed content neutrality.

We need to talk about money

As freedom of speech is a core human right, any potential constraints have to be carefully weighed up against the significance of other, competing rights. The matter is as important as it is complex, which is why it is not possible to conclusively deal with this topic here. But searching for manageable solutions for this issue, we can focus on one aspect that can help us to achieve a drastic improvement of the situation without limiting freedom of speech. Fortunately, this aspect does not concern fundamental rights, it is not the subject of controversy and it can be clarified quickly and clearly. It concerns the aspect of monetization. Let us take the above case of the student killed by IS as a starting point. When Google argues that they are primarily concerned with freedom of speech and worried about censorship, the company is concealing its first and most important motivation, namely to make money. In 1996, the first online platforms were still miles away from generating any serious revenues. At the end of 1996, there were just 36 million people online worldwide(!).[25] Of course, it made sense at the time to protect small service providers from liability lawsuits and to create a legal 'safe harbor' for the completely insignificant digital industry in which the new start-ups could test their new business models.

In the meantime, this situation has turned into its exact opposite. Digital media are the leading media. The platforms are raking in obscene profits, while analog media is becoming less and less important. And yet the platforms continue to enjoy unlimited liability privileges. The enormous profits of the digital corporations illustrate the problem. The platforms assume *economic* responsibility for content, but at the same time reject any *content* responsibility for the exact same material they are monetizing. When conflicts arise, they refer to 'freedom of speech'. We should be very careful when these unscrupulous corporations suddenly start arguing by referring to ethics. Because it is obviously one thing to allow the free expression of opinions. But it is quite another thing to earn money with content which in many cases is punishable and breaking existing laws. Typically, we quickly agree that the various incidents of online hate speech are horrible. But is it not even more horrible to use exactly this kind of content as a 'program' and earn money from it through advertising or fees?

The closer you get to the phenomenon of monetization, the more difficult it becomes to draw a clear line. At what point does it make sense to suspend responsibility for the distribution of illegal content? If Spotify pays a podcaster like Joe Rogan 100 million dollars for the content, there's a strong argument that Spotify has 'appropriated' this content and should therefore be liable like a TV station. Ethically this is the case, legally it is not. And what about a prominent YouTuber who is earning considerable revenues as YouTube pays out a share of the advertising income? Here too, YouTube ultimately pays the creator for the content, because it is specific content that generates revenue for YouTube (via advertising). Isn't YouTube then also responsible for the content? Similar to Facebook or Instagram—here too, the platform monetizes all transmitted content through advertising. Can it really be argued that the company has not 'appropriated' this content?

Of course, in democracies you sometimes have to tolerate radical voices. You may find certain statements repugnant, but you can certainly argue that democracies sometimes have to tolerate extreme and radical statements in a pluralistic spectrum of opinions. But when corporations like Alphabet or Meta generate revenues amounting to billions of dollars on the basis of 'programs' that contain criminal content, then that has nothing to do with a pluralistic spectrum of opinion.

Rejection of responsibility as a business model

We start to understand a particularly cynical pattern of behavior on the part of the tech giants, which quite simply consists of turning the problems that inevitably arise from their own business models into problems for society. To put it bluntly: First, the tech giants are openly inviting people to put potentially criminal content on their platforms, from which they earn money through advertising or fees. When critical voices come forward to question this, they say: "Really? Wow! Do you (!) really want to stop freedom of speech? Do you (!) really want to censor the entire internet?" We note: The person who even considers weighing up freedom of expression against other fundamental rights is now regarded as the one who is in the wrong. Is it not the company that is making billions in revenues with a business model that is built on the rejection of responsibility?

Once again, we have to ask the question: Is Big Tech so evil or are we so stupid? First the tech giants create a huge problem themselves. Then they tell us: well, this problem is not our problem, it's your problem. Can you please solve it? How far have you progressed with your solutions? But we, the digital companies, would find it really ethically sad if you forced us to "censor the entire web".

It is obvious that Big Tech does not care for a minute about free speech or ethical issues. Instead, it is a calculated exploitation of a regulatory loophole to maximize profits. The legal scholar Karl-Nikolaus Peifer calls this principle "distancing as a business model". To what extend should platforms be held responsible for the content they transmit? We can easily develop two opposite views. On the one hand, one could regard platforms as similar to the operators of telecommunications infrastructure and services. If terrorists exchange criminal content with each other via AT&T's telephone network, then AT&T cannot be held responsible for this content. Hardly anybody would question this stance. On the other hand, there are the editorial media: they produce the content themselves, which is why they are liable. Again, hardly anybody would question this position either.

The platforms are probably about half way in-between those two opposite positions. Of course, they do not produce the content themselves. But they do provide their users with a program of media content. The program once watched on television is now viewed on YouTube. "Intermediaries become publishers when they leave the passive technical level and rearrange, present or control content themselves."[26] The only difference is that they claim not to do this. The social media companies are effectively pretending that they are only operating telephone networks in order to be able to say: "We have nothing to do with the content." This "distancing" has only one purpose, namely to maximize profits while avoiding all conceivable liability costs. There is no better way to put it: "From the perspective of the rights holders, intermediaries specifically exploit privileges that were intended for passive and purely technical purposes of communication transmission."²⁷

The fact that the tech giants have managed to place their huge platforms full of media content in the category of 'telecommunications infrastructure' ('intermediaries') in order to avoid any liability is quite an achievement. They have always defended this on the grounds of freedom of speech. Anyone who questions this is immediately labeled as an alleged 'censor'. This is how the tech giants have managed to make their problem our problem. It is about time that we got out of this catch-22 between 'freedom' and 'control'. Luckily, there is a very simple way to do so: those who take economic responsibility must also take responsibility for the content. How precisely we can achieve this without compromising on free speech will be laid out in detail in the last chapter (☞ VI).

Right-wing extremist platforms in the name of freedom

In any case, we should no longer tolerate that entire Western societies are taken hostage by large platforms in the name of freedom of expression in order to monetize repugnant, racist, often even criminal or punishable content. This instrumentalization of freedom of speech has also spread beyond social media into rather unsavory ecosystems. Well-intentioned positions of net activists who advocate an absolutism of freedom of speech and misunderstand any kind of 'censorship' as an attack on net freedom then tragically become supporters of highly controversial figures such as Elon Musk. We should not forget that Trump's new platform Truth Social also claims ethical superiority because—according to the propagandistic narrative—it offers users the opportunity to express their opinions 'uncensored'. After being locked out of Twitter and Facebook, Trump himself provided 'proof' that 'censorship' of free speech was rampant on the established platforms. With his own platform, he can present himself as a victim ("witch hunt" et cetera). Claiming this moral high ground is not specific to Truth Social. It is common to many new platforms that spread radical right-wing positions, such as Parler, Gettr, gab, MeWe, Telegram and so on. What is even more tragic is that this extreme form of privilege means that the editorial media (whether analog or digital) are falling behind. They carry out laborious research, check their content, pay salaries and fees—and are additionally held liable if they spread false factual claims, for example. In this aspect, too, they cannot win against such massive preferential treatment by the platforms. The Spotify/

Joe Rogan case clearly shows the unequal treatment in current law, which puts editorial offerings at a massive economic disadvantage and prevents fair competition in the field of media. This only strengthens the monopolies and oligopolies of digital corporations.

3. How we are imprisoned by the platforms' legal systems

An acquaintance of mine is a live musician. As you can imagine, he suffered massively from the performance bans during the COVID-19 pandemic. From the point of view of the digital economy, you would probably say that live music is a dead dog anyway. In order to adapt quickly and future proof yourself, you would quickly have to digitize your creativity. And that's exactly what my friend did. In order to survive, he has developed new digital 'business models'.

My friend placed his bet on Spotify and streaming. Now you have to know that Spotify has been exploiting its dominant market position for years. They also want to squeeze as much of the added value from artists and their labels as possible—by organizing access to music to an ever greater extent via playlists. We are all familiar with the trend of new playlists being invented for ever new moods ("Sunday Hangover", "Winter Jazz" and so on) and also achieving ever greater shares of usage. There is a simple reason for this: the greater the proportion of music that is accessed via such playlists, the less important are the artists themselves as labels of interest and for Internet searches. They lose more and more of their brand value. Industry insiders suspect that Spotify is rather shifting to such content providers as 'Epidemic Sound' in order to increase its own profitability at the expense of the artists.[28]

My friend has now also entered this business. In order to avoid damaging his existing brand value as a live musician, he has adopted various artistic names, under which he is particularly successful in playlists. This is a common practice among artists. He has managed to build up a streaming presence with several hundred thousand monthly listeners, being able to generate four-digit monthly revenues via streaming. For years, he used Facebook and Instagram to promote his artist brands, his performances, his web presences and also his streaming offers. These channels worked well for him, because he was able to link directly to the digital content and sometimes gain 50 new followers for every euro spent.

Until, out of the blue, Meta blocked his advertising account. To this day, my friend is still wondering why. Was his credit card used for too many accounts? What did he do wrong? In a case like this, it is hard enough to find out where the support desk is hidden on Meta's domain. He finally found it, contacted it and tried everything. He was in the chat for an hour, spoke to a Meta employee on the phone for longer, emails went back and forth. Meta didn't even tell him which policy he had violated. He only received a list of seven policies that he *might* have violated. The mail concluded with the 'final decision' of a definitive blocking. Nothing more can be done about it. It is apparently no longer even possible to access the support desk. After the 'final decision', the function is then no longer visible in the account.

My friend told me all of this strictly in confidence. Like anyone who comes into conflict with the digital companies, he is scared. Because he has no alternative ways to promote his content in the future. TikTok has the wrong target group, YouTube has not delivered the desired results (which is not surprising here). Meta monopolizes access to its customers—which is now blocked for him. Which is why he asked me not to mention his name or even the genre he's active in—for fear of messing with Meta.

In Chapter III, we saw how the tech giants' mega-media are accessing ever larger areas of our lives—above all our private sphere, politics and culture, and then the economy. More and more of the reality of our lives and systems is now taking place within platforms. And whenever we move around in their digital worlds, the supposedly autonomous contractual rules of the tech giants apply. Can this even work with such an imbalance between contractual partners? After all, we have agreed to the general terms and conditions of all these digital platforms at some point in time—in most cases without understanding their implications.

The significance of this issue is immense. On the one hand, the tech giants are globally active companies, so that they can evade many obligations by using extraterritorial constructs. Most well known are the sophisticated systems for tax avoidance they have been setting up over a period of many years. On the other hand, the network effects of the platforms allow the tech giants to accumulate more and more rights, which we are constantly surrendering to them. They are replacing public State law with their own law, which applies within their ecosystems. This process is also known as the 'privatization of law'. We showed in Chapter II that digital corporations already own a large share of modern digital media genres. However, the use of media is never really voluntary—powerful network effects virtually force people to use them, as the many unsuccessful boycotts prove.

As the platforms are the owners of these media, they can use the terms of use to turn their users into their legal hostages. On the basis of the applicable contractual freedom, the terms and conditions can, to all intents and purposes, force people to contractually hand over extremely far-reaching assignments of rights to the owners of the platforms: "Either you give us all these rights, or you are no longer able to communicate with your friends—then you're out." For my live musician friend, this had very existential consequences.

Since the encroachment of platforms into the various areas of our lives is taking on ever new dimensions, this also means that the digital self-regulation amplified by market power is giving rise to a kind of second 'legal order' that is determined by the countless contracts we conclude with digital corporations.

Public State law is increasingly being replaced by the law of the platforms

However, this second 'legal order' controlled by Big Tech differs in every respect from the real public law. The public law of the State is authorized by ourselves as free citizens and in free, democratic and public processes. In the legal order of the State, we are treated respectfully as free citizens and we can count on democratically legitimized processes, procedures and sanctions. Here, the principle of checks and balances ensures that we are judged by very different people, offices and institutions in cases of doubt. Here, errors can be corrected, for example through appeal bodies, but also through the deliberate separation of powers. But in the new, second 'legal system' of the digital corporations, we have lost this freedom entirely. My friend also had to experience this. The regulations, processes, rules and sanctions that apply are determined unilaterally by the digital corporations, leading to an extremely asymmetrical balance of power.

Let's look at another example. Amazon not only has a dominant market position as the leading e-commerce retailer in the Western world. It also maintains the 'Marketplace', i.e. it bundles millions of other e-commerce retailers on the platform, who can also offer their products there. Accordingly, Amazon is both a webshop and a platform for its own competitors. Again, we find an alarming asymmetry of powers. Of course, Amazon is constantly in a position to use the various layers of its multidimensional business model to manage all parameters of the conditions in such a way that it always takes advantage of its supposed 'partners' on the marketplace. Amazon can constantly determine all levers and controllers in this digital machine (i.e. fees, commissions, prices for advertising subsidies, discounts, etc.) in a way that it earns more revenues and profits than everyone else.

All others—for a country like Germany, we are talking about almost 700,000 retailers, of which at least 90,000 are located in Germany (200,000 retailers have not specified a location).[29] The merchants can only sell on the Marketplace if they have previously agreed to Amazon's terms of use. This means that they are also subject to Amazon's internal 'legal system'. Experts from the e-commerce magazine *Etailment* have analyzed the situation of retailers in more detail. They also found that in Amazon's 'legal system', in contrast to democratic legal systems, the company is "prosecutor, judge and executioner at the same time". They compare Amazon to a state: "Sellers use its infrastructure (warehouse, financial and shipping system, the gateway to millions of customers), pay taxes (sales fees)—and must abide by its laws. [...] Amazon already has something like its own judicial system—one that seems as secretive as it is changeable."[30] *Etailment* reports that also here, sellers are repeatedly deactivated without warning. There are a number of potential reasons for this. The list is long and seems rather arbitrary. The affected retailers are existentially dependent on Amazon, but come into contact with a system that is reminiscent of Franz Kafka's "Before the Law". They face slow response times, no telephone availability, incomprehensible answers, sometimes automated communication. "The lengths to which merchants selling on Amazon will go to humiliate themselves in order to regain their right to sell is remarkable. Desperate sellers have already traveled to Seattle, others beg, as a last resort, to be 'acquitted' in a 'Jeff letter', i.e. a letter to the [then] richest man in the world. If they are very lucky, someone from Bezos's team will take pity on them."

The online retail experts recommend that desperate victims should always "confess" something, even if they consider themselves "innocent". "An admission of guilt also provides mitigating circumstances for Amazon." In Amazon's kafkaesque legal system, it apparently works best if you openly show remorse, paired with an "action plan" that illustrates how the affected retailer will achieve a future improvement of his behavior. "A level-headed approach is so important because appeals can also be rejected. Once the action plan has been officially rejected, you're out for good. Like a secular court, Amazon doesn't read the same appeal a second time." The desperate situation of many retailers has created an entire industry of consultants who deal with such cases. "On the black market, retailers are expected to pay even larger sums to have their Amazon block lifted immediately. Of course, this is only possible if someone at Amazon intervenes internally."

These examples illustrate the extent to which such a second, digital legal system is intruding in our lives. In this legal system, we are no longer free citizens who have democratically legitimized rights, through which we can rely on a fair trial, on neutral and independent judges, on a balanced and neutral separation of powers between investigation, jurisdiction and sanctions, and on appeal bodies. All instances are controlled by the respective platform, which holds all the levers in its hands on the basis of its contractual freedom to define terms and conditions.[31]

4. Is the status quo unconstitutional?

We have seen, in the course of this book, how GAFAM will take over our democratic media system. We have also outlined the various legal implications, which are alarming: Monopolies are legal under the provisions of competition law. Currently, we cannot abolish GAFAM's monopolies using the instruments of German media law. In addition, the platforms do not have to assume any liability for the dissemination of content because they are not considered media, but only 'intermediaries'. On top of that, they are allowed to set up and enforce their own 'legal order' via terms and conditions of usage, which is why we are observing a massively increasing 'privatization of the law'. How can we be so naive as to accept this?

If our media and competition law cannot keep up with digital developments, maybe we need to ask the question on a more fundamental level: Is this takeover of our democratic media system even constitutional? Intuitively, all of us would probably answer "no". But what are the facts?

Let's repeat our lab experiment from the first chapters and switch off all analog media again.

The TV screen is blank, the radio silent, there are no more newspapers or magazines. Our media system is now largely in the hands of a handful of Big Tech corporations. Editorial digital content has almost completely disappeared and the platforms dominate. User-generated content and, soon, automatically generated texts (e.g. via ChatGPT) circulate in the platforms' feeds. As a society, we have lost oversight of the mechanics by which the platforms distribute the content. GAFAM determine the flow and distribution of traffic in their ecosystems. They own the public space of media.

As a result of the digital transformation, our media reality is shifting further and further in this direction. Many young people are already using digital media more or less exclusively. This scenario therefore affects fundamental rights. This is why, in Germany, the Federal Constitutional Court has always claimed its authority on jurisdiction in the past.

The core problem is, however, that German legislation is overly focused on TV as the core media for the formation of democratic opinion, among other things due to "the wide reach, topicality and suggestive power of its forms of presentation".[32] But this way of thinking belongs to that past. Digital media are already the leading media (☞ I.2)[33], and the 'agenda setting' also takes place here (☞ III.3).

It is not justifiable that the constitutional relevance of German media law should not have the same validity for digital media as for analog media. Accordingly, the entire legal order that currently safeguards the protection of fundamental rights in analog media must also apply without any exception to the field of digital media.

Lack of media diversity due to digital monopolies

In the first chapter, we recognized that entire digital media genres are covered by monopolies or oligopolies. This is unacceptable concerning the constitutional requirement for media diversity. This diversity is a basic condition of functioning modern democracies, as the free formation of citizens' opinions can only take place on the basis of a diverse and pluralistic range of information.

It is particularly interesting to note that media diversity was already an important issue in the days of analog media. In Germany, there was initially only one program in public service broadcasting, then two (ARD and ZDF) due to the limited capacity of broadcasting frequencies and the high levels of investments required for television channels. Nevertheless, media law provided an extensive and differentiated framework to ensure that diversity was always guaranteed despite these limitations. It became the task of the public service broadcasters and the broadcasting councils to ensure a pluralistic offering from *within* the broadcasters.

After the introduction of private television in Germany in 1984, the public media authorities took on the task of safeguarding and balancing this diversity. *The diversity of media was absolutely mandatory at any point in time. The legislator paid continuous and unequivocal attention to this topic, enforcing strict regulatory control mechanisms.*

It is important that we understand the underlying legal principle: If, due to external circumstances (at that time: scarcity of broadcasting frequencies), there is no diversity of providers (lack of 'external plurality'), the diversity *must* be ensured by appropriate measures within the media concerned ('internal plurality'). For example, pluralistic committees ensured that a multi-layered program was always offered, covering the entire spectrum of opinions. The 4th Broadcasting Decision states unequivocally: "In order to achieve this, material, organizational and procedural regulations are required that are oriented towards the task of freedom of broadcasting and are therefore suitable for achieving what article 5.1 of the German Constitution is intended to guarantee."[34]

It is quite fascinating that, despite all differences, the initial situation of analog broadcasting and today's digital media are quite comparable concerning media diversity—even if the reasons are completely different. The lack of provider diversity in today's digital media is not caused by restrictions in media technology (transmission frequencies, costs, etc.). It has been caused purely by the occupation of the markets by monopolies. The problem is one created by humans due to our misguided media regulation and could also be completely avoided if we decided for a pluralistic regulation with open market access. During its evolution, German media law has created a variety of instruments, tools, authorities and institutions whose task it is to monitor the diversity of media offerings. But once again, it is a fatal mistake that, in legal terms, platforms are not being treated as media, but as "intermediaries", namely as service providers. Thus, many requirements of German media law do not apply to Big Tech platforms. As they are not counted as media, they do not need to be regulated in terms of diversity. After all, 'intermediaries' are only supposed to ensure transparency and neutrality (MStV § 93 and § 94).

Once again, a central problem created by Big Tech is 'solved' by a questionable definition—we are already familiar with this pattern from the practices of the German Federal Antitrust Office. In this case, it means that diversity is important in the media. Platforms are intermediaries and not media. So diversity is not an issue here. But what would happen in a situation where there are only 'intermediaries' left? Would it then no longer be necessary to ensure provider diversity? Let's go back to our experiment and switch off the analog media again.

We immediately recognize that these regulations are not in line with the digital age and that the concentration of digital media is much worse than it ever was in analog times. We never had monopolies covering full media genres in analog times. Why do we even accept a lack of provider diversity, which represents a clear breach of constitutional principles, even though there are no longer any technological reasons for this?

And because we have shown that provider diversity is currently not guaranteed, which authority monitors the diversity of offerings *within* the digital media monopolies? Which scientific standards and measurement methods exist to assess this diversity? How frequently are these studies carried out? Which competent supervisory committees assess the findings of these studies? Who is appointed to these supervisory boards? What legal means are available to them to enforce this diversity, even in the face of resistance?

As incredible as it is: we have no supervisory mechanisms in place. There is no authority, no measurement method, no assessments by third parties. There are no processes or procedures to scrutinize the digital media monopolies. And this is despite the fact that the digital media are the leading media of our times.

We should not live under the illusion that there are "an infinite number of offerings on the internet", that "never before have people been able to make their opinions potentially accessible to so many other people" and that "at no time in the history of mankind were more information channels available for the people", as we were told so many times. We have already demonstrated that digital diversity needs to be critically examined in three respects. Firstly, the large number of existing offerings distracts us from realising that very few of them are actually being used. Secondly, we are (in contrast to analog media) completely ignorant of the content that is transmitted *within* the platforms.

Finally, the platforms are not neutral with regard to the content they transmit (☞ III.5). The platforms modify and manipulate traffic in many different ways: through algorithms, filters, dimming and boosting, echo chambers, shadow banning, blocking, heating and so on. All of these activities have a massive influence on the structure of digital media offerings and therefore also on the diversity of offerings.

Once again, it is not justifiable that the constitutional relevance of German media law should not have exactly the same validity for digital media as for analog media.

Lack of independence of the platforms

Under constitutional law, media freedom is initially thought of as the freedom of the media from State or government influence and instrumentalization. In fact, however, this also includes freedom of control by other fields and areas beyond the State. The media must therefore never be dominated by the interests of specific groups, such as commercial enterprises or religious organizations. This was stated in the first broadcasting judgment of the Federal Constitutional Court on February 28, 1961: "In any case, Article 5 of the German Constitution requires that this modern instrument for the formation of democratic opinion is not controlled by the State or any social group."[35]

But this independence of the media has ceased to exist with the platforms. For the first time in human history, entire media genres are privately owned by corporations (☞ II.2). In particular, the Twitter takeover by Elon Musk has shown how far a single person can determine the content on a digital platform, and the extent to which such manipulation was common even before Musk. (☞ III.5) Furthermore, the platforms systematically push traffic to themselves. (☞ II.5). The owners of the platforms have a wide range of possibilities for interest-driven interventions which they can easily determine via the terms and conditions of usage (☞ IV.3).

Most of these practices are not recognizable to outside observers, which make them even more dangerous. The platforms have dozens of sophisticated and technologically proven tricks at hand. They can carry out manipulations that even users affected by them often fail to notice—for example, when posts are blocked without any knowledge of the authors ('Shadow Banning'). The same applies to the various options for 'boosting' posts positively or, conversely, reducing their visibility by 'dimming' them. Whatever we have found out in terms of malpractices in recent years—we can be pretty sure that it is just the tip of the iceberg.

Manipulating traffic by using algorithms is an integral part of the platforms' business model anyway. Every professional in online marketing knows that the platforms are constantly optimizing the visibility rules for content. Of course, they are pursuing their own economic interests. For example, the algorithms are priorizing emotional, sensational or even radical posts. This practice that has also been documented by the revelations of Meta whistleblower Frances Haugen, among others.

Another example is the reduction of organic visibility that advertisers had to experience for their content marketing campaigns. In the early years, advertisers were able to achieve high organic reach on Facebook. This is no longer the case today—because the platforms have adjusted the traffic distribution so that companies now have to invest in paid advertising to achieve sufficient reach. The platforms change all these settings quite frequently according to their economic preferences (☞ II.1).

The platforms' business model consists precisely of changing, manipulating, boosting and dimming the visibility of content and the flow of traffic in many different ways. All these measures are constantly being optimized to maximize the performance of the platform. Manipulation and traffic control is therefore not an epiphenomenon or a residual variable, as the PR-speak of Big Tech always wants us to believe when such cases come to light: "An unfortunate isolated case that we will correct". They are, to all intents and purposes, the basic principle of content monetization by platforms.

Lack of independence from the State:
Data exchange between Big Tech and the US government

Independence and distance from the State or the government is one of the basic prerequisites for the free formation of political opinion in democratic media. The long history of censorship by the State and the experience of the media being taken over and controlled by National Socialism have led us to protect the freedom of our media against access by State power in all circumstances. (☞ III.1) Where, in rare cases, State interference is necessary (for example in the prosecution of criminal offenses), we have detailed regulations and procedures that State actors must observe when accessing the media.

To what extent are the platforms accessed by various government institutions? Let's first take a look at the influence that the US government and its authorities exert on US platforms. Since the spectacular revelations by Edward Snowden, we would do well to be very suspicious in this context. In 2013, it became known that the US government had been collecting huge amounts of data worldwide for espionage purposes since 2007, which it had extracted from telecommunications transmission channels and the Internet. Digital companies played a significant role. The British newspaper *The Guardian* reported that a number of tech companies cooperated with the NSA: "In one slide [of the revealed documents], the presentation identifies two types of data collection: Upstream and Prism. [...] Prism involves: '[Data] Collection directly from the servers of the following US service providers: Microsoft, Yahoo, Google, Facebook, PalTalk, AOL, Skype, YouTube, Apple.'"[36] This means that these digital companies betrayed their customers once by spying on them and then a second time by passing on their data to the US intelligence services.

At the time, some US politicians appeased the outraged American population by pointing out that it was primarily foreigners who were being spied on (you heard correctly: it is only about people living outside of the USA, for instance here in Germany). There is no need to mention that no one bothered to obtain permission for this access in the country whose citizens were put under surveillance. Furthermore, some of the digital companies are said to have received compensation payments amounting to millions of US dollars for the costs incurred. One of the difficulties that arose during data collection was that the secret services were unable to draw a clear distinction between domestic data and information from users outside the USA—which meant an additional administrative burden for the digital companies when creating the corresponding certificates.[37]

The tech giants vehemently denied that they had cooperated with the US government. Ironically, they did so even after President Barack Obama had publicly admitted the program. As a reaction, they published statements that sounded all remarkably similar, suggesting that there may have been coordination between the Big Tech companies. "All said they did not allow the government 'direct access' to their systems, all said they had never heard of the Prism program, and all called for greater transparency."[38]

In the wake of the scandal, the tech giants increasingly distanced themselves from the US government, criticized the incumbent President Obama and demanded more transparency on various occasions, which would, for example, allow them to publish requests from the US government.[39] However, one may ask what one might think of companies that are extremely secretive at all levels of their business model and then claim to be interested in transparency in such situations.

The journalist Konrad Lischka from *Der Spiegel* wondered why tech companies did not courageously fight for the same transparency long before this revelation. It would have been open to them at any time to take legal action, similar to civil rights organizations, against the intrusive actions of the US government or against the misuse of data, for example. Nothing would have stopped them from resolutely standing up for the rights of their customers in court. They could have defended them courageously against the US government's intrusions.[41]

Here too, the affinities between digital companies and the US security authorities are not a side issue that can be neglected. Shoshana Zuboff has detailed the deep and long-term relationships in terms of exchanges between Silicon Valley and the US security authorities.

The deep symbiosis between the two worlds developed after the trauma of the attacks of September the 11th 2001, when the US security authorities were feverishly searching for ways to uncover terrorist activities through data analysis. This is why the CIA maintained its own venture capital company and financed the development of technologies itself.

Zuboff reports on Google, for example: "In late summer 2003, Google was awarded a $2.07 million contract to provide the National Security Agency with its search technology [...] In 2003, Google began customizing its search engine for the CIA's Intelink Management Office under a separate contract with the CIA [...]. In 2004, Google acquired Keyhole Inc., a company specializing in satellite mapping, whose primary funder was the CIA-owned venture capital firm In-Q-Tel. Keyhole was to become the foundation of Google Earth, and John Hanke, the company's founder, was later to take over the management of Google Maps and its controversial offshoot Street View."[42] The close connection between Big Tech and the US intelligence services was a basis for the emergence of many of today's leading digital corporations. Over the years, deep interdependencies developed between the two worlds. The 'Prism affair' should therefore not be seen as an unfortunate accident. In fact, it was the foreseeable consequence of these deep and long-term interdependencies.

Lack of independence from the State:
Traffic manipulation in exchange with the US government

Even more important for the question of the independence of the media from State instrumentalization is the question of the extent to which the State influences the content itself. The Twitter Files, which have already been discussed in detail, show that US government organizations were in active contact with the management of the platform in order to manipulate traffic flows and influence them in line with their interests (☞ III.5).

It is worth taking a closer look to gain an insight into this collaboration: "Chapter nine of the 'Twitter Files' tells us that there was a conference between CIA and Twitter employees in the summer of 2020, and that Twitter and Facebook received regular security briefings. The FBI and its 'Foreign Influence Task Force', which is responsible for counterintelligence, had not only met regularly with Twitter people, but also with Yahoo, Twitch, Cloudflare, LinkedIn and even Wikimedia."[43] As a result of the exchange, Twitter actively interfered with traffic flows using the extensive range of tools we have described above. Similar practices were apparently also common at Facebook and Google. In addition, Twitter received payments from the US government for the expenses incurred, about 3.4 million US dollars until 2019.[44] And watch out for this one: *Twitter management had consistently denied any form of such influence in the past.* If Twitter had not been taken over by Elon Musk, this influence would probably never have become public knowledge.

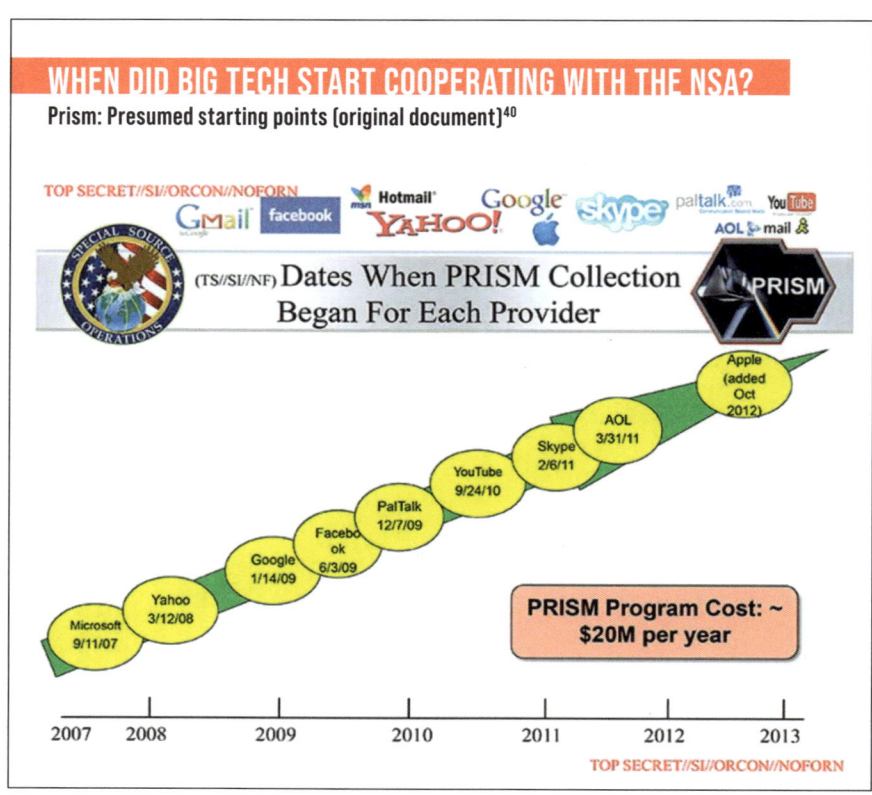

Lack of independence from the State:
Dependencies of Western governments in the field of cybersecurity

In principle, all levels of digital information flows are at risk of potential cyberattacks, i.e. the infrastructure (e.g. servers, cloud storage, etc.), transmission paths and telecommunications channels such as Wi-Fi connections, the domains as well as end devices from laptops to smartphones. The targets can be very different. For example, attacks can try to destroy software or hardware, steal data or spread manipulation through propaganda under fake profiles.

Such digital disinformation campaigns are highly dangerous for democracies. Autocratic regimes or antidemocratic groups can make use of troll armies, bots, fake accounts or human click workers for the purpose of systematically misleading the public. Platforms have the structural weakness that they can be easily misused as gateways for criminal abuse, mainly due to the lack of content curation. We should always keep in mind that this is the problem of the platforms' business model. We should hold the platforms accountable for these problems.

In the months following the US presidential election at the end of 2016, it became clear how vulnerable Western democracies were to manipulation and foreign attacks. Facebook noticed a few months after the election that the platform had been misused by Russian profiles for propaganda purposes during the election campaign. The objective was to influence public opinion in the US in favor of Donald Trump. Russian accounts had also placed advertisements. The scandal led to a Senate hearing at the end of October 2017, where Republican Richard Burr came down hard on the tech giants: "This is about national security [...]—[about a] deliberate and multifaceted manipulation of the American people by agents of a hostile foreign power."[45]

It is well known that these connections led to a massive loss of reputation for Facebook.[46] The case is interesting as it clearly illustrates the difficulty of platform owners in balancing their actions between conflicting objectives. On the one hand, they must constantly pretend to be 'only' a platform, not media. As we have learned, they must do so for regulatory reasons. If the platforms want to comply with this principle, they are not allowed to manipulate traffic.

But as the Twitter Files reveal, this is exactly what the platforms do all the time. Moreover, the entire basic principle of algorithmic selection, filtering and distribution of content also constitutes manipulation, which contradicts the alleged content neutrality of the platforms.

In this context, cybersecurity poses a serious problem, as the immense damages caused by it are not primarily suffered by digital companies, but usually by society. It tends to be innocent citizens, customers or companies that are deceived and suffer damage. Ironically, no one understands more about the potential threats to our digital information flows than the companies that operate the platforms that are used for those attacks. And this is why Western governments and their authorities are already now vitally dependent on close 'cooperation' with the tech giants that 'help' them to minimize the damage to society. The war against Ukraine can serve as an example for the role of Big Tech in this field. We will quickly discern how far-reaching the implications of this issue are. From the outset, Russia attacked Ukraine not only with tanks and soldiers, but also in the digital sphere—through concerted attacks on digital infrastructure.

In the context of this cyber war, the Ukrainian Digital Minister Mychajlo Fedorov quickly became a kind of hero figure of the resistance against the digital aggressors from Russia. He was also the one who asked Elon Musk for support in a famous tweet. Musk 'helped' him by providing the country with internet connectivity via his StarLink satellites. The access was established on the basis of a personal agreement between Fedorov and Musk. The corresponding communication on Twitter appears staged. Fedorov asks Elon Musk for support on February 26, 2022, and Musk replies on the same day, virtually as the digital savior: "Starlink services are now active in Ukraine. More terminals on the way."

Musk allegedly paid the costs of around 100 million US dollars out of his own pocket. However, CNN later reported that the vast majority of the terminals had been financed from other sources, including the US government, the UK and Po-

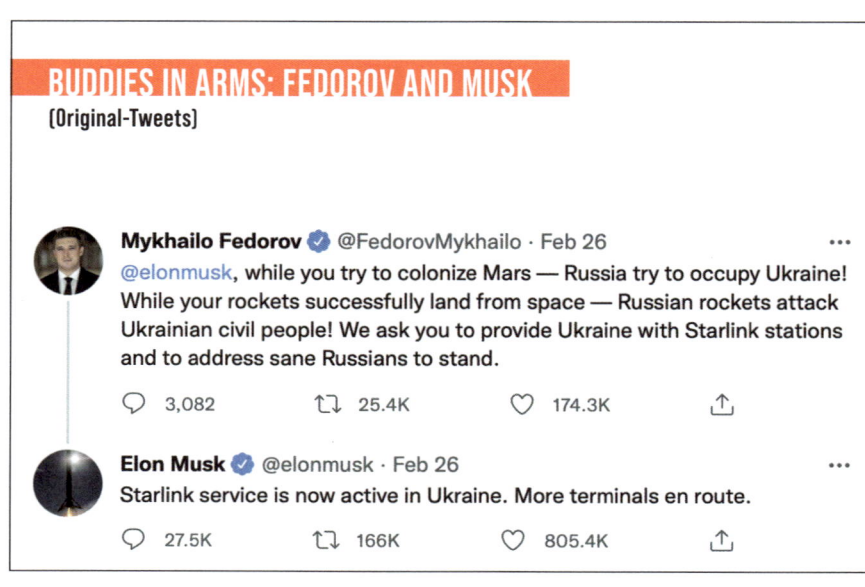

land.⁴⁷ Ukraine is completely dependent on SpaceX's satellite internet, especially for maintaining communication between the troops. Which in turn implies that SpaceX, or rather Elon Musk, has become part of this war, and that the Western governments are completely dependent on SpaceX in the context of this. If Musk shuts down the Ukrainian Internet, this could have massive consequences for the course of the war.

A detailed account in the *Süddeutsche Zeitung* (a leading German daily newspaper) is particularly enlightening. It is based on an interview with Fedorov. The article is less about the Ukrainian government's cooperation with SpaceX and more about Amazon and other tech giants: "Fedorov, 31, came to the tech conference 're:invent' in Las Vegas to deepen the partnership with cloud provider AWS [Amazon Web Services, M. A.]. The latter is investing 75 million dollars in services and humanitarian aid in Ukraine. The partnership has been extended until the end of 2023. It has been in place since mid 2021. At the beginning of the Russian war of aggression, it proved to be vital for survival: after the invasion began, Ukraine moved hundreds of terabytes of data, previously stored on thousands of servers in Ukraine, out of the country in 48 hours using the AWS data transport system 'Snowball' and from there into their data cloud. 'Tax documents, bank information, education data—all necessary to maintain the infrastructure', says Fedorov. Put simply, you could say that it is the complete knowledge of the Ukrainian government and authorities. Other companies such as IBM, Google and Microsoft also helped, and there are now dozens of petabytes (a petabyte is more than a million gigabytes) in the cloud. [...] Fedorov's circle has reported that, in Las Vegas, a new memorandum of partnership between Ukraine and AWS was signed. Furthermore, there was also a meeting with AWS CEO Adam Selipsky about long-term plans."⁴⁸

Here, we can clearly see how Big Tech companies are working, eye to eye, with Western governments. Western governments are fully dependent on them and their 'good deeds'. No one can be naive enough to assume that the digital corporations expect nothing in return for their supposedly philanthropic favors. Let's hear the original soundtrack. "Fedorow also says: 'You [Big Tech companies] are standing by us in our darkest hour. We are grateful for that, and we will do our best to ensure that we are worth every penny you have spent.' His country has big plans for the time after the war. The big goal is to make citizens fit for the digital world."⁴⁹

Once in a while, we read about Western governments and authorities cooperating with digital companies in the field of cybersecurity. Microsoft plays a leading role here. According to the digital giant's own information, the "Government Security Program (GSP)" is in use in "more than 45 countries and in international organizations represented by more than 90 institutions".⁵⁰ There are long-standing agreements with NATO and the European Union, for example.[51] German authorities are also currently using Microsoft software.[52] In general, there has been repeated criticism that this exposes governments to lock-in effects similar to those we have already described. Also here, no open standards are used which would enable governments or institutions to switch the supplier if it were to be reasonable to do so.[53] Europe's risky digital dependence on Microsoft has been repeatedly criticized[54] and has also been described in studies.[55]

Incidentally, Microsoft is also actively 'helping' in the Ukraine war with specific cyber attacks.[56] Industry experts reported that Microsoft has already provided 'support' worth around 400 million US dollars and intends to provide a further 100 million US dollars in 2023.[57] This dominance is also regarded as problematic in the USA. The fact that this dependence on Microsoft was also criticized by Google once again illustrates the ethical depravity of Big Tech.[58] Not surprisingly, Microsoft protested in a similar way when the US intelligence service NSA awarded Amazon a contract estimated to be worth 10 billion US dollars.[59] There have also been recent reports from the USA of a 'cooperation' between Big Tech (Microsoft, Google and Amazon) and various government institutions, including the Department of Justice, the FBI, the NSA (National Security Agency), the Cybersecurity and Infrastructure Security Agency (CISA), U.S. Cyber Command, the Office of the Director of National Intelligence and a specially created agency, the Joint Cyber Defense Collaborative (JCDC).[60]

We discern that Western democracies are increasingly dependent on digital companies, a situation that is being exacerbated by the war in Ukraine. In this field, Big Tech can already rule with hardly any limits. Governments are dependent on digital corporations for better or worse. Is this a potential explanation as to why Western politicians from all parties consistently refuse to tackle the problem of digital dominance with determination? Let us imagine a hypothetical case of a conflict. If a strong coalition emerged in a Western government and decided to stop Big Tech's dominance, the talks in the political backrooms would probably only last a few minutes. I imagine that it would go something like this: Big Tech's representatives will as always respond politely, friendly and professionally. "Oh, you don't like that? No problem. By the way, we've discovered some pretty scary security gaps in your IT systems. Too bad about the beautiful satellite internet in Ukraine. Yeah, they're pretty bad, the Russian hacker attacks, how are things going for you? And how many billions of Euros did Apple just plan to invest in the Munich neighborhoods? Well then, have a wonderful day."

You think that's an exaggeration? As I write these lines, the well known Munich Security Conference is taking place. As I read on Bloomberg, it "is sponsored by companies such as Microsoft and Google as well as traditional defense players

[...]. Over the weekend, Microsoft agreed to provide Ukrainian investigators with free access to its Azure cloud computing platform [...]. Last year, the meeting took place just days before Russia invaded Ukraine. Since then, the role of technology companies in supporting Ukraine has taken center stage at the conference. Technology is 'pervasive and belongs in a conversation about security', acting White House National Cyber Director Kemba Walden told Bloomberg. Apple, Amazon, Microsoft, Meta and Alphabet were all represented at the conference."[61]

With such massive dependencies, one may ask on what basis Western governments should ever implement policies directed against digital corporations when these same tech giants happily 'help' these Western governments in such fields (further areas ☞ V.4). Again, it's the same price we pay for friendly "assistance": We lose our freedom.

Elimination of public service broadcasting and the dual media system

In the first chapter, when we performed our experiment and simply 'switched off' analog media, we were also able to measure the tiny presence that public service broadcasting offers have in the digital sphere. We realized that the role of public service broadcasting content is shrinking massively when we compare it with the analog media order. National public television had a share of around 48 percent, whereas in the digital sphere, this share is only around 4 percent of digital media-on-demand (☞ I).

In this purely digital media world, public service broadcasting would have largely disappeared from the scene as a factor in shaping public political opinion. But legislation does not sufficiently define the role of public service broadcasting content as a factor in shaping political opinion under digital conditions. How would we assess a situation in which national public service broadcasting no longer has any significance? Not because these offerings no longer exist. They would still be 'on air', financed by fees, on television and radio. But in the digital sphere, they would hardly be visible, simply because media users have all migrated to the platforms.

To answer this question, we must first note that the role of public service broadcasting as a factor in the formation of political opinion is not mentioned in the German constitution. The guiding principle is merely freedom of the press and freedom of opinion, a freedom which must be guaranteed and shaped by the legislator. However, the rulings of the German Federal Constitutional Court guarantee the existence and development of public service broadcasting.[62] But under the conditions of digital transformation, it is unclear how such a guarantee of existence is to be imagined (for example, in a scenario where the offerings of public service broadcasting exist both analog and digital, but analog is hardly used anymore and digital plays practically no role). This blind spot of legislation can be easily explained. The current situation of public service broadcasting offers being 'drained' off by platforms was unimaginable at the time that these various laws were drafted. Nevertheless, the Interstate Broadcasting Treaty and the various rulings of the Federal Constitutional Court still make it clear today that public service broadcasting is assigned a central role in providing a full range media offer[63] which is "committed to the free formation of individual and public opinion and to diversity of opinion".[64] This raises the question of how the central role of public service broadcasting will be secured when younger users are already increasingly turning away from analog channels.

Even if the content of public service broadcasters is available digitally in the various media libraries, we are still faced with the same dilemma: the elimination of competition in digital media means that traffic is concentrated in the monopolies and oligopolies of Big Tech, and all other providers are largely left empty-handed. This also applies to the online presences of public service broadcasters. We cannot blame them for this issue. They are no more responsible for this weakness than the other victims of the platforms—the bloggers, the brand manufacturers, the news media and so on. At present, the penetration of the public service broadcasting offers on their own digital media centers is far too low. The same is true for the relative weight of this content in the formation of political opinion on digital channels.

But things are getting worse. In order to achieve any digital visibility at all, the editorial teams of public service broadcasters are playing out more and more content on platforms such as YouTube, Facebook or TikTok. "ARD and ZDF [the largest public service TV channels in Germany] operate 751 accounts and channels on social media, most of them on the dominant platforms Facebook, Instagram, Twitter, YouTube and Spotify. Around 27.5 percent of public service broadcasters' formats in Germany are now created exclusively for social networks."[65] This puts public service broadcasters in the vicious circle we are already familiar with: they are increasingly dependent on platforms such as YouTube to achieve relevant usage times and are thus increasingly losing their independence.

However, there is one key difference to the other players in the digital world. All privately operated market participants feed the platforms for free using their own money and resources. But in the case of Germany's public service broadcasters, this is financed by the broadcasting fee paid by the citizens in Germany. Strange, isn't it? We also pay monthly fees to feed Big Tech with high quality content and contributions for free.

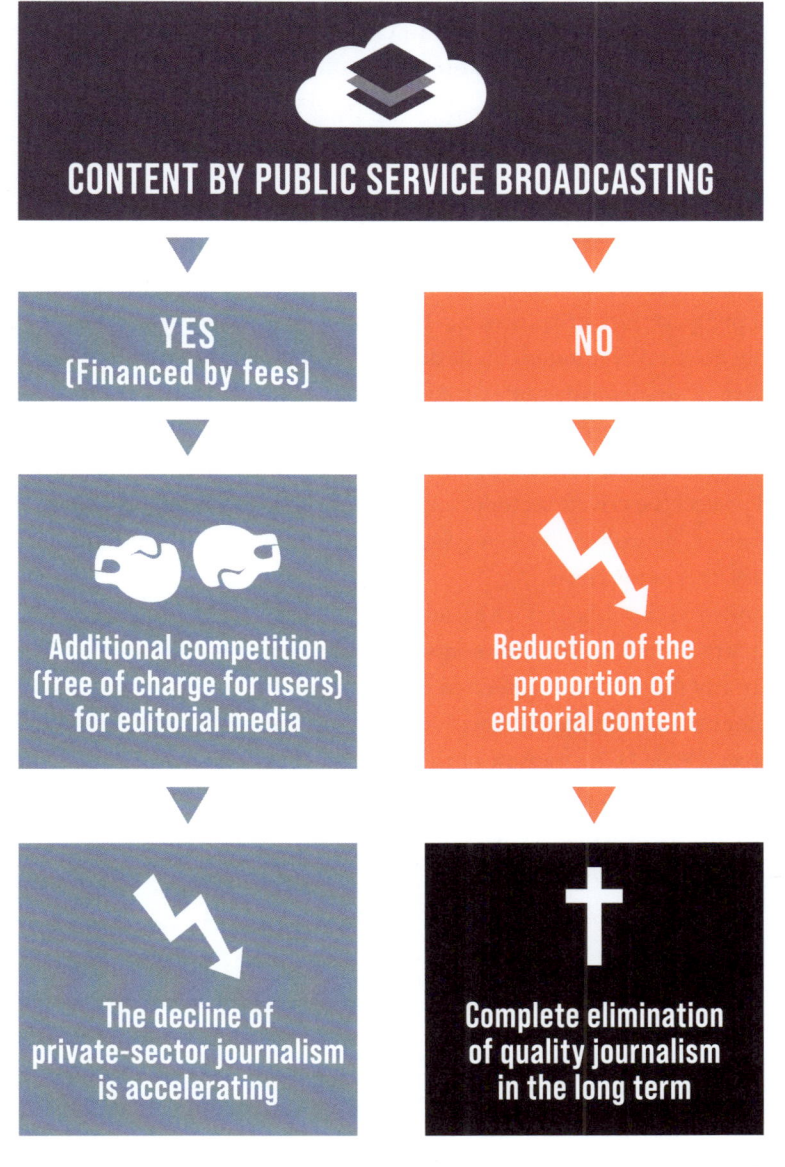

Once again, we cannot blame public service broadcasting here. All editorial offices and journalists are struggling with the same problem: Big Tech platforms are largely free from competition, they enjoy unassailable advantages and privileges. We have seen that it is the platforms that have all the levers of control in their hands to manipulate traffic at will to their own advantage, without these mechanisms being seen by the content creators. Now and even more so in the future, this will also apply to the digital offerings from public service broadcasters. Big Tech will decide what content is seen by who in Germany. And the availability of public service broadcasting content within the platforms is not free, but subject to the full control of the tech giants.

Elimination of journalism and editorial media

The constitutional situation for privately financed editorial media is similar to that of public service broadcasting. The central role of the press in the process of forming political opinion is emphasized in various German laws and judgments, but there is no guarantee of existence for the editorial media expressed in the law. The legislator protects the publishers against State authority, for example, but always presumes that it will exist. There are no legal defense mechanisms that would protect the private sector press from having their funding 'soaked up' by the platforms, as described above. Again, the current threat was not even conceivable for legislators at the time.

Compared to public service broadcasting, the private sector news media suffer particularly from a massive economic disadvantage. This is because platforms do not pay any fees for user-generated content, and they are also privileged by the legislator because they do not have to assume any liability for the content that they monetize (☞ IV.2). As a result of the network effects described above, the platforms can systematically 'soak up' the editorial media. Steadily, they simply lose their financial basis. User-generated content then becomes the generally accepted basis for forming political opinion.

5. Conclusion: Goodbye, democracy and free media

The above overview illustrates a key insight: the rapidly growing digital media monopolies are destroying entire segments of our media system and the basis of our democracy. The reason is simple: we are eliminating fair competition, equal opportunities and thus provider pluralism in the field of digital media.

We have identified major democratic policy deficits in the platforms, which even contradict the most important constitutional foundations of our media system. In my view, the following core problems have emerged:

▶ Lack of provider diversity and pluralism
▶ No independence of digital media due to monopolistic control
▶ Lack of independence from the State and governments
▶ Gradual elimination of privately financed editorial media due to the loss of their funding basis, which in turn is caused by the elimination of fair competition
▶ Gradual elimination of public service broadcasting and the dual system

In my opinion, the existing constitutionally relevant laws and rulings do not provide a reliable basis that clearly show how these problems could be solved. Accordingly, the solutions provided by these laws and judgments are no longer suitable for today's digital media world and its massive problems. Who in Germany checks that the US platforms are not manipulating traffic for their own purposes?[66] In what way and by what procedures is this controlled, and by whom and how often? Who ensures one hundred percent that the US government never gains access to these digital companies that control our digital public space? Which institutions ensure that provider diversity is guaranteed? Which processes ensure that any form of conflict of interest between tech giants and our federal government is completely ruled out—for example in the field of cybersecurity?

All of these deficits of media freedom would be completely unthinkable for broadcasting and the press. But the digital media are our leading media. Why should these democratic checks and balances not also apply to digital corporations? While these questions about digital companies remain unanswered, we are watching the editorial media die without the slightest resistance. It would be completely naive to assume that their erosion could be solved by entrepreneurial ideas, such as paywalls, digital subscriptions, media libraries, additional dimensions of monetization or other 'innovations'. Of course, all of these initiatives are both wonderful and welcome. We can also criticize many analog players for not having tackled the digital transformation with more determination in the past. But that does not free us from our democratic duty to protect the editorial media from being destroyed, in a hopeless battle, by Big Tech. Why? Because they simply cannot survive on their own in monopolistic markets without equal opportunities. No matter how great their efforts may be, the economic effects they trigger are far too small to have a lasting impact vis à vis the gigantic pull of the monopolies. With the elimination of fair competition, the editorial media are systematically being cheated on. The decline of German and European media companies will continue if we do not intervene courageously, change the framework conditions and restore fair competition.

The status quo of unchallenged digital media monopolies is already in open conflict with the regulatory objectives of German media law. Because media law affects fundamental rights, the Federal Constitutional Court has frequently ruled on fundamental issues in the past.[67] After all, it is obvious that far stricter laws and sanctions would be required to protect our media democracy than for markets in which 'normal' economic goods are traded. It is therefore surprising that the media companies, which are being put at a massive disadvantage, have not yet appealed to the Federal Constitutional Court to clarify this fundamental issue.

Jürgen Habermas raised the same question from a different perspective: "It is therefore not a political decision of direction, but a constitutional requirement to maintain a media structure that enables the inclusive character of the public sphere [...]."[68]

Legislation tackling the core problem must take a much more fundamental approach: Monopolies must be a taboo in the media sector. In the markets where they exist, they must be systematically abolished and competition must be restored. From a legal perspective, it is hard to rationalize the fact that the current leading digital media are not affected by precisely tailored regulations whereas the already collapsing analog media are systematically regulated across the entire vertical value chain and even in individual sub-segments.

Current initiatives do not deliver any substantial changes

Current legislative initiatives do nothing to change the fundamental shortcomings. The amendment to German competition law (GWB) makes it easier for the authorities to take action against the *abuse* of monopolies, which is extremely difficult to prove because there is hardly any access to the data within the walled gardens of GAFAM. The situation is very similar with the Digital Markets Act (DMA). According to the EU Commission, it is aimed at ensuring "fair and open digital markets" in the future.[69] Market-dominating gatekeepers are to be prevented from favoring their own offerings (for example, the use of Android with simultaneous registration of a Gmail account). They would be forced to open up such cross-connections to competition. For example, they would have to refrain from having an influence in terms of obliging people to use certain apps in their app stores through their gatekeeper position. Also, they would have to allow third-party providers.

However, the problem of *existing* monopolies or oligopolies is not addressed in the DMA. The legislators did not even have the courage to ban closed standards above a certain critical size. For example, they could have consistently enforced general interoperability beyond messengers. When the legislators optimistically formulate their political objective of creating "fair and open digital markets", they are showing that either they have given up or they have absolutely no knowledge of the digital reality. It will remain a secret of EU legislators out-of-touch with the real world how they can even speak about "fair and open markets", as these have already completely ceased to exist in most areas. As the core of the problem is not addressed here either, the status quo is only further cemented as a result of this legislation.

Even more bizarre than the rather fictional talk of free markets, however, is that the public reception of both the Digital Markets Act and the Digital Services Act has been consistently very positive in the German and European media. There was certainly some criticism ("more could have been done here or there"), but in general, commentators' views were positive.

When I hold presentations on this matter, I often ask the audience whether there is a person in the room who would bet a bottle of champagne that the initiatives of the Digital Markets Act will substantially reduce GAFAM's dominant market positions over a period of five years. So far, I have never found anyone willing to take that bet. That sounds strange, doesn't it? But it is in fact tragic, especially as most of my listeners are experts in this field. So everyone involved clearly knows that these measures are ineffective and will evaporate without changing anything substantial. The only difference is that politicians now have a nice 'get-out clause': "What do you want, we have done something" and "We have achieved much more here in Europe than the politicians in the USA". That's already a reason to be proud, isn't it?

As they have done something and more than the Americans (who's surprised by that?), European politicians will now want to wait and see the effects of these initiatives. The Digital Markets Act has been in force since May 2023. If we add

PROBLEMS AND SOLUTIONS?

ANALOG MEDIA

PROBLEM	SOLUTION
Lack of information	▶ Full range media offer
Scarce transmission frequencies	▶ Safeguarding of diversity
Danger of State access	▶ Distance from the State
Accumulation of Power	▶ Control bodies
Concentration	▶ Authorities/Scientific measurements

? **!**

DIGITAL MEDIA

PROBLEM	SOLUTION
Traffic manipulation by GAFAM	▶
Lack of provider diversity	▶
US government access	▶
Lack of State independence	▶
Concentration	▶

? **? ?**

three years to that, then around mid 2026, we will realize that the supremacy of Big Tech is bigger than ever. But by then it's already too late. In fact, it is already too late now, much, much, much too late. Especially because the legislative process often takes many years. Nowhere is this more true than in the field of media. After all, we have worked wonders to protect the media, which used to be in need of protection, from quick interventions and knee-jerk solutions by the State thanks to the many different responsible authorities, the separation of powers, the checks and balances. Competition law here, media law there. The federal government is responsible here, the federal states elsewhere, and now the EU is involved everywhere. This complexity was once thought up to protect journalists and editorial offices from the 'evil' State. Now it means that we are completely defenceless against overpowering and destructive digital mega-media.

Of course, the various lawyers, officials and experts know that it is a huge problem. But because it is such a huge problem, it is always great that you are never really responsible. Someone else is always responsible. The federal states can say that the federal government has to do something. The federal government would say that the EU needs to do something. Everyone can also moan together that ultimately the Americans should do something and so on. Or is there anyone out there who would like to voluntarily lift a finger and take responsibility for this situation?

If we wait until 2026, then gradually wake up and start brainstorming about what we could do against these digital corporations—well, the battle will have been completely lost long ago. We will then have to say: "Too bad for our children, our democracy has unfortunately gone down the drain. A few years ago, we could have easily prevented this." Is our constitution worth anything at all if we don't care about it? Why is there no sign anywhere that we are seriously worried? "Damn, the place is on fire!" Meanwhile, the tech giants are rubbing their hands and thinking, as they have for many years: "Dumb fucks".

ACCEPT HERE:
Why nobody cares

1. California Dreamin':
The good beginnings

The biggest mystery about our topic is this: how is it possible that the tech giants are not simply perceived as the 'Darth Vader' corporations they are? Many years ago, they had already abandoned all their ideals. Ever since, they have been operating on the 'Dark side of the Force'. Despite the obvious facts, we find the digital corporations pretty cool. Unlike Monsanto, Shell, Dow Chemical or Nestlé, nobody is ashamed to work for Facebook or Google. We adore the Big Tech CEOs. In contrast to the boring suits we know from managers of large global corporations, they have always portrayed as 'cool underdogs'. Even Bill Gates was an oddball nerd, and his massive glasses emphasized his unmistakable hacker halo for many years. "Isn't he cute?" we thought to ourselves. "This mixture of rascal, nerd and crazy genius!" Steve Jobs enchanted us with his John Lennon nickel glasses, his existentialist turtleneck sweater and his Birkenstocks. Also popular with Zuckerberg, Musk and co. are props from the hip-hop sphere, such as hoodies, T-shirts and sneakers.

Let us take a look at the videos that Mark Zuckerberg showed about the next cool digital thing on October 28, 2021—the Metaverse. We entered a cool land of adventures, everything was so diverse, colorful, hip, creative, imaginative, participative, interactive. Just *bringing people together*.

Why do we buy into this propaganda, particularly as we are fully aware of Facebook's evil machinations? This digital aesthetics that we adore so much—where does it come from? We have to penetrate the cultural center of gravity of the digital world to understand how it is possible that these pretty images cloud our senses to such an extent.

Left-wing intellectual origins: Whole Earth Catalogue (1968)

Are you familiar with the famous speech Steve Jobs gave at Stanford on June 12, 2005 ("stay hungry, stay foolish")?[1] It is possibly the most powerful document when it comes to finding out what drives Big Tech thinking at its core. In his speech, Steve Jobs picked up on the origins of his tech ideology. At the climax of the speech, he refers to a certain Steward Brand and his *Whole Earth Catalogue*

of 1968, a famous booklet that was an anarchic, creative, left-wing intellectual project, an Internet before the Internet. The authors presented content about technology, art, architecture, drug use, esotericism, cybernetics and other theories in the form of a printed collage. They created an anarchic, revolutionary cocktail that incorporated elements of Pop Art, Fluxus and Intermedia Art in its visual design. This catalog is available online as a PDF[2]—scroll through it once and it will be like scales falling from your eyes. It feels as if the entire ideology of subsequent net culture was already laid out in this impetuous document from 1968. Even the title is like a major program in its nature. It proudly announces itself as a catalog that is supposed to encompass the "whole world" like the World Wide Web later on. On its cover, we see the first published photo of the earth as seen from outer space. Thus, the catalog shows this whole world from the perspective of futuristic space travel (just think of Elon Musk's Mars mission and the galactic ambitions of tech bosses).

The inside of the cover is adorned with a highlighted text field with the heading "Purpose", anticipating, back in 1968, the now popular mission statements that have migrated from the digital sector to most companies. The text begins with a self-assertion, "We are like gods …"—reminiscent of Nietzsche and his Zarathustra. We should bear in mind here that the same Nietzsche was also the inspiration for the model of 'creative destruction', which today we also call 'disruption'.[3] The *Whole Earth Catalogue*'s mission statement is based on a revolutionary claim to overcome the old order of the State and institutions, including their commercial heteronomy. In the new age, the individual will be freed from these shackles.

It is remarkable how closely this document mirrors key values of today's digital culture. It seems as if Zuckerberg's PR agents have put together the various proclamations on the Metaverse from very similar texts. However, there is one crucial difference: The authors of the *Whole Earth Catalogue* were genuine underdog hippies from left-wing communes in San Francisco. They experimented with an alternative, anti-commercial lifestyle in a colorful mix of subculture, art, drug use, New Age and esotericism. Meta, on the other hand, is a monopolistic billion-dollar corporation with ethically unacceptable practices that threaten democracy.

In 1968, the *Whole Earth Catalogue* provided information on suitable products for the utopian new forms of life that were being tried out by the various left-wing communes in California. The publishers were already recommending the use of computers and other IT products for the purpose of personal development and social change for private domestic use. This catalog thus became the starting point for a unique cultural transmission. The *Whole Earth Catalogue* is nothing other than the nucleus of a positive digital ideology that continues to have a massive impact on us today.[4] The epochal achievement consisted in the then truly revolutionary reinterpretation of technology. In earlier times, this had been quite different—the cultural left had commonly viewed technology through a negative ideological lens. For decades, technology in general and computers in particular were typically understood as the mechanical apparatus of oppressive, capitalist exploitation. A corporation like IBM, for example, was still seen as a symbol of this oppression at the time. It would have been completely unthinkable to attribute any kind of coolness to such a company. Technology was blamed for the increasing dehumanization of the living world, for increasing bureaucratization, for the division of labor into hierarchies, for war and oppression in the modern age.

The *Whole Earth Catalogue*, on the other hand, created a radical re-evaluation of such values. The very same technology that had previously been held responsible for the alienation of modern man from his natural and spiritual environment was reinterpreted by the lens of this logic as a positive catalyst for social liberation from an outdated establishment. Technology no longer appeared to be evil and capitalist. It was transformed into the exact opposite. From then on, it was seen as *anti*-capitalist. From this new perspective, technology enabled emancipation and liberation, collaboration and community, a spiritual rebirth of the networked individual in a cyberspace that was as free as it was boundless, a digital new economy that stood for transparency, individual initiative, diversity and openness.

Beyond the law: The hacker as digital outlaw

Back then, the hippie originators of the *Whole Earth Catalog* already saw themselves as outlaws. This provided the ideological interface for an equally fascinating extrapolation. After all, it was only a few millimeters from here to the symbolic figure of the hacker. Facebook's headquarters have the address '1 Hacker Way'. Cool? We'll see.

Hackers have always glorified themselves as outlaws.[5] Originally, they imagined themselves as superheroes who had to live undercover in the formerly evil IT industry. Behind the inconspicuous facade of their dull office job (at IBM, for example), the hackers were secretly engaged in ingenious, superhuman tasks. If it served their good cause, they also broke the law. They were not interested in financial incentives, marking their contempt for all things commercial with their negligent apparel. The only thing that mattered to them was the heroic act of hacking and the recognition for their deeds in the world of hackers. At the heart of the hacker narrative, we can identify a deep narcissistic injury. The nerdy child prodigy, despised and bullied from an early age, takes revenge for all the humiliation through radical self-empowerment. In his secret hacker identity, he stands above the State and the society of the unsuspecting, who are all unaware that he is like the chosen one, an undiscovered messiah in a nerdy plaid shirt. What is also fascinating is that these bruised egos are almost all male. The hacker breaks laws, but he does it for a good cause. And like the superhero in the Marvel comics, he acts in secret. Ordinary people have no idea of his superhuman abilities.

The figure of the hacker is often combined with that of the 'dropout'. Do you remember, for example, how Steve Jobs repeatedly emphasized the biographical element of his adoption, as well as the fact that he dropped out of university and was fired from his own company? Since then, dropping out of university has been an integral part of a proper digital biography. This is how the magical founder figures mark their break with the old order: they cross a threshold and become heroic outcasts. In all these cases, we are dealing with narcissism: a child's soul has been injured and cries out for recognition.

The Hacker's Manifesto (Lloyd Blankenship; excerpt)[6]

This is our world now... the world of the electron and the switch [...]. We make use of a service already existing without paying for what could be dirtcheap if it wasn't run by profiteering gluttons, and you call us criminals.

We explore... and you call us criminals. We seek after knowledge... and you call us criminals. We exist without skin color, without nationality, without religious bias... and you call us criminals. You build atomic bombs, you wage wars, you murder, cheat, and lie to us and try to make us believe it's for our own good, yet we're the criminals. Yes, I am a criminal. My crime is that of curiosity. My crime is that of judging people by what they say and think, not what they look like. My crime is that of outsmarting you, something that you will never forgive me for. I am a hacker, and this is my manifesto. You may stop this individual, but you can't stop us all... after all, we're all alike.

2. Digital Darth Vaders dress up as philanthropists

Casual clothing, non-conformist dropouts, cool hackers: here, we can see the first outlines of the powerful digital ideology that is shaping our present, regardless of whether we are talking about digital creatives, net activists, the various facets of a digital bohemia, IT freaks, agency nerds or start-up founders. The starting point is always an old and outdated analog world that is being replaced by a new and better digital order. This is precisely why the association with revolution works so well. Revolutionaries traditionally like to use the *manifesto* as a form of expression.

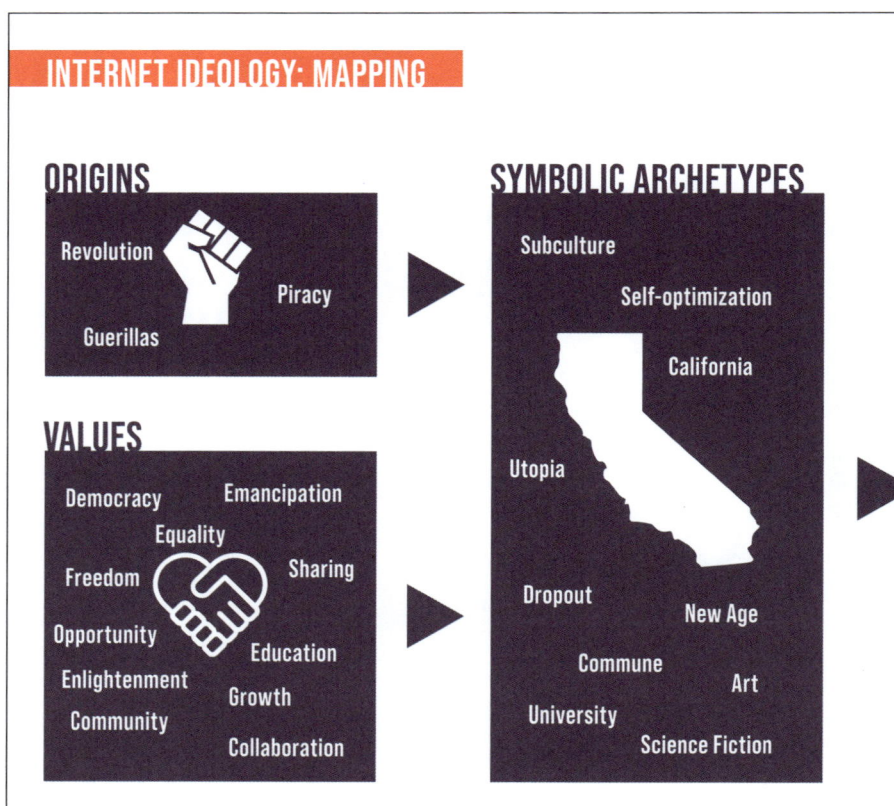

They love such pompous declarations in which they tell the whole of humanity what the new and better world will look like in the future. In such upheavals, the 'good revolutionaries' usually care little about law and order, which, for them, is just old junk that has to be thrown away anyway. The same applies to the symbolic figure of the pirate or buccaneer (just think of the name of the early platform PirateBay, the skull as early symbol of the German Chaos Computer Club or Germany's Pirate Party). The pirates also put their own anarchic order in place of old and boring structures. Pirates sail the world in their wild adventures across the oceans (which is why we also find many words from the field of navigation in the digital world, such as Explorer, Netscape Navigator, Log-in, Port et cetera).[7] Real pirates simply take what they want. They don't ask for permission, they act just like today's digital pirates and hackers. In their world of wild 'Ad-Ventures', the conspiratorial communities of pirates and revolutionaries fought against established, overpowering countries and rulers, just like the adventurous ventures

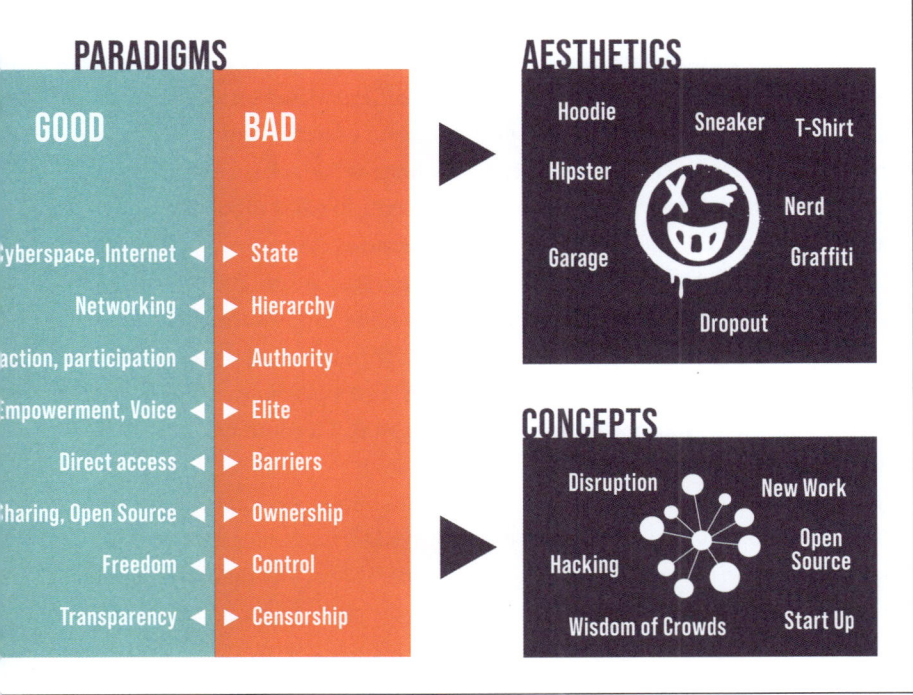

of the modern digital industry. In their courageous fight against much stronger opponents, they also styled themselves as guerrillas—outwitting their opponents with unconventional tactics and tricks.

The digital upheaval is driven by democratic and enlightened motives. People are fighting for freedom, equality and fraternity in the new, better order, for the community, for cooperation, for the sharing of goods (with anti-capitalist undertones), such as in the 'sharing economy', for the emancipation of the weak, for equal opportunities, education and diversity. Yes, the law is broken from time to time for these good causes. They do it with the same nonchalance as pirates would, wildly, anarchically, with a magnanimous gesture ("Oh really, that was yours? We didn't even notice ..."). Even if you break the law, you can say: "Oops, there was a law?" or: "It was just a game."

Pirates love the open horizon, beyond which is the sphere of the unknown, the undiscovered. California has a very similar aura: a kind of mythical eldorado, the gold-rush country par excellence, the dream of the Wild West, the sphere of the pioneers, the land of dreamers, idealists, madmen and utopians who were always in trouble with the boring establishment. California provided the big stage for the 1968 generation: drugs, rock'n'roll, dropouts, hippies, artists with all kinds of penchants for esotericism, New Age, self-optimization, experimental communes. And last but not least, the activity most associated with California, surfing. Those who sailed the digital oceans as pirates were now surfing the Internet.

Every ideology draws a clear distinction between good and evil. This also applies to the ideology of the internet that clearly differentiates between friends and foes. Let's take a look at these opposites: The new, anarchic and lawless space of cyberspace, the Internet, is great, whereas the State is bad. Networks are great, hierarchy is rejected. Even metaphorically, the decentralized symbol of this network is always opposed to orders with top-down structures. The new digital world will be characterized by equality, interaction and participation. The old authorities and elites will be abolished. The new media provide 'empowerment' and 'voice' for the oppressed who previously had no voice. Through direct 'access', they can now participate on all levels of society. 'Sharing' and 'open source' are the future, replacing the old imitations of property and capital. Freedom and transparency have finally triumphed over control and censorship.

The symbolic programming of net culture resembles a cocktail in which very different ingredients are mixed together and stirred (revolution, pirates, California, underdog, utopia, networking, surfing and so on). This is why today, we see such a specific digital aesthetic—with elements such as the start-up garage, graffiti, hoodies, nerds, hackers, hipsters and so on. The same ideological cocktail is also used to mix concepts that characterize our working world today. 'Disruption' then becomes synonymous with digital revolution, companies hold 'hackathons', develop new ideas 'open source'. Finally, we end up in the current manifestation of 'new work', its bean bags and soccer tables, the digital 'innovation labs' and so on.

One key insight is important: all the props on this ideological map are not 'innocent'. Just like clothing, they are always part of a struggle for domination. We, the good guys, sit on bean bags and go surfing. You, the bad guys, work in corporate cubicles.

How ideology distorts our perception

This chapter on ideology is perhaps the most important one in this book. Only the ideology of the 'good internet' can explain the mystery of why we accept the status quo and don't fight back against the hostile takeover of our society by Big Tech. Moreover, we even allow them to present themselves in the guise of left-wing intellectual benefactors or cool revolutionaries. This wrong categorisation is fatal, as these symbols of philanthropy and counterculture point to deeper values. And the digital corporations not only ignore or disregard these values with which they want to be associated. Their entrepreneurial activities largely pursue the exact opposite of these ethical values, as the illustration on the following page shows.

They cooperate with the US secret service. They deceive their customers, monitor our data and spy on our private lives. They manipulate traffic according to their own interests. They make money also with criminal content. They algorithmically boost hate and polarization. They do not pay ethically adequate taxes, they aggressively destroy competitors. They exploit miserable working conditions, they fire their own employees in a disrespectful manner, they lie and deny, they aggressively establish their own legal systems, they systematically exploit us. Do we really want to allow these companies to present themselves as left-wing and well-meaning benefactors?

Let's imagine the worst companies on the planet. Companies that make you sick just hearing their name. Where nobody would want to work. What comes to mind? Shell, Nestlé, BlackRock, for example. I'd have to be tortured to work there.

What would we actually think if BlackRock CEO Larry Fink or Nestlé CEO Mark Schneider suddenly presented themselves in cool hipster outfits and incessantly talked about how their companies were all about empowerment and sharing "to make the world a better place", about access, about giving a voice to the oppressed, about freedom of course, "to bring people together", about empowerment. We would feel that they were making fun of us. We would tar and feather them. We would kick them off all stages, we would nail them down on this and ask them can how they can dare to tell us such nonsense. So why do we let the tech giants get away with it?

Because a few early founders started out as hippies in Californian garages thirty years ago? Because they have a certain street credibility to present themselves here in the masquerade of casual underdog culture? Because they also decorate this style nicely with further 'purpose-washing'—i.e. placing a few good PR stories here and there on topics such as sustainability and diversity? Apparently, we adore them so much that they can do whatever they want. We just love them anyway. There is a mysterious force at work in our brains *that systematically distorts our perception and impairs our cognition. This is exactly what ideology does.*

'Ideology' refers to unconscious patterns of perception, world views and attitudes that have become so ingrained that we can no longer recognize them any more. Since Karl Marx and Friedrich Engels, we have known that ideologies have fulfilled an essential function for thousands of years: They legitimize power and domination. This is because ideologies create a kind of *systematic deception* that leads oppressed people to believe that this reality of exploitation is completely normal. The unbelievable happens: they accept reality and submit instead of rising up against the oppressors. An unmistakable sign of the presence of ideology is when even the oppressed groups adopt the argumentative position of the oppressors. The state of oppression thus appears to *all members* of society as completely normal, natural, inevitable and even desirable, although the opposite is the case. Because we do have a choice and can shape the world completely differently.

In our case, the oppressors would have to deceive the exploited people into believing that the whole mechanism of digital exploitation is a great thing for everyone. And this is exactly what the tech giants have achieved through the ideology of the good Internet. Otherwise, the many popular bestsellers from the years between 1995 and 2010 would have been unthinkable, in which intoxicated digital evangelists unilaterally praised models such as swarm intelligence, crowdsourcing, peer production and open source as liberation and empowerment. They did not realize that they were dancing to the ideological tune of Big Tech.

Many digital enthusiasts promoted all this and thus enabled the maximum conceivable exploitation of people working for free for Big Tech, from *Being Digital* (Nicholas Negroponte, 1995), T*he Age of Access* (Jeremy Rifkin, 2000) and *The Long Tail* (Chris Anderson, 2006) to *Wikinomics* (Tapscott/Williams 2008) or *What would Google do?* (Jeff Jarvis, 2009).[8] The digital corporations must have laughed hard at the legions of volunteer supporters who worked hard for them for free, simply because they took these digital utopias at face value—while Big Tech raked in the profits quarter after quarter.

The creation and shoring up of this ideology plays an absolutely central role in the chess game of Big Tech. You think that's an exaggeration? Read the following quote from the then CEO of Google, Eric Schmidt: "the multidimensional result[...] will be more egalitarian, more transparent and more interesting than we can even imagine. As in a social contract, users will voluntarily relinquish things they value in the physical world—privacy, security, personal data—in order to gain the benefits that come with being connected to the virtual world".[9] Of course—it is only for our own good if Big Tech rules the world.

IDEOLOGY LEGITIMIZES POWER

The new ruling class must ...

"... present its interest as the common interest of all members of society, i.e. in ideal terms:

express their thoughts in a universal form, present them as the only reasonable, generally valid ones."

Marx, Engels: The German Ideology

3. The destruction of freedom in the name of freedom

"The Internet is free—regulation is useless anyway and only restricts digital freedom!" Sounds reasonable, doesn't it? We have often heard these and similar sentences in debates on net politics. We can use this example to show how strongly digital ideology affects the status quo—without us even realizing it.

An infinite number of political activities are carried out by, for example, net enthusiasts, NGOs and bloggers. The common denominator is often to protect the freedom of the Internet from State access and, above all, censorship. There is actually a consistent thread of tradition here from John Perry Barlow's *Declaration of the Independence of Cyberspace* to the German Chaos Computer Club or the European dispute over digital copyright violations some years ago. But this preservation of net freedom has a dark side—surprisingly, it leads to a much more fundamental destruction of freedom without us realizing it. To understand what this is all about, we need to reflect briefly on the concept of freedom.

First of all, it should be clear that absolute freedom cannot exist under the rule of law. Every freedom is limited if other people are harmed by certain actions. We can quickly explain this using the example of freedom of expression. It is correct that freedom of opinion in Germany is covered by the Constitution. But people are not free in the sense that they can simply say anything they want. If, for example, they knowingly claim false facts about another person that destroys that person's reputation, then that is not covered by the right to freedom of expression. Such statements are then punishable as defamation. You are not allowed to incite other people to break the law, you are not allowed to discriminate against people or call them racist names. Denying the existence of the Holocaust is banned in Germany. Interestingly enough, the same principle applies to freedom in the economy. Of course we have a free market economy, but this freedom is not limitless either. For example, companies are not allowed to knowingly sell defective or harmful products. They are not allowed to dump toxic waste into rivers, child labor is prohibited, people are not allowed to pay with counterfeit money, and so on.

Freedom therefore only exists as a theoretical ideal. In reality, we always balance freedom against other aspects and also the freedom of our peers. Hardly anyone would dispute the usefulness of these restrictions. Our laws represent a democratically legitimized framework within which our liberal actions can unfold without harming other people. Or to put it another way: There are no spheres in our society that are free of rules and limitations to freedom.

However, the early days of the digital transformation represented a special situation. There was a largely unregulated, 'free', anarchically wild and exciting digital adventure space. There was still no legal framework for the new network

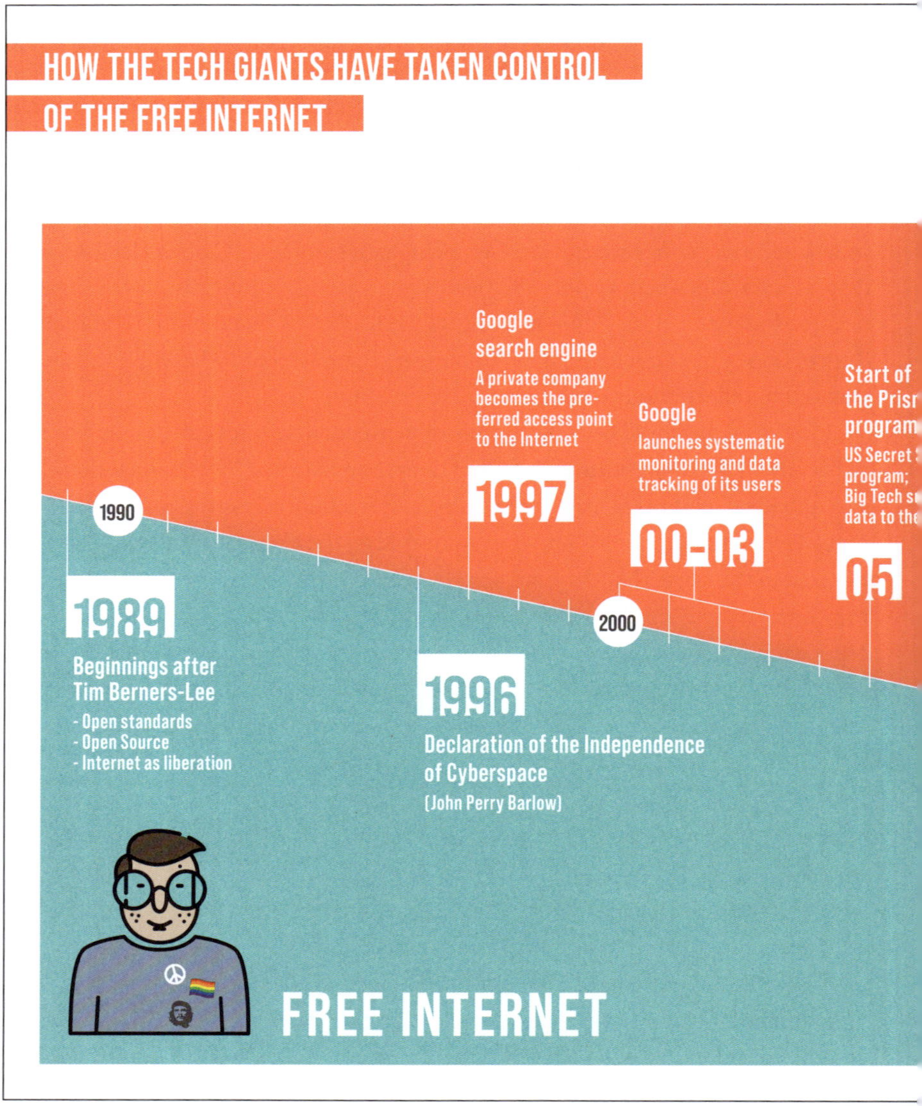

HOW THE TECH GIANTS HAVE TAKEN CONTROL OF THE FREE INTERNET

1989
Beginnings after Tim Berners-Lee
- Open standards
- Open Source
- Internet as liberation

1990

1996
Declaration of the Independence of Cyberspace
(John Perry Barlow)

1997 Google search engine
A private company becomes the preferred access point to the Internet

2000

00-03 Google launches systematic monitoring and data tracking of its users

05 Start of the Prism program
US Secret Service program; Big Tech sends data to the

FREE INTERNET

reality. This was not a major problem at the time, because the net was only used by a few digital nerds and was barely being used for commercial purposes. A typical problem was the infringement of copyrights—for example, when creative people made videos from existing materials and then published them on social networks, but ignored the intellectual property rights of the authors. It was also a question of

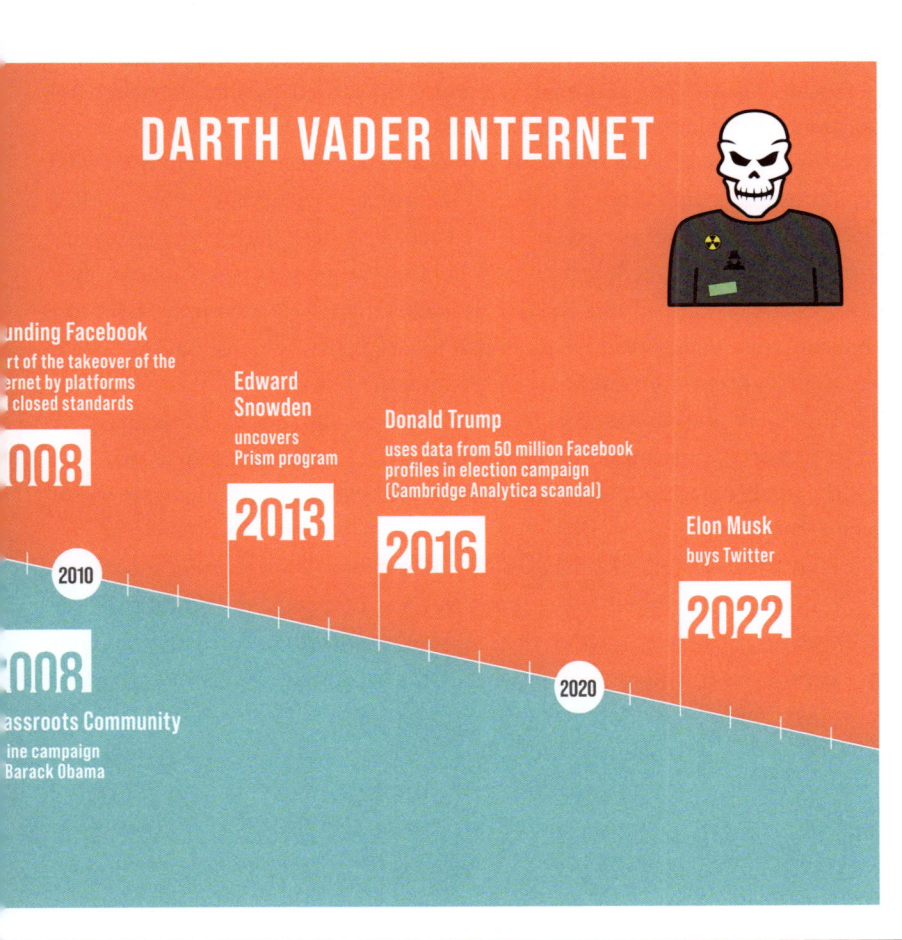

whether the operators of early chat forums could be held responsible for criminal content. We have already dealt with this aspect when discussing liability. It would go beyond the scope of this book to investigate this development in detail. But one key detail is important: In the early digital days, all the initiatives in favor of a 'free' and largely unregulated Internet were voiced by creatives, hackers and network enthusiasts as well as by the early digital companies, which were still on the 'Good side of the Force' during those days. Nobody in those days could have foreseen that these insignificant start-ups would turn into corporations that engage in 'Darth Vader' like activities within a few years.

In the years that followed, the largely unregulated Internet proved to be an eldorado for the companies concerned. They grew into the tech giants they are today. In the course of various scandals, from Prism to Cambridge Analytica, the platforms were increasingly criticized for not taking any responsibility. Their answer to the public was always the same. The platforms referred to the regulatory advantage they had been granted many years ago under entirely different circumstances. They repeated again and again that were not media at all and that they were not responsible for the content on their platforms.

We now understand the mechanics. In order to achieve their economic goal of exploiting their digital monopolies undisturbed by regulation, they hijacked the ideology of 'freedom of speech'. Since then, they have been consistently appearing in the guise of freedom fighters defending the people's rights against 'evil' State interference. They appear on stage as noble knights who just want to protect the Internet from widespread censorship. It is completely obvious that the 'Darth Vader' digital corporations were no longer interested in any ethical issues at this point. They were not interested in freedom of expression, but in defending their freedom to harvest maximum profits against every conceivable restriction. And that is the intellectual fraud committed when tech giants constantly make use of the word 'freedom'.

We start to understand the magic power of ideology. With their most trusting look, the digital corporations tell us about 'freedom of speech' and how much they fear censorship. They raise their eyebrows and express their sincere concern about excessive State intervention and regulation on the Internet. And what happens? Bloggers, net enthusiasts, intellectuals and journalists collectively take a stand *against* regulation. Why is this surprising? Because the same crowd would *never* even think of rejecting State intervention in any other area of the economy. They would never seriously question regulations that protect the rights of consumers, mitigate the aggressive encroachments of gigacorporations or prevent the exploitation of customers. People who are otherwise more likely to vote for left or green political parties argue against regulation *only when it comes to the Internet*—even

THE NET ENTHUSIAST: SAM, 44

AGE
44

GAMING
NET CULTURE
DIGITAL ART
EXCHANGE WITH OTHER DIGITAL NERDS

regulat
and c

VALUES AND GOALS
- Politically left-wing and active
- Appreciates creativity and art
- Loves boundless freedom
- Fights for minorities
- Takes a stand against discrimination
- Acts as an underdog and nerd

PAIN POINTS
- Against all conceivable forms of regulation, especially restrictions on civil liberties (copyright, freedom of expression)
- Against the oppression of minorities
- Against data surveillance

OCCUPATION	PLACE OF RESIDENCE	STATUS	INCOME
Blogger	Berlin	Single	US $ 28.000 per year

"...ernet is FREE— ...seless anyway ...tricts freedom."

TOUCHPOINTS

- ▶ Twitter ● ● ● ● ●
- ▶ Blogs   ● ● ● ● ○
- ▶ Discord ● ● ● ● ○
- ▶ Twitch   ● ● ● ○ ○

MOTIVATION

- ▶ Positive connection with digitalization, experienced as a departure into an anti-hierarchical, networked and diverse world
- ▶ Lifestyle of a 'digital bohemian'
- ▶ Laissez-faire: tolerates violations of the law for 'good causes' (e.g. creativity vs. copyright)
- ▶ Anarchist tendencies

though they would certainly reject similar positions in other areas as quite unsavory. Many agree with the general attitude: "The State should not intervene on the Internet—regulations have never achieved anything."

Fortunately, more and more bloggers and net enthusiasts are realizing how badly they have been deceived by the digital corporations for years. They have been instrumentalized for purposes that are the opposite of what they believe in. Of late, the takeover of Twitter by Elon Musk has made it clear where the journey is heading and who owns the web. Musk had also dressed himself up as a self-proclaimed "absolutist of freedom of speech"—but more and more enthusiasts are no longer willing to fall for that line.

Markus Beckedahl, Germany's most prominent net activist and editor-in-chief of *Netzpolitik.org*, has also expressed his concerns and questioned how "such an enormous concentration of power can be monitored, controlled and limited by democratic institutions".[10] Hopefully, we will see a turnaround in net politics. After all, our society needs the digital expertise of net activists now more than ever. They catalyzed the emergence of the Internet like no other group. They were often the ones who made our Internet possible, through open source initiatives and free collaboration. They provided the creative content, they worked tirelessly and helped shape our digital world with all their positive and creative energies. The digital corporations have skimmed all the profits at their expense for all these years and decorated the whole exploitation machine as a philanthropic project.

Net enthusiasts have always been on the good side of power. If there's one group that could claim to hold some kind of intellectual 'copyright' on the internet, it's them. If anyone has the authority to rip the mask of left-wing intellectual philanthropy off the tech giants' faces, it's the net activists. It's time for them to take a stand against the digital corporations and help to free the internet from their rule.

4. Promote versus punish: Big Tech's lobbying machine

While ideology ensures that the hostile takeover of our society is concealed by a deceptive veil of philanthropy and coolness, Big Tech maintains a gigantic lobbying apparatus to infinitely reinforce this wonderful staging and at the same time nip any form of resistance in the bud. Big Tech has long since replaced suspect lobbyists from earlier industries that engaged in 'Darth Vader' like behavior. According to a study by Corporate Europe Observatory and LobbyControl from 2021, digital companies now account for the lion's share of investment in lobbying and are now the leading investor, well ahead of the automotive industry, the pharmaceutical segment or the banking sector, with investments of around 100 million euros annually in Europe alone.[11] Big Tech maintains an apparatus of no less than 140 lobbyists in Brussels alone, who try to manipulate and shape European politics in the interests of the digital corporations. In total, there are 1,500 active lobbyists in Europe. Big Tech is operating behind a huge network of around 600 different associations, agencies, think tanks, law firms, NGOs and consultancies.[12]

It is often impossible for outsiders to tell at first or even second sight whether some of these organizations are independent voices or mere facades that are actually backed by Big Tech. In the worst case, policymakers may think they are hearing authentic recommendations from idealists whereas, behind the scenes, the NGO that they are talking to is in fact funded and controlled by Big Tech. This was the accusation made by prominent EU politicians from the Netherlands, Germany and Denmark in 2022: "Large US technology companies such as Google, Meta and Amazon have deceived lawmakers during consultations on the new rules for online platforms by lobbying through smaller front organizations. [Members of parliament] are also pushing for a ban on cooperation between these companies and the EU institutions."[13]

The arguments that Big Tech lobbyists try to disseminate always run along the same lines: regulation threatens innovation, only the digital companies have the required digital expertise, know their way around the internet and can deliver great solutions for us users. On top of that, all they do is for the good of mankind. Finally, they claim that we can only escape a hostile takeover of the Internet by the 'evil Chinese' if we accept their digital leadership.

Even worse than the massive lobbying is the intensive exchange between Big

Tech and leading US government institutions and other political offices. Jonathan Taplin provides a series of examples of former Big Tech managers who have been hired by politicians and, conversely, politicians who have been drawn to Big Tech: "There have been 53 revolving-door moves between Google and the White House. These moves involved 22 White House officials who left the administration to work for Google and 31 Google executives (or executives from Google's main outside firms) who joined the White House or were appointed to federal advisory boards". For Google alone, Taplin cites 28 additional cases from the US defense and security agencies and 23 cases for the State Department.[14]

The fact that Big Tech has almost infinite financial resources at its disposal has enabled it to build up a complex system in all areas of our society. Through this system, Big Tech massively promotes specific stakeholders where this plays into the hands of its digital takeover. On the other hand, critical voices or parties are punished. Ultimately, they are transferring the same system of dimming and boosting that is at work in their platforms to the field of lobbying. The subtlety and efficiency of 'promote versus punish' can best be illustrated with a concrete example. Let's take a deeper look the German media system again, especially as we can expand on many of the insights we have already gathered.

Divide and rule: How Big Tech is playing editorial media off against each other

The main impact of Big Tech on the media lies in the gradual elimination of existing editorial media companies that we already described in detail. The tech giants were only able to succeed by facilitating the approval of legislation that systematically eliminates fair competition in the digital media. The fact that the many legal platform privileges are not called into question despite the huge collateral damage for our society is simply the result of their successful ideological work and their massive lobbyist investments.

But now things are getting wild. Big Tech is running a promotion program for the editorial media on a nicely decorated stage in the foreground. That's right: Big Tech is systematically eliminating the editorial media, but at the same time the digital corporations are brazen enough to present themselves as promoters of that same media they are eliminating. Of course, the amounts that they invest are ridiculously small compared to the gigantic territorial gains that are achieved in parallel through the systematic elimination of editorial competitors. Metaphorically speaking, it would be like the same unscrupulous occupation powers who seize huge territories giving former inhabitants a few nice presents.

We can take a closer look at this using Google as an example, because an excellent study on the topic was executed by Ingo Dachwitz and Alexander Fanta.¹⁵ Between 2015 and 2019, Google gave around 150 million euros to the media in Europe through its 'Digital News Initiative' (DNI). A clear pattern can be identified. In Europe, preference is given to large countries and here, the established, leading news media corporations are treated with special favors by Big Tech.

From a lobbyist's point of view, this strategy makes a lot of sense. After all, the small and regional media offerings are already weak and battered; to put it bluntly, you could say that they are 'already gone anyway'. But the big, traditional news media brands are still highly relevant in terms of opinion power. These still attract so much attention that they must be 'contained' in a positive sense. This is why it is precisely these leading editorial media that are being promoted and supported. But behind this pretty stage of support and favors, a fierce battle for money is raging in the background. The reason is simple: Google, for example, has been using publishers' content for years without paying the publishers an appropriate amount of financial compensation. This topic of ancillary copyright for press publishers is difficult to understand even for experts. Put simply, Google's strategy is to divide the industry and conclude deals with individual, mostly leading news media companies that are highly advantageous for the publishers in the short term ('Google News Showcase'), but which will probably lead to significantly lower prices for the industry in the long term. A market insider called these payments "hush money".¹⁶

This leaves the weak publishers even worse off ('punish'), while the strong ones are strongly rewarded ('promote')—through voluntary support programs (DNI), the payments from the Google News Showcase and additionally through the placement of advertising. This is because Google provides "the major news publishers with disproportionately high advertising investments. An analysis of Nielsen figures shows that seven large media companies alone, all of which are also part of Showcase, received a gross amount of 28 million euros between 2019 and 2021. DvH Medien (*Handelsblatt*, *Tagesspiegel*, 50 percent of *Die Zeit*), for example, received around 8.3 million euros (gross) between 2019 and 2021. *Der Spiegel* was awarded 5.3 million euros (gross)."¹⁷

It is easy to grasp that this is well invested money for Google. Through its advertising, the company presents itself to the public in the guise of the philanthropic benefactor that we described above. Readers who are capable of digesting extremely hypocritical content without violent physical reactions should spend some time reading the Google magazine *Aufbruch* (German for "Dawn") which is often used as an insert in the press—it's all about the dawning of a great digital new age, diversity, sustainability, education, participation, and so on.¹⁸

Of course, it's not just Google that uses such instruments. We could also find similar examples from other Big Tech companies. Facebook, for example, concluded a deal with the media publisher Springer in 2021. According to media sources, it is assumed that the deal will deliver revenues worth hundreds of millions over several years.[19] Internationally, Facebook is said to have 'supported' 2,600 publishers with more than 600 million US dollars.[20] Through the Bill & Melinda Gates Foundation of the Microsoft founder, several hundred million euros of 'support' have been distributed to the media worldwide,[21] with the leading German news magazine *Der Spiegel* receiving around 5.4 million euros of this money.[22] And we could go on like this for a long time. The same applies to advertising gifts. In addition to Alphabet, Meta is pleasing the big German news media companies with huge advertising investments. *Zeit*, *Spiegel*, *Süddeutsche* and *FAZ* each received around 4 million euros (gross) from Alphabet and Meta combined in 2021, i.e. a total of around 16 million in just one year.[23] The sums distributed are so equal that one might even come to the conclusion that Alphabet and Meta have coordinated this 'support' with each other. Can the ailing media companies be blamed for accepting these payments? Revenues in the industry have been stagnating for many years. Many publishers have their backs to the wall and have little choice in the fight for survival.

Another crucial question is whether Big Tech expects something in return from the publishers for the 'support'. Structurally, the journalists are independent thanks to the separation of editorial and commercial departments in the publishing houses. In the interviews from the study by Ingo Dachwitz and Alexander Fanta, there was no evidence of GAFAM directly influencing the editorial content. However, also here individual journalists expressed concern about "corrupting proximity", which could lead to "people practicing a kind of self-censorship, saying: 'No, come on, they've given us so much money, this is a great project. Let's not get all up in arms about it!'"[24]

But fortunately, I have been able to identify one case where a tech giant has demonstrably tried to stop critical reporting by an editorial team through direct intervention by threatening to withdraw advertising budgets (see box). I cannot say how widespread this blackmailing practice is. However, the case clearly and unequivocally demonstrates Big Tech's expectations: we support you, so we expect you to behave in a tamely manner. If not, you will suffer the consequences. And this is exactly what happened in this case.

Big Tech cracks down on independent journalism and tries to stop a critical publication

Blackmailing an editorial office by threatening sanctions

During my research, a journalist of a print news publisher told me the following story: They were planning to publish a comprehensive investigation on the threats posed by Big Tech. Two tech giants were among the advertisers of the publisher. They heard about the planned editorial focus from their contacts with the publisher's advertising department.

One of the tech giants then tried to influence the publication by threatening to cancel an already planned advertising campaign if the extensive reporting with the criticism of Big Tech were to be published. A second campaign was also under threat at the time. The editors were not impressed by this and published the articles anyway. In fact, the publisher was punished immediately: after the publication, the threat was carried out and the planned advertising campaign was canceled by one of the tech giants.

The journalist also reported intensive debates within the editorial team in the run-up to the publication. There were fears that this critical report would also result in sanctions at other levels, for example with programs such as 'Facebook News'. It is obvious that Big Tech favors media that are particularly willing to cooperate through these programs while disadvantaging media that report critically. This dependence on traffic from the large platforms means that editorial teams are afraid to report critically on Big Tech because they also assume that they could be punished.

This means that an editorial office will fear potential sanctions by Big Tech as a punishment for such critical publications (whether explicitly threatened or not). Thus, publishers are always in danger of losing considerable amounts of their funding—which, due to the difficult economic situation in the editorial offices, inevitably leads at least to the consideration of self-censorship. It is significant that the journalist only gave me this information on the assurance that I would not reveal his name or the name of the blackmailed publisher—again for fear of possible sanctions by Big Tech.

The 'promote versus punish' game is odd, isn't it? Let's put ourselves in the shoes of an industry that has been steadily declining for years. Many editorial teams have to give up, are being merged or restructured. Circulations are declining, editors are losing their jobs and there are hardly any positive prospects. In the digital field, you are dependent on the platforms for better or worse anyway. You always live in fear of being downgraded by Google's search engine, for example, or of not being included in a digital program (Facebook News, Google News Showcase). In many cases, innovative digital projects can often only be funded accepting the 'help' of Big Tech. On top of that, GAFAM provides 'support' by allocating millions in advertising budgets. Let's not forget about all the cool sponsored events. Thus, Big Tech is able to destroy the last remnants of the publishing landscape in two stages. In the first phase, they dry up the funds of regional publishers, who are already starving. In parallel, they silence the big publishing houses, who tolerate this because they benefit considerably in the short term. In phase two, profits are also extracted from the large, supra-regional competitors—by massively worsening conditions. We recognize the desperate situation of the media houses in a market without any fair chance of success. Common sense thinking would immediately make us realize that this is a systematic abuse of dominant market positions, because the victims are barely able to defend themselves. Companies in Germany are supposed to be protected from such practices by the State—and this is true especially for the media. Once again, this is the domain of the Federal Antitrust Office. Our example is so illuminating precisely because the affected news media publishers filed a joint complaint in the fall of 2020 about precisely this 'Google News Showcase' case.

The Federal Antitrust Office launched the investigation in summer 2021. It was one of the first applications of the revised competition law (GWB, paragraph 19a). Therefore, the case could have set a precedent for a new era of decisive crackdowns on Big Tech by German authorities. But this was far from what actually happened. Shortly before Christmas 2022, i.e. more than two years (!) after the original filing, the authority announced that it was discontinuing the proceedings. This is particularly frustrating because *all* market participants from the publishing houses had protested—interestingly enough, even Google's willing cooperation partners! To quote one commentator: "The remarkable thing about this objection is that it comes from everyone—from all publishers, from publishers who do not have contracts with Google and from those who do. Their joint statement shows that, despite their contracts with the digital giant, even they seem to be uneasy and fear that Google is pursuing a plan to fob off the entire German press with a few pennies."[25] And then the Antitrust Office closes the case. The Big Tech executives must have had a good laugh that day.

Infiltration and manipulation of science

Big Tech is also following the same tried and tested 'promote versus punish' pattern in the field of science. When we ask ourselves how we as a society will generate our knowledge in the future, we should have sleepless nights anyways. Because every day, platforms collect gigantic amounts of data on every conceivable aspect and area of our world, giving them unbeatable advantages in understanding our digital world. This has significant consequences for our future. The institutions, authorities and persons who have been responsible to explain our world up to now, such as universities, scientists, journalists, do not have access to this data. At the other end of the scale, the digital giants aggregate and own more and more data. In addition, only they understand how the data was created. Only they have full access. In future, we will understand the digital world increasingly as it is shown to us by the digital companies.

As if that were not enough, Big Tech is also encroaching ever more deeply into the sphere of science, attempting to manipulate it to play to its tune. One particularly instructive case was uncovered by investigative research by the *Wall Street Journal*. By analyzing thousands of leaked emails, these investigations were able to prove that Google had systematically 'sponsored' US scientists over a period of around ten years. They financially 'supported' the creation of hundreds of research papers in order to "sway opinions and public policy" and "defend against regulatory challenges of its market dominance", according to the authors.[26] The individual grants ranged from 5,000 to 400,000 US dollars, and the funded institutions included top-class universities such as Harvard and Berkeley. In many cases, the 'funding' of the scientists was not disclosed in the research papers.

FUN FACT: Google has financially supported hundreds of research projects in the USA—in order to manipulate public opinion on regulatory issues.

Google apparently had a massive influence on the choice of topics. It even compiled "wish lists of academic papers that included working titles, abstracts and budgets for each proposed paper. Google then searched for willing authors", reported a former employee and a former Google lobbyist. The funded 'research' papers took funny positions—that Google's spying on user data was only a fair exchange for the free use of its services (of course!), that Google did not use its market dominance to redirect users to its own products or services (nope, never ...), that Google should be allowed to use intellectual property without paying royalties (what else?) and so on. According to the authors, specific studies from this program were used "to deflect antitrust allegations against Google by the Federal Trade Commission (FTC)".

The digital corporations also support universities, institutions and think tanks. In the case of Google, for example, the 'New America Foundation' made headlines after receiving more than 20 million US dollars in support from the company. The then Google CEO Eric Schmidt himself was Chairman of the Supervisory Board of this think tank until 2016. After the European Commission imposed a fine on Google, one of the think tank's researchers, Barry Lynn, who ran a project called 'Open Markets' on tech dominance, posted a positive comment on the website—and was fired shortly afterwards by the foundation's president, Anne-Marie Slaughter (that is her real name).

"Mr. Lynn, in an interview, charged that Ms. Slaughter caved to pressure from Mr. Schmidt and Google, and, in doing so, set the desires of a donor over the think tank's intellectual integrity. 'Google is very aggressive in throwing its money around Washington and Brussels, and then pulling the strings', Mr. Lynn said. 'People are so afraid of Google now'. Google rejected any suggestion that it played a role in New America's split with Open Markets."[27] Of course.

Once again, we see that Big Tech is playing the game of 'promote versus punish' in a way similar to how it manipulates traffic through boosting or dimming on its platforms. Voices that are useful for enforcing one's own positions are 'promoted', while critical voices are downplayed. This is also shown by two recent cases on Facebook.

Facebook stops critical scientific studies

In August 2021, it was revealed that Facebook had blocked profiles of two New York University researchers and around two dozen other accounts. Previously, "The company served the pair cease and desist letters just weeks before the 2020 election, calling on the team to disable an opt-in browser tool called Ad Observer and unpublish their findings."[28] The installed tool enables researchers to find out which mechanisms Facebook uses to display specific ads to users. In this case, it was mainly about political advertising in the context of an election. The tool had been developed for the Firefox browser. Interestingly enough, Mozilla (the company who owns Firefox) had confirmed that it had carefully checked the tool twice to ensure that it complied perfectly with all conceivable data protection regulations. The case took a particularly interesting turn because AlgorithmWatch in Europe heard about these revelations and decided to go public with previously unknown information. It had experienced similar reprisals (i.e. also being blocked by Facebook) in relation to a similar study, as I explain now.

The NGO had also launched a research project to find out exactly how Instagram's algorithms are manipulating which content people watch: Which posts do users get to see and which ones are not shown? To this end, voluntary participants of the study had to install a browser add-on that could read and save all the content of their news feed. The project was supported by high-profile institutions. "In early May 2021, Facebook asked us for a meeting. Our project, said Facebook, breached their Terms of Service, which prohibit the automated collection of data. They would have to 'move to more formal engagement', if we did not 'resolve' the issue on their terms—a thinly veiled threat".[29]

The case also shows the extent to which the 'privatization of law' (☞ IV.3) allows digital companies to block such investigative research quite easily, because they can update the terms of use at any time. AlgorithmWatch writes: "the company could forbid any ongoing analysis that aims at increasing transparency, simply by changing its Terms", and continues: "On 13 July [2021], we took the decision to terminate the project and delete any collected data [...]. Ultimately, an organization the size of AlgorithmWatch cannot risk going to court against a company valued at one trillion dollars."

And here is another strange incident: When *Der Spiegel* reported on this and asked Facebook for a statement, the company replied: "We contacted AlgorithmWatch because the browser extension they were using was collecting information from users in a way that violated our Terms of Service and potentially jeopardized the privacy of our users." Just for the record: Facebook is fighting for the privacy (!) of its users, which is said to be threatened by AlgorithmWatch's research (!) Of course.

An editor's notice was apparently placed below the article after its publication: "On Friday afternoon, after the editorial deadline for the printed edition of *Spiegel*, Facebook announced in an 'updated statement': "We have not threatened to sue them." Nah, sure, Facebook, of course the people at AlgorithmWatch got that completely wrong.[30]

'Promote versus punish' means: On the one hand, science that supports the interests of Big Tech receives financial support. On the other hand, 'unpopular' research is actively stopped by the tech giants—as I was able to experience it myself (☞ Knockout). And I can confirm that they often act indirectly. None of the things they do are punishable by law. They intimidate by hinting at possible consequences or they make use of intermediaries working for them. When in doubt, the victims always got it wrong. It was all meant quite differently.

Big Tech 'supports' science in Germany

Also in Germany, Big Tech is highly active 'supporting' science that fits its own interests. Here are just a few examples: Google/Alphabet is sponsoring the Alexander von Humboldt Institute for Internet and Society in Berlin. After initial funding of 4.5 million euros, the company has now provided around 14 million euros and a representative of Google Germany is on the supervisory board.[31] Facebook is currently paying the Technical University of Munich 7.5 million euros for a new ethics institute for AI (you might think "that's so absurd, it must be a joke". But no: ethics deals with morally good behavior, and Facebook is indeed supporting that institute). Facebook apparently pays 1.5 million euros per year here and awards millions more in funding to specific research projects. Facebook is also 'helping' to decide which projects are funded. And Facebook's approval is required for future appointments to the institute's management.[32] Amazon invests 700,000 euros a year in the Max Planck Society for research into data analysis using artificial intelligence (the amount is probably renegotiated annually). Amazon also provides data from its own platforms. Scientific research would otherwise not have access to such data (great, isn't it?). Here too, Amazon has a say in which dissertation projects are funded. It is apparently unclear who owns the research results—the contract between Amazon and the institute is not public.[33]

We are systematically being brainwashed

We could go on like this forever and illuminate the 'promote versus punish' game that Big Tech plays in every conceivable part of our society. The digital corporations are just applying the same principles they use in their platforms to the field of lobbying. Just as they boost and dim content at will on their platforms to maximize their own interests, their lobbying machine does the same in every part of our society.

We could for instance investigate this for the field of business. 'Promote' means here inviting managers to cool events (preferably on ethical topics such as diversity or sustainability), hip team training sessions on digitalization, inspiring trips to Silicon Valley for top managers or board members, participation at VIP chimney talks, plus free publicity and fame that comes along with the participation at conference talks or panels, and so on. On the other hand, the tech giants can always play the digital transformation joker. Because they virtually own the digital world, they can always say something like: "What, you're not investing enough of your money in digitalization? Then just go down." All of this is embedded in ready-made ideological narratives that they can exploit for their own purposes: You are lagging behind in digitalization, Germany is missing the boat, if we digital companies don't do it, the 'evil Chinese' will take over and so on: "But no problem at all. Everything is easy. Because we know how to run the show. We can help you. Just sign here—and become part of our shared digital future."

They can only proceed like this because we have made three fundamental mistakes: First, we have allowed Big Tech to become synonymous with digitalization, so to speak. Or to put it another way: We are so brainwashed that we can no longer even imagine a digital world without the dominance of Big Tech. This is precisely ideology "in action". And this is precisely the deeper meaning of our book title: 'Big Tech must go!' Big Tech must not only be broken up and unbundled materially. Above all, we need to emancipate ourselves *mentally* from Big Tech. There is *nothing* to stop us from imagining a better digital world that serves people and not primarily the digital corporations.

Our second mistake is that we have become completely addicted to the ideology of the good Internet. Through the power of these wonderful aesthetics, the symbols and values, we suffer from a mental distortion due to which we can no longer perceive the systemic oppression, exploitation and domination that emanates from Big Tech. We would reject it if the CIA were to sponsor an ethics institute in Germany. If Facebook does it, there is no uproar.

Big Tech constitutes the largest existing accumulation of power and wealth in the Western world. Certainly, there have always been obscene concentrations of power—the Pharaohs, the Roman Empire, the Sun Kings of French absolutism. But never before in human history has such domination dared to appear publicly in the guise of an underdog counterculture. They are tyrants who pretend to have only good things in mind. And this type of tyrant has always been the very worst in the history of mankind. As soon as we manage to take distance from this ideology, we will realize that this is just a masquerade. We will immediately recognize how the tech giants here have appropriated formerly left-wing intellectual counterculture symbols even though their actions betray the values of this counterculture on a daily basis. Once we see through this, their mental power over us will instantly crumble.

Third, we have subjected ourselves to the 'promote versus punish' game, which Big Tech has put in place to achieve only one goal: To divide us all and keep us down. 'Divide and rule' is probably the most important principle of success for autocratic rulers. The Romans had an elaborate system of treaties, privileges, sanctions and drastic punishments to prevent the invaded and defeated peoples from joining forces against the exploitative empire. The dominance of Big Tech is established by similar principles.

CAUGHT IN THE WEB OF THE TECH GIANTS

PROMOTE

MEDIA/ PUBLIC SPHERE
- ▶ Financial 'support'
- ▶ Deals (copyrights etc.)
- ▶ Advertising donations
- ▶ Sponsoring conferences, trainings, courses etc.

POLITICS/ LAW
- ▶ Financial 'promotion'
- ▶ Content-related 'promotion'
- ▶ Lobbying
- ▶ Cybersecurity

ECONOMY
- ▶ Cool events and workshops
- ▶ Top management trips to Silicon Valley
- ▶ 'Cooperation', 'partnerships' in fields such as diversity, sustainability, etc.

SCIENCE
- ▶ 'Support', 'promotion' and 'cooperation'
- ▶ 'Buying' GAFAM-friendly research
- ▶ Creating publicity for GAFAM-friendly scientists

PUNISH

- Monopoly abuse
- Elimination of competition
- Stopping investment in the event of unfavorable reporting

- Exploiting dependencies
- Conflicts of interest

- Monopoly abuse
- Lawsuits against disliked competitors
- Killer acquisitions

- Suppression of 'unpopular' research
- Control and blocking of data access

V ACCEPT HERE

We just have to recognize that we are all, without exception, being deceived by Big Tech: Creators and companies, private and public service broadcasters, influencers and editors, academia and politics, the left and the free market advocates, progressives and conservatives, the rich and the poor, Big Tech 'partners' as well as opponents and NGOs. In Germany as well as in all other countries of the Western world. Without exception, we are all being done over by them.

We can see from the above example of the news media companies how far Big Tech has succeeded in pitting all parties against each other, even within such a limited field. It would be easy for us to stop GAFAM immediately—if only we could see that we are all in the same boat and if we were to join forces to liberate the web.

CHAPTER VI

COUNTDOWN 2029: How can we liberate the Internet?

1. A glimmer of hope: The people do not want Big Tech monopolies

After having analyzed the hostile takeover of our society by Big Tech, we can start this final chapter with some really good news. First of all, despite the gigantic efforts of digital corporations to disguise themselves as philanthropic organizations, people in Germany see through the scam. I conducted a study on this with 1,000 respondents. To be honest, my goal was extremely modest. Because our topic is not on the current agenda of the media, I just wanted to illustrate: "Look, an aspect like data surveillance has been filling the headlines in the media for ten years now—but our topic is also important to people, even though there is no debate about it." My assumption had been that many people in Germany are concerned, but at a much lower level. I was quite stunned when the results came in: our topic is highly relevant for people. And above all: almost all of the citizens polled (82 percent) in this country reject the status quo.

> **FUN FACT:** Big Tech has already been voted out: 82 percent of Germans polled criticize the dominance of the tech giants

The second piece of good news is that we do not live in a dictatorship, but in a democracy. In China, we would have to put up with the media system and the digital offerings that the autocratic government presents to us. Not here in Europe. Fortunately, we are in charge ourselves. We are free to shape our media system as we citizens would like to have it. No one can force us to accept the rule of the digital corporations. If we the people decide so, Big Tech must go.

The third piece of good news is that we have a broad parliamentary majority in Germany to abolish the dominance of Big Tech immediately. Fortunately, based on their political programs, all the major political parties should categorically reject Big Tech. On the one hand, it is inconceivable that left-wing parties such as the SPD, the Green Party and even the Left Party would allow Big Tech to continue as they have done until now given that they are among the most exploitative monopolies in the world. No person with a sensibility for social equality can support the

THE PEOPLE REJECT BIG TECH
Rejection by the German people in percent[1]

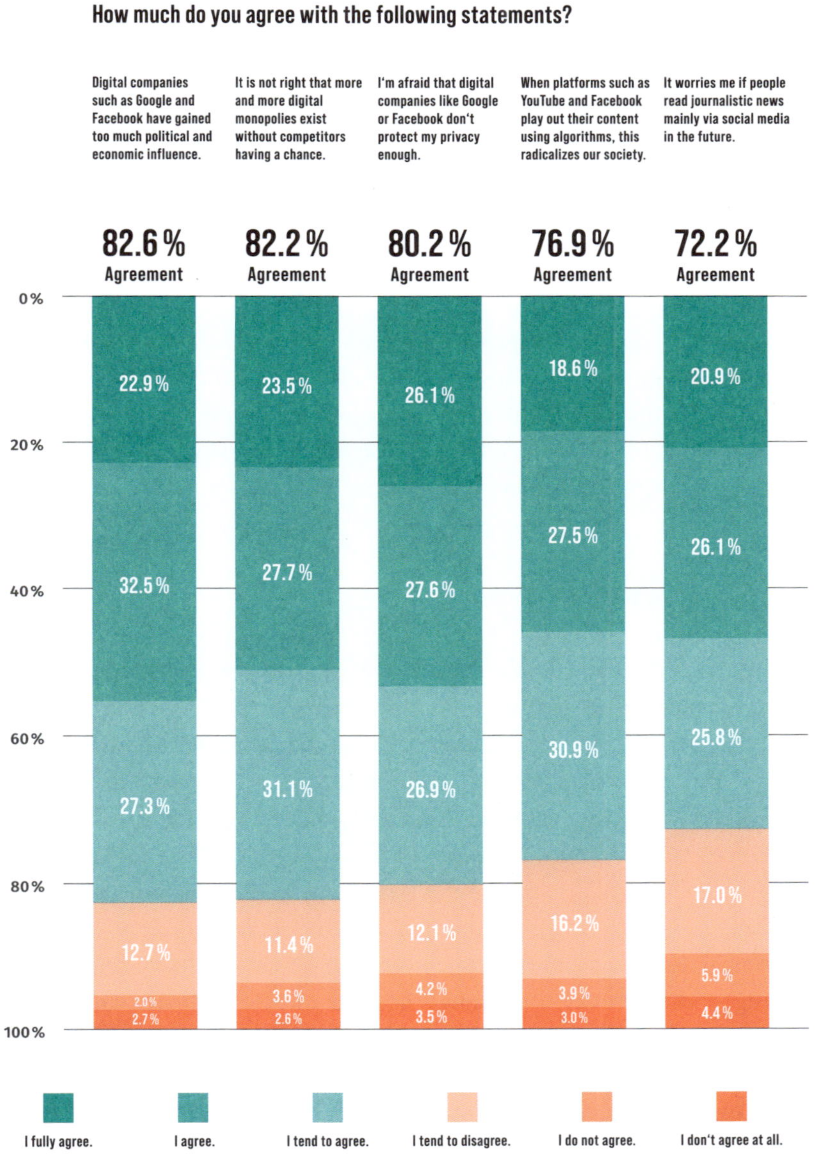

How much do you agree with the following statements?

Digital companies such as Google and Facebook have gained too much political and economic influence.	It is not right that more and more digital monopolies exist without competitors having a chance.	I'm afraid that digital companies like Google or Facebook don't protect my privacy enough.	When platforms such as YouTube and Facebook play out their content using algorithms, this radicalizes our society.	It worries me if people read journalistic news mainly via social media in the future.
82.6 % Agreement	**82.2 %** Agreement	**80.2 %** Agreement	**76.9 %** Agreement	**72.2 %** Agreement
22.9 %	23.5 %	26.1 %	18.6 %	20.9 %
32.5 %	27.7 %	27.6 %	27.5 %	26.1 %
27.3 %	31.1 %	26.9 %	30.9 %	25.8 %
12.7 %	11.4 %	12.1 %	16.2 %	17.0 %
2.0 %	3.6 %	4.2 %	3.9 %	5.9 %
2.7 %	2.6 %	3.5 %	3.0 %	4.4 %

 I fully agree.
 I agree.
 I tend to agree.
 I tend to disagree.
 I do not agree.
 I don't agree at all.

tech giants. On the other hand, parties in favor of free markets such as the FDP, but also the CDU/CSU in Germany, should be extremely allergic to the total abolition of competition, fair market access and equal opportunities. Big Tech is the exact opposite of what they believe in at heart. And so we have a fantastic parliamentary majority of 89 percent against Big Tech in Germany! What would stop us? We can immediately disempower the digital corporations in the interests of the voters. In a few months, all the fears would be in the past—and the Internet would be liberated!

I understand, politics is not quite ready yet. We can easily explain why given that, for many years, politicians in all parties are consistently acting in favor of Big Tech and *against the will of the voters*. We can also explain it by referring to the dependence of Western governments on Big Tech (☞ IV.4) and the lobbying efforts of digital corporations (☞ V.4). The situation is very similar in the USA. There, too, politicians consistently act in the interests of digital companies and against the will of the people. Depending on the survey, 75 to 80 percent of the people in the USA are concerned about the dominance of Big Tech, and still nothing happens.[2] That is why we must hold the politicians and authorities accountable from now on. Why are they artificially and needlessly maintaining the miserable status quo? The majority of people rejects Big Tech. The status quo is unconstitutional (☞ IV.4–5). We must explain to politicians now that the time has come to act and save our Western democracies.

It's easy to solve the problem

Perhaps the hostile takeover of our society by the tech giants is the second most important social problem for our society after the climate crisis. But it is precisely this comparison with climate change that should fill us again with hope. Climate change is a problem that is very difficult to solve. There is a solution, but it is extremely complex, lengthy, time-consuming and expensive. We need astronomical levels of investment to reduce emissions. Everyone in the world will have to give up many things in order to accomplish this task. We will all have to make Herculean efforts together and globally, over decades, to save the planet.

In comparison, our problem is ridiculously easy to solve. All we need is the will, the courage and the creativity to change the status quo for the better. Currently, we are all being cheated on: Journalists, creators, companies, artists—and, ultimately, all of us users. But together, we could all free the Internet of Big Tech before it is too late. This solution can be implemented in the short term: by agreeing on clear and transparent rules that restore fair competition, open markets and diversity in the field of digital media. And the best thing is (unlike climate change): *Liberating the Internet doesn't cost us any money at all.* We don't have to give up *anything*. On the contrary, we can even assume that restoring competition will quickly lead to more diversity, better products and a more dynamic economy. We just need to have the confidence to work all together and bring about a tiny little revolution for a better world. At no cost and without sacrifice.

Isn't that fantastic? After struggling with problems and annoyances for hundreds of pages, we can still have a happy ending!

In order to preserve this visionary spirit of optimism and to convince you that it is worth fighting together for this better world, I will now show you a few measures with which we can quickly free our digital world from the rule of Big Tech. We have to learn again to imagine a digital world that is no longer owned by digital giants. We must learn to be digitally courageous again and to dream. Let's be just as courageous now as we were once enthusiastic about a better digital world. Let's stop being resigned to the status quo! Let's roll up our sleeves, get to work and do away with Big Tech.

2. How can we liberate the Internet

The first step on our journey is the most simple, but also the most important one. You may be confused for a moment, but wait and see. I promise you, there will be a surprising punch line when you least expect it. So please join in.

We start our journey with a mini self-test in which we examine our attitude towards democracy in the context of digital transformation. Don't worry, it's really quick—all you have to do is check whether you agree with the following three statements:

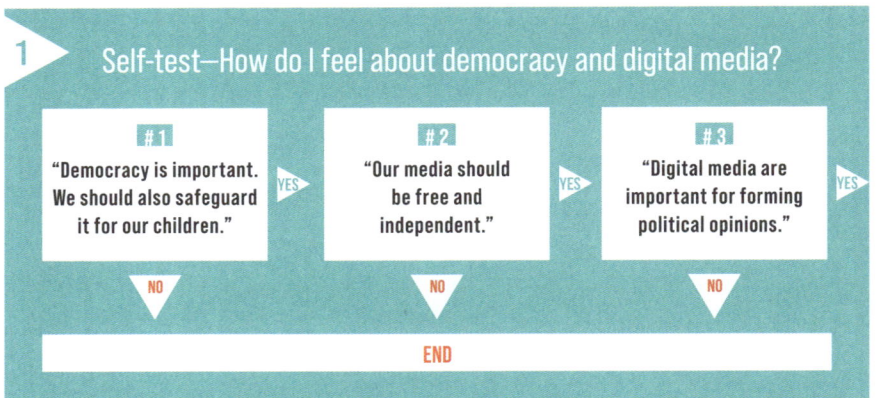

If you have answered "No" to any of these questions, I am truly sorry, because you have probably bought the wrong book. I also don't know how it happened that we only noticed this here at the very end, but I hope you won't hold it against me and I sincerely wish you the very best.

But if you answered "Yes" to all three questions, then congratulations! You are a democrat and believe in the democratic relevance of digital media. That makes me particularly happy, because we can derive a pretty clear and positive target image from this starting point.

It's time to tell Big Tech: Enough is enough!

If we are truly democrats and want freedom, then almost everything that follows in the next few pages is almost self-evident. If we are democrats, then we do not want a future in which the Internet is dominated by a handful of Big Tech corporations who can do whatever they want thanks to their obscene accumulation of wealth and power. We want a diverse, pluralistic and open digital future. We are longing for a digital world in which a colorful variety of different providers compete for our attention.

That's why we are now taking our fate into our own hands. Not by boycotting Big Tech's offerings. That would be counterproductive. Not by trying to develop state-funded public alternatives as would be done in a planned economy. That would be completely pointless. No, our approach is different. Fortunately, we have learned a lot from you, Big Tech.

You tech giants think hacking is so cool (☞ V.1)?³ How about we change the rules now? Surely you don't mind if we hack *you* for a couple of years now? We will just take what we want from you—exactly the same way as you have been doing with us for so long. We simply take everything back in the same style that you have been stealing it from Western democracies for decades. Wasn't the 'sharing economy' a great idea of yours? Great, we adopted your great idea straight away. Now it's *your* turn to share—and to share your platforms as a common good with the people who create them for you. That's our hack: we could hack the platforms and give control back to the users.

Currently, we users create and develop the platforms for their owners. In return we are being spied on, betrayed and deceived. This is going to be over now. Thanks to our hack, we could put the digital corporations in their place through democratic processes. We will take our share of these media. And we'll do it just like the hackers: we'll take what we want, regardless of whether the owners like it or not. You never asked us in the past. We won't ask you either. The Internet will once again serve the people and not the people the digital corporations.

Mark Zuckerberg will be thrilled with our hack. In his own manifesto *The Hacker Way* under the heading "Build Social Value", we can read: "Facebook exists to make the world more open and connected, and not just to build a company. We expect everyone at Facebook to focus every day on how to build real value for the world in everything they do."⁴

They will happily freak out when they realize that our Internet hack is fully synchronized with their wonderful digital visions and values. They will certainly quickly embrace our new Internet, which will then be open and fair again, just as they themselves have been demanding for a long time. It will be decentralized and anti-hierarchical, it will be participative and interactive, it will be wonderfully

Big Tech must go!
How we free the web

START — Darth Vader corporations dominate the web

1 Self-test—Democracy and digital media

#1 "Democracy is important. We should also safeguard it for our children." — YES → **#2** "Our media should be free and independent." — YES → **#3** "Digital media are important for forming political opinions."

NO / NO / NO → **END**

WHY?

6 Mission Statement

"Digital corporations, you tired giants of closed standards and manipulation, I come from the liberated web, the future home of the mind. In the name of the future, I ask you, as representatives of an outdated past, to leave us alone. You are no longer welcome here. Where we gather, you no longer have sovereignty. ..."

ADAPTION — adapted to the digital situation in 2023

INSPIRATION — Submission by John Perry Barlow (1996)

WHAT?

7 How we reclaim the Internet—Measures

GOAL — We have freed the Internet!

#1 General enforcement of open standards

↓

#2 Full outlink freedom for content creators

↓

#3 Disclosure of usage, sales, profit and taxes

↓

#4 Payment of the full tax burden

→ **#5** Disclosure of government interactions

↑ **#6** Separation of business areas with conflicts of interest

↑ **#7** Stop traffic manipulation and self-preferencing

↑ **#8** Maximum of 5 algorithmic traffic distribution schemes

→ **#9** Communitization of all data

↓ **#10** Unbundling the tech giants

↓ **#11** Separation of channel and content for democratic relevance

↓ **#12** 30 % market share cap in case of democratic relevance

→ **#13** Stop the monetization of criminal content

↑ **#14** Terms & conditions created by communities

↑ **#15** Oversight Boards through communities

Purpose—The free Internet

#1
Freedom and diversity are fundamental democratic values—not only in the analog world, but also digitally.

▶

#2
That is why we must free the Internet from the rule of the digital corporations.

▶

#3
Private companies should never become gatekeepers for the free web: Big Tech must go!

HOW?

Internet liberation—slogan

MEANING
This is precisely the style in which we will unbundle the digital monopolies—for freedom, diversity and democracy.

SLOGAN
"We smash Big Tech with its own weapons ("move fast and break things")"

◀

Principles

#1
Monopolies are taboo in the field of media. Where they exist, they are abolished.

▼

#2
Digital media are important for our society. And of course they are media.

The values of the free Internet—briefly explained for Big Tech

#7: TRANSPARENCY
Platforms disclose information on sales and usage.

▲

#6: SHARING
Tech giants share their data and algorithms with users and society.

▲

#5: PARTICIPATION
Tech giants participate in taxation in the countries in which they are active.
They contribute the same percentage contribution as other media companies.

▲

#4: EMPOWERMENT
We users are allowed to have a say in our own digital media.

#1: FREEDOM
All media are free.
The Internet is also free and should never be dominated by individual tech giants.

▼

#2: OPENNESS
All standards in big platforms must be open and interoperable.
This also applies to offerings from the tech giants.

▼

#3: COMMUNITY
Digital media belongs to the communities that produce it—not the tech giants.

◀

diverse, exciting, wild, a real eldorado of new potential. Above all, it will no longer be owned and ruled by the tech giants.

We can also show exactly *how* we will change the distribution of online traffic. The current, misguided regulation that breeds digital feudalism will be abolished. By doing so, we will restore diversity and create a new, pluralistic web. The distribution of traffic on the web will look completely different. In a hundred years' time, people will be talking about it: In the very past, dark forces tried to take ownership and full control of our media. Thank God that was averted.

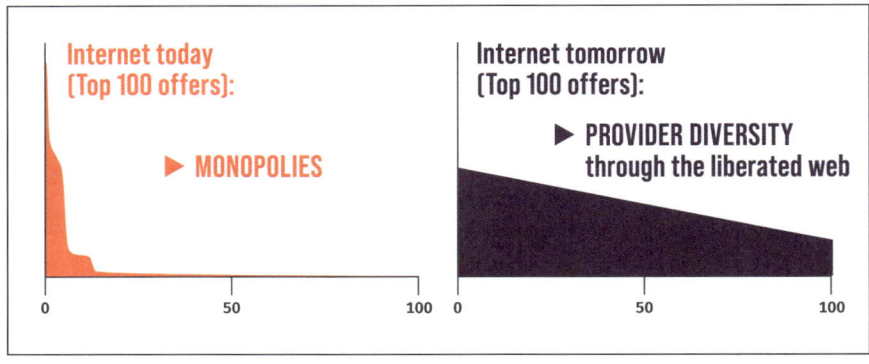

This results in our target image and our vision:

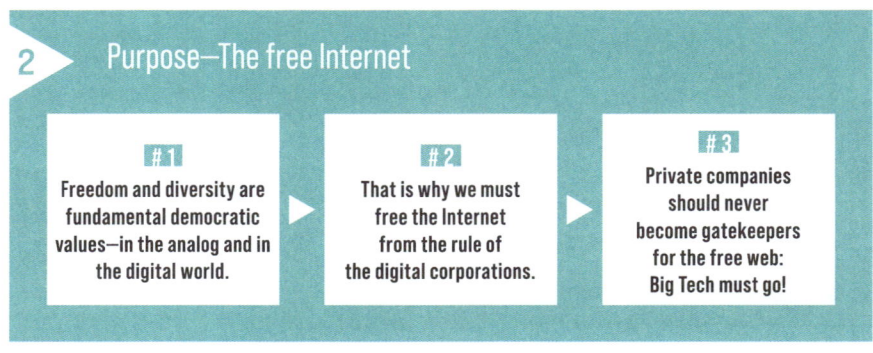

We are guided by two basic principles:

3 Principles

#1
Monopolies are a taboo in the field of media. Where they exist, they are abolished.

#2
Digital media are important for our society. And of course they are media.

The basic values of the free Internet

As long as they have existed, the tech giants have been falling back on ethical values and ideals that originally emerged in left-wing intellectual ecosystems (☞ V.1–2). In the future, we will no longer let them get away with such hypocritical masquerades. That's why we briefly explain the implications of these values to them. This is an integral part of our tech hack. It allows us to interrupt them every time in their ongoing ethics bullshit talk and hand them a signature-ready template of their own digital core values. Thus, they can prove on the spot how serious they are about these values. Here we go:

4 The values of the free Internet—briefly explained for Big Tech

#1: FREEDOM
All media are free.
The Internet is also free
and should never be dominated
by individual tech giants.

#2: OPENNESS
All standards in big platforms must
be open and interoperable.
This also applies to offerings
from the tech giants.

#3: COMMUNITY
Digital media belong to the
communities that produce it—
not to the tech giants.

#4: EMPOWERMENT
We users are allowed to have a say
in our own digital media.

#5: PARTICIPATION
Tech giants participate by paying the same tax rates
as other media companies.

#6: SHARING
Tech giants share their data
with users and society.

#7: TRANSPARENCY
Platforms disclose information on sales
and media usage to society.

Net liberation claim

Every good movement needs a slogan that gives it strength, that drives it forward, that ensures that you have a kind of compass to follow at all times. Here, too, we have taken inspiration from the tech giants—by hacking their own game. We choose the famous saying from Mark Zuckerberg:

> **5** Internet liberation—slogan
>
> "**Move fast and break things.**
> Unless you are breaking stuff, you aren't moving fast enough."
>
> *(Mark Zuckerberg)*

Yay! We will break up and unbundle the digital monopolies Zuckerberg style in order to restore freedom, diversity and democracy. We will build whatever structures, processes and organizations that are needed to free the Internet. Gone will be the days when tech giants could rely on cumbersome provincial authorities. We will build teams of digital experts, net activists, hackers, idealists, and proceed at the speed of light when we break up Big Tech. Don't worry, digital corporations: we will move fast enough. We will move at such high speed that you will only see us from behind for the next few years. We know the clock is ticking. We only have a few years left.

Mission Statement

If we want to liberate the web, we need a good mission statement. A kind of "declaration of independence" in which we emancipate ourselves from the domination of the occupying power. Fortunately, we don't have to look far. We can build on the most famous manifesto ever written on the Internet: A Declaration of the Independence of Cyberspace by John Perry Barlow.

John Perry Barlow was not only a songwriter for the Grateful Dead, he is also a cult figure of the free internet and one of the founders of the Electronic Frontier Foundation. His declaration of independence dates back to a time when the young digital movement was emancipating itself from the established forces of the analog corporate world and its large corporations. At the time when he wrote his manifesto, there were only around 20 million people using the internet—worldwide.[5] The Internet was still completely insignificant in relation to the analog world. And that is precisely why the tone of his presumptuousness at the time is so fascinating. We should use exactly the same presumptuous tone of voice today, because our starting position is also completely hopeless in the face of the tech giants' powerful monopolies. But no matter how hopeless our endeavor is today, one day we will have made it and liberated the Internet.

No one would like that more than John Perry Barlow. Like Tim Berners-Lee, he belongs to the group of early idealists who always fought for decentralized structures and democratic open source philosophies. John Perry Barlow firmly believed in an Internet that could improve the world through its democratic potential. The current takeover of the Internet by the tech giants breaks with all of these values. That's why it makes a lot of sense to study his thoughts today. His ideas have never been more relevant. And that's why I wondered what his Declaration of Independence would actually look like if we rewrote it today—with the same spirit, but adapted to the new threats.

6 ▶ Mission Statement

Declaration of independence of the Internet

*Inspired by the original by John Perry Barlow (1996),
freely adapted to the digital situation in 2023*

Digital corporations, you weary giants of closed standards and manipulation, I come from the liberated web, the future home of Mind. On behalf of the future, I ask you, as representatives of an outdated past, to leave us alone. You are no longer welcome among us. You have no sovereignty where we gather. I declare the global social space we are building to be naturally independent of the tyrannies you have imposed on us for many years. You have no moral right to rule us, nor do you possess any methods of enforcement we would have true reason to fear. You claim there are problems among us that you need to solve. You use this claim as an excuse to penetrate ever deeper into our territories and to dominate and exploit us in every corner of our private sphere. Many of these problems don't exist. We are in the process of forming our own digital contract. This new digital world will arise according to the conditions of our world, not yours. Our world is different.

We are creating a new digital world in which even small and insignificant players can participate without being sucked up and swallowed by your gigantic traffic silos. We are creating a world in which everyone can move freely without fear of being spied on, monitored and controlled by you everywhere.

We reject your outdated legal concepts according to which you own our social media and platforms; they no longer apply to us. From now on, all digital media should be treated as common goods, because they are created by us users, not by you. And that is why we will take back our own media that you have stolen from us.

Throughout the world, you have established your monopolies that betray the democratic spirit and insult the dreams of Jefferson, Washington, Mill, Madison, DeToqueville and Brandeis. These dreams must now be born anew in us.

You are terrified of the users of your own platforms because you know that you have been ripping them off and cheating on them for many years on a daily basis. That is why you have taken precautions to nip even the smallest sparks of digital freedom in the bud everywhere. You have set up guards everywhere on the Internet, which may delay the liberation of the internet for a short time, but cannot prevent the dawn of a new era.

Your outdated ideas of wealth, compulsion and manipulation lead to arrangements in which you claim to own the media themselves all over the world. In our world, however, all media belong eternally and solely to the people who create them. Your rules are no longer necessary for the global exchange of our thoughts.

Your increasingly hostile measures of the digital world put us in the same position as those previous lovers of freedom and self-determination who had to reject the authorities of distant, uninformed occupying

> powers. We must declare ourselves immune to your sovereignty.
> We will create a digital civilization of the Mind in a liberated Internet.
> May it be more humane and fair than the world your platforms have
> created so far.

How do you feel when you read it? Take a look at the original text[6]—you'll be amazed at how little I had to change. I am sure that John Perry Barlow is looking down on us from heaven and forgives us for this playful reinterpretation of his thoughts. Hopefully he will be pleased that we are finally doing something against the dark forces who have occupied the free Internet and will give us his blessing.

7 How we reclaim the Internet—15 simple steps

We have a claim, a mission statement and the right spirit—now it's time to take concrete actions to free the web immediately from the rule of the tech giants. I will put forward 15 suggestions. Some of them are easier to implement, others are much more difficult to execute. They are suggestions—if you have better ideas, please let me know. On most ideas, we should be able to find an agreement easily. Others might be more complicated to implement, especially in cases where other fundamental rights are affected. But there's still no reason to complain. On the contrary. Remember our comparison with the climate crisis: All these measures cost nothing, and most of them could be implemented immediately if we really wanted a solution. If we lock a dozen experienced lawyers in a conference room for a weekend, they should quickly be able to translate these points into legislation. That would solve a large part of the problem. Because that's the beauty of legal frameworks: They are completely under our own control and we can change them instantly by our own beliefs and convictions. The best thing is that we can also correct past mistakes immediately. So let's get started, let's forget about our inner paralysis and turn on this digital amplifier to free the Internet from the rule of Big Tech!

1. General enforcement of open standards and interoperability

A reliable method of creating monopolies is to establish *closed standards*, which bind users to a particular manufacturer or service provider and massively restrict people's freedom to change. Conversely, *open standards* offer a simple and proven method of quickly creating competition and diversity. In a world of open standards, no player has an insurmountable advantage in the market.

Tim Berners-Lee, the godfather of the free global Internet, was also a strong advocate of interoperability. We should therefore introduce rules that force all digital companies with a global turnover of 500 million dollar or more to offer all their content exclusively via open standards so that it can be used regardless of the corporation who operates it.

This would mean that users could share all content such as videos, images and texts seamlessly from one platform to another. These open standards should also make it possible to migrate followers across platforms—so that, for example, you could invite your Facebook followers to follow you on a new network at the touch of a button if you no longer feel like using Facebook.

2. Full outlink freedom for content creators

The issue of open standards is directly linked with the permeability of platforms. If all content is based on the same standards, it is possible to share it between different platforms. We should therefore force all platforms with an annual turnover of 500 million dollars or more to enable outlinks at *every* level of content, i.e. at headline, image or video and text level. We would also have to ensure that users seamlessly leave the in-app browser when an outlink is called up and that the selected offer is then used outside the platform. Every click on content must be respected as a decision that the user wants to leave the platform.

We would also have to strictly prohibit platforms from reducing the visibility of posts if they contain outlinks. Every structural barrier for outlinks, no matter how small, and also the slightest disadvantage or dimming of posts with outlinks would have to be legally assessed as a severe abuse of monopoly. Any such action of self-preferencing and the abuse of dominant market positions should be punished as severely as serious and intentional antitrust offenses. Platform operators should be forced by strict rules to make their offerings open and permeable in accordance with the free and open principles of the Internet.

The underlying rule would be the following: If you want to be an open platform that is maintained by the work of its users, you must enable those same users to attract traffic for their own offerings outside your platform without any discrimination. If you don't like this, you are welcome to change the business model (e.g. hire content creators who produce the content for you).

3. Disclosure of usage, sales & profits, taxes

Many tech giants list transparency among their core values. However, due to their extraterritorial structure, it is unknown what turnover or profits they generate in a country, how much taxes they pay and where. We also have no access to the platforms' usage data, which we as a society could use to determine the degree of monopoly power and media concentration.

The legal barriers to the disclosure of such information might currently be insurmountable due to the legal protection of trade and business secrets. Nevertheless, we must find solutions here. Ultimately, the protection of our constitution and democracy is the greater good. We should therefore create specific rules for all internationally active digital companies in the media sector with a turnover of more than 300 million euros in Germany and 10 billion dollars worldwide. These companies would have to disclose their turnover and profits generated in the country as well as their usage data on a quarterly basis to a supervisory authority to be determined. The information would be stored there confidentially, but would also be available on demand by tax, antitrust or media concentration authorities and the like.

The usage data provided should be sufficiently detailed: How many people have visited the platform (unique users)? How many sessions? How long were these sessions? How much aggregated usage time did the platform achieve (total duration)? By these measures, we would immediately create a reliable data basis for the appropriate taxation of big tech and the assessment of media concentration. The tech giants, who are constantly calling for transparency, could of course disclose this data voluntarily to the public already now. But as long as they act in an anti-democratic manner, they are unlikely to do so without legal enforcement.

4. Payment of full taxes in the country of economic performance

Digital corporations like to talk about the ethical value of 'participation' that their products are supposed to enable for a better digital world. We remind the tech giants of the opportunity to become active participants themselves and to support the societies they exploit economically by paying significantly higher taxes.

This is why, in the future, they should pay taxes on all profits that they generate in the specific country of operational business at exactly the same rate as the average for all editorial media companies in the same country. Once again, this is an aspect relevant to democracy: We cannot accept that editorial media, for example, are massively disadvantaged quarter by quarter in the competition with Big Tech corporations. The relatively higher tax burden endured by Big Tech's competitors is itself a factor that Big Tech is using to dry up and systematically destroy our democratic media system.

5. Disclosure of government interactions and conflicts of interest

Tech giants that maintain offerings in the field of digital media (such as Facebook, Instagram, Google, YouTube, WhatsApp) must transparently document every form of interaction with and influence by State institutions as a basic condition of their economic presence in Western democracies such as Germany.

6. Separation of business areas with conflicts of interest (from 5)

Furthermore, tech giants must no longer be allowed to be commercially active in the field of media in Western democracies such as Germany if they are also commercially active in the field of cybersecurity in connection with State institutions, or if they carry out other business, services or transactions with State institutions.

If tech giants want to operate such businesses, they must spin off separate, independent companies. If they are not prepared to do so, they must completely shut down their business activities in the field of media in Western democracies such as Germany. In the field of media, we cannot tolerate any conflicts of interest that arise when media companies receive payments or instructions from State institutions, or any other dependencies between them and State institutions.

7. Abolition of traffic manipulation and sanctions for self-preferencing

In addition to putting an end to practices whereby tech giants dim posts with outlinks (see point 2), tech giants may not actively manipulate traffic in any form (☞ III.5). This applies in particular to self-preferencing through own gateways (☞ II.5). Potential self-preferencing must be checked by independent institutions through scientific measurements at regular intervals. Such traffic manipulation also constitutes an abuse of dominant market positions and must therefore be punished in future in the same way as serious antitrust offenses.

8. Neutral algorithmic traffic distribution schemes (maximum of five factors)

Nobody except the platforms currently knows by what algorithmic principles people receive content. We must stop also this lack of transparency. Platforms will be allowed to distribute traffic according to algorithmic distribution schemes based on a maximum of five factors. They must disclose these factors transparently to their users.

9. Communitization of data—level playing field for competition

The services offered by the tech giants are essentially created through the cooperation of their users. A law that is at the cutting edge of digital technology must take this fact into account and identify ways of harvesting the value of data not only for the tech giants, but also for society, which produces and generates this data in the first place.

Or to put it the other way around: A fair legal framework must ensure that the tech giants do not gain any competitive advantages over potential competitors through their exclusive possession of the data. The tech giants would therefore have to make aggregated and anonymized data available to the public and the scientific community. In this way, competitors or start-ups could develop products that can compete with those of the tech giants and start directly on the basis of fair competition.

Once again, platforms that do not want to share this data could, as an alternative, change their business model and produce their own content. This opening up of data would also explicitly apply to all content published by users on social media—all companies would therefore have the same starting conditions here as Meta or Alphabet, for example. This in turn would enable competition in the field of generative AI (ChatGPT et cetera) (☞ II.6).

10. Unbundling the tech giants

The various offerings of the tech giants would have to be unbundled according to category and separated into different companies. Categories whose boundaries must not be crossed would be:

- ▶ Infrastructure (e.g. cloud services, satellite internet, telecommunications networks, et cetera)
- ▶ End devices (e.g. smartphones, tablets, laptops, wearables, et cetera)
- ▶ Social media (for example Facebook, Instagram)
- ▶ Media-on-demand (for example YouTube, Netflix, Amazon Prime)
- ▶ Search engines (for example Google)
- ▶ E-commerce (for example Amazon)
- ▶ Marketplaces (for example Ebay, Amazon Marketplace)
- ▶ Ad Tech

This separation of the tech giants into different categories would serve to completely eliminate any cross-platform network effects and synergies that currently put potential competitors and challengers at a massive disadvantage and exclude them from these markets. Accordingly, we would have to consider any exchange of information across these categories as a serious antitrust offense.

11. Separation of channel and content for democracy-relevant platforms

The strict separation of channel and content has proven itself in terms of safeguarding fair competition and in creating effective checks and balances (☞ IV.1). Digital platforms with a dominant market position in categories that play a central role in shaping political opinion (such as Google, Facebook, Instagram, YouTube) would therefore have to be broken up into two levels at company level. The two entities would then separately monetize the distribution channel on the one hand and the content on the other.

For example, YouTube would have a company for YouTube Platform Services and a company for YouTube Content Services. The video platform itself would have to be fully interoperable (see point 1). From this perspective, YouTube Platform Services would be transformed into an operator that enables various content providers (beyond YouTube) to host channels independently, i.e. in competition with YouTube Content Services, and to monetize them through advertising.

This would also emancipate the many creators and influencers. They could then easily switch from one provider to another—and possibly find that they can generate significantly higher payments there, all this without leaving the platform itself (here: YouTube).

By enabling competition, we would also create transparency with regard to cost and profit structures within the respective platform. It would be possible to compare key indicators between providers in order to immediately eliminate any form of exploitation of dominant market positions.

12. 30 percent market share cap in democracy-relevant categories

In many democracies, media categories with a high relevance for the democratic public are protected against monopolies by maximum market share thresholds. In Germany, the Interstate Media Treaty for editorial media (☞ IV.1) fixes the maximum share at 30 percent of the usage share in the respective media category. This should also apply for digital platforms with dominant market positions in categories that play a central role in shaping political opinion such as Google, Facebook, Instagram, YouTube. By separating channel and content (point 11), it would be easy to allow additional competitors access to the same platform and ensure that no single competitor exceeds this 30 percent limit.

The 30 percent threshold would be applied in all digital categories with high democratic significance (search engines, free video-on-demand, social media). As in analog media, dominant market positions would be reviewed by an independent institution and determined by equally independent periodic scientific measurements. These analyses would have to be carried out on the basis of real usage measurements and be based on aggregated usage time (reach considerations are not sufficient here). They can be compared with the data provided to us by the platforms (see point 3).

13. Prohibition of monetization of criminal content through advertising or fees

This proposal is solving the problem we discussed on the case of Joe Rogan (☞ IV.2). How can we find a fair solution for the unequal treatment of platforms and editorial media in terms of liability? This is a sensitive issue. On the one hand, it seems unsatisfactory that platforms transmit criminal content with impunity (we are not talking about trivialities here, but about false factual claims, defamation, incitement to commit crimes, defamation, Holocaust denial in Germany, et cetera). On the other hand, it is also not desirable to restrict freedom of speech online.

However, a balanced consideration of the various rights can be achieved if we include the aspect of monetization into our consideration. It is one thing to enable freedom of expression (at least according to the narrative of the digital companies). However, it is a completely different matter to use punishable and criminal content as a program shown to users with the intention to monetize the content via advertising or fees.

It would be easy to interpret specific forms of monetization as a clear signal that a platform has appropriated the content used and has to take responsibility. To put it simply: Whoever assumes economic responsibility for content must also bear responsibility for the same content. Or vice versa: If you do not bear a basic level of responsibility, you are not allowed to cash in.

We could mitigate feared effects such as 'overblocking' through balancing regulations. For example, we could set certain thresholds above which such regulations apply. First of all, we could restrict validity to platforms with a global turnover of more than 1 billion US dollars. Sensible limits can also be set at the level of the content concerned—for example, posts from profiles with more than 5,000 followers or profiles with an annual monetization of more than 10,000 US dollars and so on.

Such rules do not only create limitations. On the contrary, they could also unleash a new and innovative dynamic on the social media market. The platforms would finally be forced to grow up in line with their current market position and take responsibility. They could also propose innovative solutions themselves. For example, they could introduce alternative offerings or additional feeds on their platforms that do not assume any liability (such as 'Facebook/YouTube/Spotify unfiltered'). However, in such a program or feed, there should also be no economic monetization of content through advertising or fees. In this way, it would remain open to every user to freely (and in an 'unfiltered' way) express their opinion on such platform feeds—even in the case of potentially criminal content (in such feeds, the usual notice & takedown procedures would then be applied in the case of criminal content).

In any case, we should reconsider the current practice that allows the major platforms to hold Western societies hostage in the name of freedom of speech, just for maximizing profits and monetizing criminal or racist content. The Spotify/Joe Rogan case clearly shows the unequal treatment in current law, which puts editorial offerings at a massive economic disadvantage, prevents fair competition in the field of media and thus only strengthens the monopolies and oligopolies of digital corporations.

The advantage of including the aspect of monetization in the debate is obvious: it helps to break the current stalemate between control and freedom. It would enable new, constructive and innovative solutions.

14. Platform terms and conditions must be approved by the community

We have already seen how the advance of the tech giants into every conceivable area of our lives is leading to a second 'legal system' increasingly replacing our democratic legal system (☞ IV.3). These rules and regulations are currently being shaped entirely by the tech giants, who also determine the entire 'legal system' within their platforms—for example, the possibilities of objection, appeal bodies, processes and the organizational composition of the 'judges'. With the important flaw that there is no separation of powers here: Plaintiffs, judges, the judiciary and law enforcement are all controlled by the respective digital corporation.

This is just as legal under the applicable laws as a supermarket setting up its own house rules. But as the value of these platforms is created almost exclusively by the network of users and the network effects they 'create', it is not legitimate that these communities are not at all empowered to have a voice in the self regulation of the network that they themselves create.

An innovative solution could be to force platforms with a global turnover of 500 million dollars or more to develop their terms and conditions as well as their community standards together with democratically elected representatives of their users and to have the community vote on key questions of platform governance. In case of doubt, platforms would also have to accept decisions that run counter to the economic interests of the platform owners.[7]

Platforms that massively benefit from the many advantages of this business model would have to accept certain disadvantages. If they do not want to accept that, they can switch to other business models—but then they would also have to pay employees to create their platform content.

By this delegation of control to the community, the platforms would reconnect with the participatory basic idea of the Internet. At the same time, they would prevent our liberal, democratically legitimized legal system from being increasingly replaced by the legal systems of the tech giants. Or in the terminology of the digital corporations themselves: The affected people would now have a 'voice' again. Through this voice, we would 'empower' them to defend themselves against unfair practices—against the actual platforms.

15. Introduction of appeal bodies/oversight boards via the community of users
Along the same lines, platforms should also create independent and neutral appeal bodies that are recruited from the community of their users. These independent oversight boards made up of users should monitor the various policies of the platforms and intervene in case of doubt. We would introduce 'empowerment' and 'voice' here too.

3. Seriously?

We see that we could easily free the Internet from the rule and control of the tech giants. The experts and institutions that are familiar with this area will no doubt object that these ideas are completely naive and and say that none of this is feasible, that some measures can only be solved internationally, or that they are completely utopian due to constraints X, Y and Z. Besides, they will no doubt add, we are not responsible ourselves, the EU would have to do something and we are not powerful enough, the Americans would have to sort it out. And so on.

Of course, we all know that even the smallest attempts to change the dominance of Big Tech are immediately crushed by the gigantic lobbying efforts of the digital corporations. Let's take just one example, namely the discussion about tightening antitrust regulations in the USA (mind you, this is not about breaking up the monopolies, but merely about the first tentative attempts to restrict self-preferencing). Big Tech then launched its gigantic lobbying machine, even sending out advertising campaigns worth 36 million US dollars, as the *Wall Street Journal* found out in mid-2022.[8] Facebook even used a front organization called American Edge as the basis for a campaign, as the *Washington Post* reported.[9] It looks like Big Tech has won here once again. So far, virtually nothing has happened.

Point taken. But I'm not giving up that easily. Let's repeat our experiment one last time: let's switch off the analog media so that we're left with a purely digital media universe.

Let's be clear about our goal once again: we want to free the web from the rule of the digital corporations. For real. Not just tell some PR story as the EU does when the officials there talk merrily about "fair and free markets", which have long since been completely destroyed. These markets apparently only exist in the imagination of the out of touch Brussels technocrats. We want to reject all of this: No nonsense. Because then we can save ourselves the trouble.

Let's be very clear about our goal: we don't just want to take some bureaucratic actions so that we can say afterwards that we have done something ("We tried it— unfortunately it didn't work"). We want to solve this problem in such a sustainable way that our children will be sure to still live in a free democracy with free digital media, so that, in 100 years' time, people will look back and say: in 2025, the threat of the tech giants taking over Western democracies was completely prevented.

Let's take another look at the 15 proposed actions. And let's examine these actions one by one: Are there any actions where you would say: "Well, that's not really so important now. We could do without it and still maintain a functioning media democracy under purely digital conditions."

Try the exercise. I'm looking forward to your assessment. To be honest, I was quite frustrated when I tried it out for myself.

We can also give up

It is possible that only now are we becoming aware of the huge scale of the digital misery. Now that we are being forced to come up with solutions, at least in the flowery fiction of these imaginative lines, we start to understand. We now realize how big the problem is that we have created for ourselves through years of inactivity. And perhaps we come to the conclusion: we can't do it.

So if it becomes too difficult for us to implement these measures together, there is an easy way out. We can go all the way back to the beginning of our plan, back to the democracy self-test. Maybe now you understand what we were talking about when we said that this is the most important part of our plan. Because it really is. At this point, we can simply change our attitude and say: "Perhaps democracy is not so important to us after all." We're experiencing a democratic crisis anyway (well, who's surprised? Perhaps it's gradually becoming clear where it's coming from 😉).

Then it will sound something like this: "It's not certain where it's all going anyway. There's even a war in Europe now. Damn, I'm tired and exhausted after this pandemic anyway. Then there's climate change on top of that. Surely we could just muddle on for a few more years and then see what happens. Leave me alone with the digital monopolies now. It'll work itself out."

If we decide to give up now, then so be it. But even under these circumstances, which would be depressing for me personally, we would be enriched by an important insight. We would know as a society that it is not so important for us to really fight for our democracy and our freedom after all. That Facebook and Google are more important to us than our democracy and our free constitution. We might then look each other in the eyes. Then, we will recognize in the tired, empty, sad looks of our fellow human beings that the tech giants have long since managed to extinguish our free will with billions of behavioral manipulations and nudges.

We would have certainty that it is unfortunately already too late. That as a society, we have signed the deal with the tech giants at some point years ago when we agreed to their terms and conditions, apparently without realizing it. That we have long since moved out of the free world and into the wonderful, brightly colored cyber prison into which they have invited us and where they are always surprising us with new and wonderful amenities.

So if we are prepared to give up democracy, then our goal will also change. Then we no longer need to fight the rule of the tech giants. On the contrary, then we might as well give up completely.

4. A free Europe between US digital feudalism and China's online dictatorship?

No, we're not going to let this book end in such a frustrating manner. I have one more thought for you. Indeed, if we see the project of liberating the Internet only as a painful ordeal that we need to go through because we got into this terrible situation through our own misconduct, it would be a kind of punishment for our own stupidity. If this is true, then, from a psychological perspective, it will not work out and so we might as well just give up. But is this purely negative view necessary? Is our project only a 'liberation' in the sense that we are just removing an evil with lots of effort? If so, our Internet liberation would actually have the sex appeal of a root canal procedure.

The opposite is the case. We recognize that immediately if we just visualize the day after. Imagine that: We've finally done it. The internet is freed from the rule of the tech giants. What will happen?

No matter how we have implemented the various measures, if we have been successful, we have achieved one thing for sure: there will be massively less traffic on the platforms, which conversely means that all independent content providers have a much better chance of getting their messages out and offering their content to interested users.

The dynamic from this will unleash the full potential of the digital funnel for all participants. We have shown above (☞ III.2) that, in future, all content in a digitized society will be offered via this digital funnel. It is important that we understand that this applies to all offerings without exception—not just media content and economic goods and products, but also political parties, politicians, programs, music, art, influencers and so on. In future, everyone who offers something will do so via this digital funnel anyway, regardless of whether it is goods, culture or politics. If we do nothing, all of this will take place on the platforms in the future and the tech giants will completely control our society.

However, if we change the rules as described, it will become much more attractive for everybody to place their content, products and programs outside of the platforms. Let's take a YouTuber as an example. The simple truth is that no YouTuber is on YouTube voluntarily. I mean that in the sense that no YouTuber prefers to work in Alphabet's digital prison, i.e. being fully dependent on Alphabet.

If YouTubers had a free choice and achieved the same or better results in terms of attention (i.e. viewers, sessions, impressions, et cetera) and financial revenue on an independent website, they would never entrust their entire existence to a platform for better or worse and move into such a cyber prison. We can study this dependency scientifically in cases where unsuccessful platforms have been shut down after bankruptcy, such as was the case with Vine. The affected creators or influencers have to start completely from scratch. Their economic existence collapses from one day to the next. This would not be the case if they had built up an independent existence on their own domain.

Over the last two decades, most bloggers have given up their free, independent domains. The boom in influencers and YouTubers was only possible because the platforms have drained the independent traffic on the net. Accordingly, they barely have a choice. They are only on the platforms because that's where the traffic is (or the other way around: if there was no traffic, they wouldn't be there either).

This digital dependency would change fundamentally if we liberated the Internet because, in a liberated Internet, our exemplary YouTuber would have many more options. He could already find a better provider even within the same platform to monetize his content (because there would now be competing content operators). Because the standards would be completely open and he could set outlinks at will, he can also offer his content elsewhere, also on other competing platforms. Maybe there's a new platform that performs much better—great, then as a creator he will get more attention and more money there and can take all the followers with him.

The dynamic created by this scenario will immediately create strong competition between the platforms. The platforms will automatically earn less and less money. Content will have a value again. The platforms will have to desperately search for the best artists, and the artists can earn more and more in relative terms. Why? As we have hacked Big Tech, we have also turned the tables. First, content creators now have much more resources to invest in their content. Second, by freeing up outlinks, they can link much better to their own sites, i.e. their own domains. The decisive difference is that the entire traffic on their own web presences belongs to them alone and no longer to the platform. For the first time, YouTubers are no longer the dependent vassals of YouTube.

As a result, it will become increasingly attractive for creators to take the risk of producing innovative formats and content on their own sites. And the best thing is: the platforms can no longer change the rules of the game at will, which currently means that content creators are always caught on the wrong foot. In the future, this would be different. In any case, the traffic on your own domain always belongs to you—the tech giants have no access to it.

The day after: What we could gain

This technological unleashing of the digital funnel would almost automatically trigger a tremendous dynamic. We would experience a liberation across all conceivable categories. This unleashing of the funnel would affect *all* (!) areas of society equally. What would apply to YouTubers would also apply to everyone else who is active online:

Politicians would be less reliant on platforms such as X/Twitter. In this scenario, they can build up their own strong presences in parallel and also monetize them as they wish, as an attractive option for political campaign funding, for example.

Editors can post their fantastic content on platforms and, by freeing up outlinks, direct traffic to their own domains and monetize it there. Bloggers, artists and creatives could create powerful digital spaces of their own and earn money independently.

The same applies to companies, but especially challengers and start-ups. Do you remember the early days of social media, where companies got millions of views for free by creating funny and entertaining videos? Where posts from company pages had very strong organic reach? That would be possible again in the future. By freeing up outlinks, they can build strong communities and content on their own sites. No platform would be allowed to discriminate against posts with outlinks. And everyone would also be treated equally when it comes to traffic. Platforms would no longer be allowed to prioritize specific content according to their own economic interest (the approach under which platforms might say: "This is a company that should rather advertise with us, so they get massively less organic reach—we simply dim it down."). We would also liberate the good idea that used to be behind content marketing: That companies are able to easily build up their own reach with *relevant* content, for example on their own domains.

Imagine if we liberated the web in Europe in this way—what an incredible global impact it would have! Young digital creatives from all over the world would come to us. "Have you heard what's going on in Europe right now?" Off to Berlin, to Paris, to Warsaw, to Prague! It would be immediately clear to all market participants that this 'unleashing of the funnel' would make it much easier to get traffic in Europe. This could trigger a huge dynamic of innovation. In addition, we would have achieved a communitization of data in Europe. This could fuel science applications on the one hand and provide enormous support for the start-up scene on the other. Europe is a huge market with a lot of purchasing power. More and more companies would certainly launch their ideas on the market here first, simply because the probability of success would be much higher here. Who would then want to waste their time in the USA trying to launch new products under the rule of the tech giants? Europe could thus become an innovation incubator. This is where the best new ideas would be tested.

> I have been studying digital concentration for 15 years. Since then, futurologists and digital evangelists have been constantly announcing new digital breakthroughs that will supposedly soon destroy GAFAM's supremacy—such as NFTs, cryptocurrencies, Web3 or blockchain in recent years. However, nothing has changed in all these years. I therefore remain skeptical. Firstly, Big Tech can exploit every technological leap for itself through investments and takeovers and further expand its monopolies. Secondly, the quality of future generative AI (which is a real game changer) will depend on access to the largest possible data corpora. This will be an easy game for the digital corporations, as they possess infinite resources of texts, images and videos via the platforms as training data for every conceivable generative AI. This will only further increase Big Tech's unassailable lead. And that is precisely why we must take responsibility now and liberate our Internet ourselves.

No more gatekeeper silos:
Establish direct connections with users (D2C)

I hope it becomes clear how much potential could be unleashed with this dynamic. The principles correspond to the original ideology of the free Internet created by Tim Berners-Lee. A new version of it has been circulating in the press for a few years now as the 'Direct-to-Consumer' (D2C) revolution. D2C means that under digital conditions, every participant can establish a much better and deeper relationship with their 'customer' by being in direct contact with the users, processing all possible transactions with the users directly.

The problem at the moment is that many D2C innovations and business models do not work because the tech giants control the rules of the game. They are in control and can withdraw traffic from D2C players at will or multiply transaction costs. Anyone who relies on D2C currently runs the great risk of ending up in the graveyard of unused content we showed in the first chapter. This would change immediately if we liberated the Internet.

D2C could boom almost without limits under these new conditions, quite simply because much more traffic takes place outside the platforms. And again, this applies to all categories: Politicians will communicate D2C, bloggers and editors will publish D2C, musicians and artists will be able to sell their products D2C and so on—without having to keep 'paying' the platforms like feudal lords at every turn.

Our structural changes would have a surprising impact on the quality of content. It is true that all content providers will continue to be tempted to achieve more short term impact on platforms than on their own domains. But because the opportunities on their own domains are now significantly improved, they can risk the trade-off and try to increasingly transform short-term impressions and annoying clickbait into intensive, long-lasting relationships on their own domain, which they would maintain with particularly high-quality content. This could catalyze a decisive change.

Let's compare this to the current situation to illustrate the difference. The current platform economy mainly incentivizes the distribution of ever-increasing amounts of increasingly worthless content (which is precisely what is currently killing editorial teams). "Flood the zone with shit" was the mantra of Trump propagandist Steve Bannon, which could also serve as the logical media-economic imperative of the platforms: *Flood the platform silos with shit.* More and more, no matter what, just get out as much crap as you can! This is exactly how ChatGPT and generative AI are now tying the noose around the neck of the editorial media. It's up to us to change this immediately.

By freeing traffic from the platforms, we enable all content providers to win over users with high-quality content and retain them in long-term, intensive relationships.

I bet I can now pull a rabbit out of the hat that you didn't expect at all. I'm talking about at least a partial solution to what is probably the most difficult problem of all, and that is the issue of liability. If things happen as described here, there will be a self-reinforcing dynamic: More and more traffic is 'emancipating' itself from the platform silos, more and more new, dynamic high quality content is being published by creators on their own domains. This content can be monetized by the owners themselves, regardless of whether it is news, culture, influencers or films, webshops or podcasts. Do you notice what happens automatically without us having to do anything? The decisive side effect would be this: *Authors automatically assume full liability for content on their own domains.* So this shift in traffic alone will lead to an increased balancing and pacification of content.

It is tempting to estimate the economic potential that the opening of the digital markets would yield. Once again, let's use our ranking of the current aggregated attention on the Internet as a starting point and benchmark. From this ranking, we can define an upper limit with the only German digital company in the top ten, United Internet (ranked 8th and 12th with web.de and GMX) with an annual turnover of around 5.6 billion euros. From the few existing German players, we can pick out some companies in the middle of the ranking (ranked between 27th and around 220th) for which the turnover is published. Examples include Zalando (around eight billion euros in sales), Check24 (around 500 million euros), Payback (around 280 million euros) and spiegel.de (more than 100 million euros). If we now assume that, in the future, the top 50 percent of total online usage is no longer generated by seven companies as is currently the case, but instead by 50 different companies, we can estimate that this dynamic could result in 43 companies with annual sales in a corridor between one and three billion euros in Germany (this is a very conservative estimate). Just for reference, a single company like United Internet has around 10,000 employees—we can guess how many jobs could be created in the short term by liberating the Internet. Just imagine the extent of the digital boom for all of Europe!

Simply by breaking up the monopolies and reintroducing competition into the field of digital media, we are protecting our democracy and our free economy from being controlled by US digital corporations. By freeing up the digital markets and enabling various competing offers, the defense of dominant market positions through killer acquisitions would also be made considerably more difficult in purely structural terms, simply due to the large number of alternatives on the market.

As ironic as it sounds, in the mid term a liberated Internet would also be a blessing for the tech giants themselves. For at least ten years, the focus of digital corporations has been solely on securing their monopolies, on copying, killer acquisitions and lobbying, which explains their pathetically low success rate when it comes to own innovations, and this despite huge investments. Their successful 'new' products were almost always just acquisitions (☞ II.4).

Ultimately, however, our main goal would be achieved with all these side effects: our free democracy, our free market economy would be saved. By opening up the digital markets, through diversity and competition, we would continue to live in an open and pluralistic world. The diversity and the principle of separation of powers, which form the basis of our democracy, would be fulfilled with the breadth of the various offers. With a multitude of checks and balances, it would no longer be possible for the tech giants to dominate the various functional systems in our society and 'rule' them.

Final objections

Because these killer comments keep cropping up, I want to take them up briefly at the end, especially as we don't have to fear them either:

1. *"The rescue must come from the USA."*
2. *"Regulating tech has never worked."*

The first point:
With everything we hear from experts, we can assume that no help will come from the USA, neither in the short term nor in the medium term. I heard from an insider that US digital NGOs are even increasing their funding in Europe because they see the situation in the US as desolate, which is why they hope to achieve more through European initiatives. There could be several explanations for this.

First: US selfishness in economic matters is well known from historical analysis. Currently, the tech companies are the most successful export products of the US economy. From a purely economic point of view, the hostile takeover of Western democracies by US platforms is a profitable affair for America.

Second, the infiltration of American politics with former managers of tech giants is extremely far reaching.

Third, the digital transformation process is already more advanced in the USA than in Germany or Europe. In the US, we are already much closer to the 'point of no return', which I have estimated to be the year 2029 for Germany.

Fourth, digital companies in the US have managed to build symbiotic relationships with both Republican and Democrats. We should therefore be careful not to overestimate US initiatives, which are often just placebo actions that typically achieve nothing ("We tried it—it didn't work, the bill wouldn't have achieved a majority in the Senate" et cetera).

This development is tragic insofar as people in the USA are also becoming increasingly critical of the accumulation of power by the tech giants.[10] Big Tech currently seems to have such a strong grip on the political elites in the USA that they are making decisions that contradict public opinion. Many policymakers are making common cause with the digital corporations. That is why we Europeans are now standing on our own two feet here (as in other areas). Of course, it would be awesome if the US pioneered and liberated the Internet from the grip of their Big Tech corporations. But if the US flakes out, we will have to step up to the challenge in Europe.

On the second point:

Anyone who thinks that regulation has never achieved anything should look at this point from a different perspective. I would argue the opposite: the tech giants have already been regulating *us* for many years. Let's remember, for example, how the platforms are constantly changing the rules on the networks in their favor or turning down the outlinks (☞ II.1). Big Tech has long since taken control successfully. We have handed over the control of the digital machine room to the tech giants without any fight or even defense.

If regulatory initiatives from the past have achieved nothing, it is probably because they were implemented miserably and incompetently by bureaucrats who were overwhelmed by the entrepreneurial aggressiveness of the digital champions. They had too little knowledge of digital markets and business models. Take a look at an ecosystem like Amazon, for example. Analyze how Amazon uses dozens of rules, incentives, performance indicators, sanctions and 'tips' to optimize this system so that it is always two to three steps ahead of its supposed 'partners'—so that it always benefits more from the framework conditions set than the 'partners' who are active in it (☞ IV.3).

Just imagine for a second if we regulated digital companies with the same cleverness and rigor as Amazon regulating its own marketplace. That's exactly how we could hack Big Tech. Here, too, we will confront them with their own inhuman methods. I am already looking forward to a wonderful hotline that we will set up for them, where they will urgently try to reach us if they have lost a license or market access, for example.

> **FUN FACT:** Without any objection or defense, we have given away our digital sovereignty. We don't regulate Big Tech—Big Tech regulates us.

This also shows that the idea of unregulated markets is a contradiction in itself. In fact, no one uses the power of regulation better than the tech giants. We therefore need to completely rethink regulation and adapt it to the new digital realities. In fact, the Internet is currently also regulated, but in the *wrong* way. Metaphorically speaking, the existing regulation has led to a huge desert with no traffic on the Internet, whereas a few tech giants are supplied with an abundance of water. This misguided regulation is actively creating the current digital feudalism. We should therefore abolish this wrong regulation. We should find new, fair rules that ensure that not only the tech giants get the water—and that the irrigation creates a diversity of providers. By abolishing this false regulation, we open up the digital world to provider diversity, pluralism, competition, fair and open markets.

In order to rethink regulation, we must no longer leave this sphere to technocratic organizations that are mentally overwhelmed by the speed of digital corporations and are being overrun by developments. We need creative, entrepreneurial, innovative organizations that can quickly free the digital world from the monopolies.

These teams must always be superior to those of Big Tech in terms of speed, precision and aggressiveness. And they must ensure with the same determination that every single framework condition always leads exclusively to one and the same goal: That Western democratic societies affected benefit disproportionately more from these framework conditions than the digital corporations. In other words, we will proceed on the basis of the similar principles that Amazon applies in its own ecosystem.

This is a huge opportunity. Because if we liberate the digital markets, Europe could blossom digitally. As the guardian of the free world—with a free democracy and a free economy. With a fantastic, unique appeal to a suffering world full of crises and misery that is searching for real (!) values, thirsting for meaning, freedom and orientation. It could also help and support developments in the USA, which is experiencing the most serious democratic crisis in its history.

A European liberation of the Internet and the resulting economic and social dynamics could immediately show everywhere in the Western world that the propagandistic fear-mongering of the tech giants is completely unfounded ("Small businesses will suffer", "The Chinese will overtake us technologically" and the like). On the contrary: the digital transformation will unleash new potential, and we will all finally participate in it: companies, creators, editors, artists, politicians, start-ups. We would finally put into practice the central values of the new digital world together. Freedom, openness, community, empowerment, participation, sharing and transparency would no longer be hypocritical masquerades, but would be reinstalled as true and genuine values.

If only we could get our act together and say:
IT'S ENOUGH.

If we would have the courage to fight together:
THEN WE WILL STOP THEM.

Thanks

This book has been written over the years as a result of hundreds of enriching encounters and countless conversations with inspiring people, for whom I am extremely grateful and for whom I cannot pay enough tribute—which is why I am only mentioning the most important sources of inspiration and contributors here:

First and foremost, I would like to thank Prof. Karl-Nikolaus Peifer, Director of the Institute for Media and Communications Law at the University of Cologne. Without his selfless professional support and continuous encouragement, this book would never have been written.

I would like to thank Robert Habeck, Vice Chancellor of Germany, who patiently listened to my theses despite his busy schedule, as well as Claudia Roth and the Federal Ministry of Culture and Media for inviting me to speak on these topics at the Federal Government's Digital Summit, and Wolfgang Büchner, the Federal Government's deputy spokesperson, for exciting discussions.

I would like to thank Prof. Stephan Packard from the University of Cologne for his tireless, continuous support of my research, as well as Prof. Peter Marx and Prof. Benjamin Beil. Without their trust, also the *Atlas of the Digital World* could not have been created. I would like to thank Prof. Damian Tambini from the London School of Economics for the fruitful exchange.

I would like to thank many inspiring people for their professional input and advice, including Jens Jenssen from the State Chancellery of Rhineland-Palatinate, Prof. Werner Schwaderlapp, the Chairman of the Media Commission of the State Media Authority of North Rhine-Westphalia, Wolfgang Kreißig, the President of the State Office for Communication Baden-Württemberg, Michael Ellwanger from the Baden-Württemberg State Ministry, Prof. Christoph Neuberger from the FU Berlin and also Director of the Weizenbaum Institute, Prof. Thomas Höppner, Prof. Otfried Jarren from the University of Zurich, Dr. Michael Seemann, Prof. Christian-Mathias Wellbrock and Stephan Grulert.

I would like to thank Aycha Riffi and Lars Gräßer from the Grimme Institute for the enriching collaboration. I would like to thank Prof. Martin Gläser, editor of the journal *MedienWirtschaft*, for his trust and interest in my texts, the media entrepreneur Sebastian Turner for his commitment and support, Carla Hustedt from the Mercator Foundation and Hermann von Engelbrechten-Ilow for enriching professional discussions.

I would like to thank Andreas Mundt, President of the German Federal Antitrust Office, and Dr. Sebastian Wismer, Head of the Digital Economy Division at the German Federal Antitrust Office, for the respectful and constructive exchange we have always had, even when we do not come together on the matter—controversial discussions are also part of our endangered pluralistic democracy. I would like to thank Constantin Krückels for his reliable support with research and analysis. I would also like to thank Waltraud Berz and Dr. Judith Wilke-Primavesi from Campus Verlag for their expert support and the editor, Andrea Dietrich, for her professional supervision. I thank Julian Hale for kindly checking the English translation.

But above all I would like to thank my family, my children and especially my wife, who had to spend many weekends and vacation days without me—without their boundless understanding I would not have been able to write this book.

Notes

A All references in the text that use the superscript letter 'A' refer to measurements published in the scientific study 'Atlas of the digital World'; see also Note 6 in Chapter I; additional information under www.atlasderdigitalenwelt.de/en

Knockout

1 In this book, 'Big Tech' essentially refers to the five largest digital corporations Alphabet (Google), Amazon, Meta (Facebook), Apple and Microsoft, which are also known as GAFAM after the initial letters of their (former) company names. Because the acronym 'GAFAM' is commonly used for Google, Apple, Facebook, Amazon and Microsoft, the term is also used here after the renaming (Alphabet, Meta) as a collective term for the major US digital corporations.

2 Which, by the way, is denied with the same regularity by the tech giants—see also the cases in Chapter V.4. In most cases, they get away with it because, firstly, they often act through dependent intermediaries and, secondly, they express their blackmailing threats of sanctions indirectly, along the lines of: "I wouldn't do X— it would be a shame if Y happened". The threats are always skillfully formulated ambiguously. In the event of a conflict, it is always a case of statement against statement ("we never said that", "we meant it differently" etc.).

Chapter I—GAME OVER 2029

1 Cf. **McLuhan, Marshall:** Understanding Media. The Extensions of Man. London, New York: Routledge 2001 [1964].

2 Cf. u. a. **Janke, Klaus:** "Digitale Spendings liegen erstmals über nicht-digitalen Investments", in: Horizont online, 7.10.2021. https://www.horizont.net/medien/nachrichten/werbemarkt-2021-digitale-spendings-liegenerstmals-ueber-nicht-digitalen-investments-194918; **Janke, Klaus:** "Warum die Mediaagenturen so viel Wachstum bei den digitalen Plattformen erwarten", in: Horizont online, 14.2.2022; https://www.horizont.net/medien/nachrichten/werbemarkt-warum-die-mediaagenturen-so-viel-wachstum-bei-den-digitalenplattformen-erwarten-197781

3 Detailed background information can be found at www.bigtechmustgo.com

4 Figures according to **Brandt, Mathias:** "Anzeigen-Einnahmen haben sich seit 2010 halbiert"; in: Statista, 28.7.2021; https://de.statista.com/infografik/25420/anzeigen-und-beilagenumsaetze-der-zeitungen-in-deutschland/ (data BDZV); "Entwicklung der verkauften Auflage der Tageszeitungen in Deutschland in ausgewählten Jahren von 1991 bis 2022"; in: Statista, 24.2.2023; https://de.statista.com/statistik/daten/studie/72084/umfrage/verkaufte-auflage-von-tageszeitungen-in-deutschland/

5 The figures are based on **Navarro, J. G.:** "Advertising Expenditure in Western Europe from 2017 to 2024, by Medium."; in: Statista, checked on 6.1.2025; https://www.statista.com/statistics/799801/ad-spend-in-western-europemedia/. The growth rates of the last eight years has been extrapolated for each media genre into the future, leading to a share of 76.1 percent for digital media and a share of 23.9 percent for analog media. For the year 2024, the report states a share of digital media of 63.3 percent.

6 Cf. **Andree, Martin,** and **Timo Thomsen:** Atlas der digitalen Welt (= 'Atlas of the Digital World'). Campus 2020. Further information can also be found at www.atlasderdigitalenwelt.de/en. All figures from our atlas are marked below with footnotes showing the letter 'A'. This atlas is to my knowledge the only existing, holistic scientific measurement of media usage across all devices for a full country that exists globally (smartphone, tablets, desktops). The raw data was kindly provided by the leading German market research company GfK in a cooperation with the University of Cologne (GfK Cross Media Link Panel, n = 16.000). The data is from the third and fourth quarters of 2019; usage across all devices (smartphone, tablet, desktop), total population. A detailed appendix in the 'Atlas' spells out the scientific framework of these data measurements. It may be argued that these figures are slightly outdated—however, we are primarily using relative shares here. Experience has shown that these shares remain quite stable over time. In any case, the high measurement accuracy speaks for the descriptiveness of the data. With regard to our topic (concentration), I would not expect any serious shifts, even with current figures.

7 **Anderson, Chris:** The Long Tail. Nischenprodukte statt Massenmarkt. München: Deutscher Taschenbuch Verlag 2009 [2006].

8 According to a study by GroupM, the share of the top 3 (Alphabet, Meta, Amazon) in total digital advertising expenditure worldwide (excluding China) is between 80 % and 90 %; **Adgate, Brad:** "Agencies Agree; 2021 Was A Record Year For Ad Spending, With More Growth Expected In 2022"; in: Forbes, 8.12.2021; https://www.forbes.com/sites/bradadgate/2021/12/08/agencies-agree-2021-was-a-record-year-for-ad-spending-with-more-growth-expected-in-2022/?sh=3dc3a7257bc6; In the USA, the figure is already as high as 90 %; cf. **Hagey, Keach,** and **Suzanne Vranica:** "How Covid-19 Supercharged the Advertising 'Triopoly' of Google, Facebook and Amazon"; in: Wall Street Journal, 19.3.2021; https://www.wsj.com/articles/how-covid-19-supercharged-theadvertising-triopoly-of-google-facebook-and-amazon-11616163738; A study by business consultants Ebiquity puts the global share of the top 3 at 74 %; cf. n.a.: "Google, Meta and Amazon are on track to absorb more than 50 % of all ad money in 2022", in: Ebiquity, 4.2.2022; https://ebiquity.com/news-insights/press/google-meta-and-amazon-are-on-track-to-absorb-more-than-50-of-all-ad-money-in-2022/; In Germany, industry experts estimate the share of the top 4 (Alphabet, Meta, Amazon and Apple) at 80 %.; Cf. **Scheppe, Oliver:** "69 Prozent mehr Umsatz: Google und Co. gewinnen am Werbemarkt, Klassische Medien fallen zurück"; in: Handelsblatt, 11.11.2021;

9 Source: Atlas der digitalen Welt (cf. note 6), p. 96.

PROVIDER	TOTAL DURATION (HOURS/MONTH)	NET REACH	DURATION PER UNIQUE USER
bild.de	18.897.739	53,7 %	00:36:06
wetter.com	13.793.040	48,5 %	00:29:06
spiegel.de	8.616.478	48,5 %	00:18:31
t-online.de (Homepage)	7.243.708	37,0 %	00:20:06
focus.de	7.168.160	59,3 %	00:12:24
chefkoch.de	5.120.149	51,9 %	00:10:07
web.de (Homepage)	2.878.632	37,5 %	00:07:53
sueddeutsche.de	2.134.246	25,3 %	00:08:39
chip.de	2.110.831	59,6 %	00:03:38
Stern News	2.016.302	35,4 %	00:05:51

10 Cf. z. B. **Moorstedt, Tobias:** Jeffersons Erben. Wie die digitalen Medien die Politik verändern. Frankfurt/M.: Suhrkamp 2008.

11 Source: Atlas der digitalen Welt (s. note 6), p. 232

PROVIDER	TOTAL DURATION (HOURS/ MONTH)	NET REACH	DURATION PER UNIQUE USER
achgut.com	69.600	2,0 %	00:03:39
borncity.com	23.845	1,4 %	00:01:49
bildblog	19.716	0,6 %	00:03:33
langweiledich.net	16.548	0,2 %	00:08:03
grenzwissenschaft-aktuell.de	16.443	0,5 %	00:03:43
netzpolitik.org	11.931	1,3 %	00:00:59
mitvergnuegen.com	10.715	1,9 %	00:00:36
zugreiseblog.de	6.582	1,1 %	00:00:37
mobilegeeks.de	5.012	0,9 %	00:00:33

12 Source: Atlas der digitalen Welt (cf. note 6).
To the selection of brands and other categories (e.g. automobiles, sport, luxury) cf. ibid., S 239–243.

PROVIDER	TOTAL DURATION (HOURS/ MONTH)	NET REACH	DURATION PER UNIQUE USER
Nivea	322.694	11,6 %	00:02:52
Pampers	229.914	4,1 %	00:05:44
Nestlé	226.416	11,6 %	00:02:00
Ferrero	147.109	4,2 %	00:03:37
HiPP	146.843	5,0 %	00:03:01
Dr. Oetker	122.397	6,7 %	00:01:52
HARIBO	65.800	3,9 %	00:01:45

13 Source: Atlas der digitalen Welt (cf. note 6), p. 76, among others p. 96

14 Audience ratings based on studies by AGF in cooperation with GfK/TV Scope/ media control GmbH, cf. https://www.meedia.de/video/tv-monat-juli-zdf-und-rtl-bauen-vorsprung-als-marktfuehrer-aus-the-masked-singer-und-das-sommerhaus-der-stars-sind-die-sommerhits-daff836a7094d480fabd006cd9ecd0da; https://www.meedia.de/video/tv-monat-august-promi-big-brother-pusht-sat1-und-sixx-nitro-holt-dank-eintracht-frankfurt-neue-alltime-rekorde-8a0e9aa87d2407bb995b5f0675fb7489; https://www.meedia.de/video/tv-monat-september-die-hoehle-der-loewen-pusht-vox-auf-den-besten-monats-marktanteil-seit-zweiein-halb-jahren-6be8b2ea1fb42db25b6511c27eff9914.

15 Cf. additional background information on the unreliable results of surveys at www.bigtechmustgo.com.

16 Cf. **Mantel, Uwe:** "Angebliche Reichweiten von Zeitungen und Zeitschriften. Neue Print-MA sorgt vor allem wieder für Fragezeichen"; in: DWDL, 27.7.2022; https://www.dwdl.de/zahlenzentrale/88945/neue_printma_sorgt_vor_allem_wieder_fuer_fragezeichen/?utm_source=&utm_medium=&utm_campaign=&utm_term=

17 - *Alphabet:* "Gewinn von Alphabet weltweit in den Jahren 2011 bis 2022", in: statista.de, 07.02.2023; https://de.statista.com/statistik/daten/studie/76456/umfrage/nettogewinn-von-google-seit-2001/;
- *Bertelsmann:* "Bertelsmann verzeichnet 2021 zweistelliges organisches Umsatzwachstum und operatives Rekordergebnis"; in: bertelsmann.de, 31.03.2022; https://www.bertelsmann.de/news-und-media/nachrichten/bertelsmann-verzeichnet-2021-zweistelliges-organisches-umsatzwachstum-und-operatives-rekordergebnis.jsp?atn=&abp=;
- *ProSiebenSat.1:* "Konzernergebnis der ProSiebenSat.1 Media SE in den Jahren 2006 bis 2021"; in: statista.de, 27.05.2022; https://de.statista.com/statistik/daten/studie/183316/umfrage/gewinn-von-pro-sieben-sat-1-seit-2006/;
- *Springer:* "Gewinn der Axel Springer SE in den Jahren 2007 bis 2021"; in: statista.de, 17.04.2023;https://de.statista.com/statistik/daten/studie/523532/umfrage/gewinn-der-axel-springer-ag/;
- *Holtzbrinck:* "Gewinn bzw. Verlust der Georg von Holtzbrinck GmbH & Co. KG in den Jahren 2014 bis 2021"; in: statista.de, 19.12.2022; https://de.statista.com/statistik/daten/studie/1279845/umfrage/gewinn-der-holtzbrinckpublishing-group/;
- *G&J:* Hanfeld, Michael: "Beim Boostern sind nicht alle dabei" in: faz.net, 30.03.2023; https://www.faz.net/aktuell/feuilleton/bertelsmann-steigert-umsatz-zerschlaegt-gruner-jahr-18788440.html

18 **Hachmeister, L., C. Wagener, & T. Wäscher:** Wer beherrscht die Medien? Die 50 größten Medien- und Wissenskonzerne der Welt, Köln: von Halem 2022; **Hachmeister, Lutz:** Wer beherrscht die Medien? Die 50 größten Medienkonzerne der Welt. 1. Aufl. München: Beck 1997. The ranking only shows the turnover of the corportions in the media market— (i. e. not the total turnover).

Chapter II—THE END OF THE FREE INTERNET

1 **Doctorow, Cory:** "Tiktok's Enshittification", in: Wired, 23.1.2023, https://www.wired.com/story/tiktokplatforms-cory-doctorow/

2 **Carlson, Nicholas:** "Well, These New Zuckerberg IMs Won't Help Facebook's Privacy Problems", in: Business Insider, 13.5.2010; https://www.businessinsider.com/well-these-new-zuckerberg-ims-wont-help-facebooksprivacy-problems-2010-5?IR=T

3 **Fishkin, Rand:** "In 2020, Two Thirds of Google Searches Ended Without a Click", in: SparkToro, 22.3.2021; https://sparktoro.com/blog/in-2020-two-thirds-of-google-searches-ended-without-a-click/

4 Cited in **Gertner, Jon:** The Idea Factory. Bell Labs and the Great Age of American Innovation. New York: Penguin 2012, p. 368.

5 Cited in **Höppner, Thomas,** and **Tom Piepenbrock:** Digitale Werbung und das Google Ökosystem. Frankfurt/M.: R&W 2023, p. 295.

6 **Berners-Lee, Tim:** Weaving the Web. The Original Design and Ultimate Destiny of the World Wide Web. San Francisco: Harper 1999, p. 16.

7 Ibid., p. 36.

8 Additional background information on the various boycotts can be found at www.bigtechmustgo.com.

9 Cf. **Heinrich, Jörg:** "Twitter: Kaum jemand wechselt zu Mastodon", in: Werben & Verkaufen, 6.12.2022; https://www.wuv.de/Themen/MarTech-CRM/Twitter-Kaum-jemand-wechselt-zu-Mastodon

10 Cf. u. a. **Economides, Nicholas,** and **Ioannis Liano:** "The Elusive Antitrust Standard on Bundling in Europe and in the United States in the Aftermath of the Microsoft Cases.", in: Antitrust Law Journal 76/3 (2009); https://www.ucl.ac.uk/cles/sites/cles/files/economides_lianos_antitrust_microsoft_cases.pdf

11 Cf. **Knight, Daniel:** "The Rise of the Microsoft Monopoly", in: Low End Mac, 20.3.2008; https://lowendmac.com/2008/rise-of-microsoft-monopoly/

12 Cf. https://de.statista.com/statistik/daten/studie/77226/umfrage/internetnutzer-verbreitung-von-officesoftware-in-deutschland/#:~:text=Laut%20einer%20Studie%20zur%20Nutzung,laut%20Studie%20auf%20Google%20Docs.

13 Cf. "EU-Gericht bestätigt Milliardenstrafe gegen Google", in: Spiegel, 14.9.2022; https://www.spiegel.de/netzwelt/netzpolitik/kartellrecht-eu-gericht-bestaetigt-milliardenstrafe-gegen-google-a-59ddfed2-b493-421c-895c-3f256aba1ed8

14 Cf. **Herwartz, Christoph:** "Europas Kartellwächterin kämpft mit neuen Waffen gegen Google", in: Handelsblatt, 2.5.2022; https://www.handelsblatt.com/politik/international/margrethe-vestager-europaskartellwaechterin-kaempt-mit-neuen-waffen-gegen-google/28287774.html;
"Erneute Milliardenstrafe für Google", in: Legal Tribune Online, 20.3.2019; https://www.lto.de/recht/kanzleien-unternehmen/k/eukommission-wettbewerbsstrafe-missbrauch-marktmacht-google-adsense-for-search/

15 "Kartellrecht: Kommission verhängt Geldbuße in Höhe von 2,42 Mrd. EUR gegen Google wegen Missbrauchs seiner marktbeherrschenden Stellung als Suchmaschine durch unzulässige Vorzugsbehandlung des eigenen Preisvergleichsdienst", in: ec.europa.eu, 27.6.2017; https://ec.europa.eu/commission/presscorner/detail/de/IP_17_1784.

16 "Kartellrecht: Kommission übermittelt Apple Mitteilung der Beschwerdepunkte zu Apple-Pay-Praktiken", in: ec.europa.eu, 2.5.2022; https://ec.europa.eu/commission/presscorner/detail/de/ip_22_2764

17 Cf. "EU-Kommission schränkt Wettbewerbsvorwürfe gegen Apple ein"; In: Horizont, 28.2.2023; https://www.horizont.net/marketing/nachrichten/app-store-eu-kommission-schraenkt-wettbewerbsvorwuerfe-gegen-apple-ein-210188

18 Cf. **Mussler, Werner:** "Amazon vermeidet mit Zusagen eine EU-Kartellbuße", in: FAZ, 20.12.2022; https:// www.faz.net/aktuell/wirtschaft/amazon-vermeidet-mit-zusagen-eine-eu-kartellbusse-18548469.html.

19 Cited in **Höppner, Thomas,** and **Tom Piepenbrock:** Digitale Werbung und das Google Ökosystem. Frankfurt/M.: R&W 2023, p. 345.

20 All values were determined to the best of our knowledge and belief from the various studies available:
- *Search engine*
De.statista.com "Marktanteile von ausgewählten Suchmaschinen bei der Desktop-Suche und bei der mobilen Suche in Deutschland im Dezember 2022"; https://de.statista.com/statistik/daten/studie/301012/umfrage/marktanteile-der-suchmaschinen-und-marktanteile-mobile-suche/
De.statista.com "Marktanteile der Suchmaschinen weltweit nach mobiler und stationärer Nutzung im Januar 2022"; https://de.statista.com/statistik/daten/studie/222849/umfrage/marktanteile-der-suchmaschinen-weltweit/
- *Gratis Video-on-Demand*
Atlas der digitalen Welt (Own measurements, basis: aggregated usage time)
- *Online map service*
Atlas der digitalen Welt(Own measurements, basis: aggregated usage time)
- *E-Mail*
De.statista.com "Bei welchem Anbieter haben Sie Ihre am häufigsten genutzte E-Mail-Adresse?" https://de.statista.com/statistik/daten/studie/170371/umfrage/nutzung-von-e-mail-domains/
De.statista.com "Marktanteile der Top 8 E-Mail-Clients weltweit im Oktober 2022" https://de.statista.com/statistik/daten/studie/688163/umfrage/marktanteile-der-e-mail-clients-weltweit/
- *Browser*
"Marktanteile der führenden Browserfamilien an der Internetnutzung in Deutschland von Januar 2009 bis Januar 2023", in: de.statista.com, 2.2.2023; https://de.statista.com/statistik/daten/studie/13007/umfrage/marktanteile-der-browser-bei-der-internetnutzung-in-deutschland-seit-2009/
"Marktanteile der führenden Browserfamilien an der Internetnutzung weltweit von Januar 2009 bis Januar 2023", in: de.statista.com, 2.2.2023; https://de.statista.com/statistik/daten/studie/157944/umfrage/marktanteile-der-browser-bei-der-internetnutzung-weltweit-seit-2009/
"Marktanteile der führenden mobilen Browser an der Internetnutzung mit Mobiltelefonen in Deutschland von Januar 2009 bis Januar 2023", in: de.statista.com, 2.2.2023; https://de.statista.com/statistik/daten/studie/184297/umfrage/marktanteile-mobiler-browser-bei-der-internetnutzung-in-deutschland-seit-2009/; "Marktanteile der führenden mobilen Browser an der Internetnutzung mit Mobiltelefonen weltweit von Januar 2009 bis Januar 2023", in: de.statista.com, 2.2.2023; https://de.statista.com/statistik/daten/studie/13120/umfrage/marktanteile-mobiler-browser-bei-der-internetnutzung-weltweit-seit-2009/
- *Android*
"Vergleich der Marktanteile von Android und iOS am Absatz von Smartphones in Deutschland von Januar 2012 bis Dezember 2022", in: de.statista.com, 8.2.2023; https://de.statista.com/statistik/daten/studie/256790/umfrage/marktanteile-von-android-und-ios-am-smartphone-absatz-in-deutschland/; "Mobile operating systems' market share worldwide from 1st quarter 2009 to 4th quarter 2022", in: statista.com, 17.1.2023; https://www.statista.com/statistics/272698/global-market-share-held-by-mobile-operating-systems-since-2009/
- *App Marketplace*
"Schätzung zur Anzahl der Downloads von Apps nach App-Stores weltweit in den Jahren 2017 bis 2021", in: de.statista.com, 16.6.2022; https://de.statista.com/statistik/daten/studie/993352/umfrage/anzahl-der-downloads-von-apps-nach-app-stores-weltweit/; „Bruttoumsätze mit Apps nach App Stores weltweit in den Jahren 2016 bis 2022", in: de.statista.com, 16.06.2022; https://de.statista.com/statistik/daten/studie/802760/umfrage/schaetzung-des-umsatzes-mit-apps-nach-app-store-weltweit/
- *All Ad Tech products* (Ad servers for advertisers, ad servers for publishers, advertising networks, demand side platforms, supply side platforms, tracking tools): **Höppner, Thomas,** und **Tom Piepenbrock:** Digitale Werbung und das Google Ökosystem. Frankfurt/M.: R&W 2023, p. 187.

21 Ibid. p. 203

22 **Sawers, Paul:** "UK closes 'Jedi Blue' antitrust collusion case against Google and Meta", in: Tech Crunch, 10.3.2023; https://techcrunch.com/2023/03/10/uk-retreats-from-jedi-blue-antitrust-collusion-case-against-google-and-meta/

23 There are often different figures on the number and purchase prices of takeovers. The figures given here have been aggregated to the best of our knowledge from the following data sources:
- *Wikipedia:* List of mergers and acquisitions by Meta Platforms. https://en.wikipedia.org/wiki/List_of_mergers_and_acquisitions_by_Meta_Platforms
- *Wikipedia:* List of mergers and acquisitions by Apple. https://en.wikipedia.org/wiki/List_of_mergers_and_acquisitions_by_Apple
- *Wikipedia:* List of mergers and acquisitions by Microsoft. https://en.wikipedia.org/wiki/List_of_mergers_and_acquisitions_by_Microsoft
- *Wikipedia:* List of mergers and acquisitions by Amazon. https://en.wikipedia.org/wiki/List_of_mergers_and_acquisitions_by_Amazon
- *Wikipedia:* List of mergers and acquisitions by Alphabet. https://en.wikipedia.org/wiki/List_of_mergers_and_acquisitions_by_Alphabet
- Tracxn. https://tracxn.com/
- mergr. https://mergr.com/
- crunchbase. https://www.crunchbase.com/
- CB Insights, https://www.cbinsights.com/
- **Alcantara, Chris; Schaul, Kevin; De Vynck, Gerrit;** und **Albergotti, Reed** in Washington Post, veröffentlicht am 21.4.2021. https://www.washingtonpost.com/technology/interactive/2021/amazon-apple-facebook-google-acquisitions/

24 In our own measurements, we were able to quantify the share of aggregated usage time of Facebook and Instagram within social media at 83 %; cf. **Andree, Martin,** and **Timo Thomsen:** Atlas der digitalen Welt. Frankfurt/M.: Campus 2020, p. 146.

25 The network analyses are published and explained in detail in **Andree, Martin,** and **Timo Thomsen:** Atlas der digitalen Welt. Frankfurt/M.: Campus 2020. Cf. for Alphabet p. 215f., for Meta p. 204–206.

26 This is a recommendation from Google for the search engine optimization of websites, but the original link is no longer available. Cited in **Höppner, Thomas,** und **Tom Piepenbrock:** Digitale Werbung und das Google Ökosystem. Frankfurt/M.: R&W 2023, p. 127.

27 Cf. also author: Medien machen Marken. Eine Medientheorie des Marketing und des Konsums. Frankfurt/M.: Campus 2010, p. 125ff. und p. 175ff.

28 Cf. **Hindman, Matthew:** The Internet Trap. How the Digital Economy Builds Monopolies and Undermines Democracy. Princeton, Oxford: Princeton University Press 2018; ders.: The Myth of Digital Democracy. Princeton, Oxford: Princeton University Press 2009.

Chapter III—HOSTILE TAKEOVER

1 **Fechner, Frank:** Medienrecht. 21. Aufl. Tübingen: Mohr Siebeck 2021, p. 247.

2 The three areas are meant conceptually. It is certainly possible to discuss in detail what to include and what not to include. Market sizes according to Statista; additional background information on www.bigtechmustgo.com

3 Cf. **Rabe, L.:** "Online-Umsätze von ausgewählten Warengruppen in Deutschland bis 2022"; in: Statista, 31.1.2023; https://de.statista.com/statistik/daten/studie/253188/umfrage/umsatzstarke-warengruppen-im-online-handel-in-deutschland/

4 Cf. also **Kolf, Florian, Michael Scheppe,** and **Katrin Terpitz:** "Heinz, Nestlé, Henkel: Warum jetzt viele junge Marken der Konzerne scheitern", in: Handelsblatt, 6.3.2023; https://www.handelsblatt.com/unternehmen/handel-konsumgueter/heinz-nestle-henkel-warum-jetzt-viele-junge-marken-der-konzerne-scheitern-/28946620.html

5 Detailed background information can be found at www.bigtechmustgo.com

6 Cf. **Fries, Trutz:** "Amazons Eigenmarken 2022, Analyse und Liste", in: Amalytix, 1.5.2021; https://www.amalytix.com/blog/amazon-eigenmarken/

7 **Staab, Philipp:** Digitaler Kapitalismus. Markt und Herrschaft in der Ökonomie der Unknappheit. Frankfurt/M.: Suhrkamp 2019, p. 227 und p. 221.

8 Cf. **Habermas, Jürgen:** Strukturwandel der Öffentlichkeit. Untersuchungen zu einer Kategorie der bürgerlichen Gesellschaft. Frankfurt/M.: Suhrkamp 1990; zu den Effekten der digitalen Transformation cf. ders.: Ein neuer Strukturwandel der Öffentlichkeit und die deliberative Politik. Frankfurt/M.: Suhrkamp 2022.

9 Cf. **Meyer, Thomas:** Mediokratie. Die Kolonisierung der Politik durch die Medien. Frankfurt/M.: Suhrkamp 2001, p. 75ff.

10 An excellent overview of the use of social media in the last German election campaign can be found at https://interaktiv.tagesspiegel.de/lab/social-media-dashboard-bundestagswahl-2021/

11 **Oborne, Peter,** and **Tom Roberts:** How Trump Thinks. His Tweets and the Birth of a New Political Language. London: Head of Zeus 2017, p. vii.

12 Ibid.

13 Cf. general **Biblin, Rebecca,** and **Cory Doctorow:** Chokepoint Capitalism. How Big Tech and Big Content Captured Creative Labor Markets and How We'll Win Them Back. Boston: Beacon 2022.

14 The 'Digital Dependence Index' indicates the dependencies on digital technologies in individual countries; with a value of 0.82 (2019), Germany is in the 'high vulnerability' range; cf. "Vermessung der digitalen Dependenz"; https://digitaldependence.eu/; cf. auch eine aktuelle Studie von Forschern der Uni Bonn zur digitalen Abhängigkeit Europas, veröffentlicht: Konrad Adenauer Stiftung: "Auf dem Weg zur digitalen Selbstbestimmung?"; https://www.kas.de/de/einzeltitel/-/content/auf-dem-weg-zur-digitalen-selbstbestimmung.

15 Detailed background information can be found at www.bigtechmustgo.com

16 **Duffy, Clare:** "Facebook's dream of creating its own global cryptocurrency officially comes to an end", in: CNN, 1.2.2022; https://edition.cnn.com/2022/02/01/tech/facebook-diem-association-dissolving/index.html

17 Cf. **Kleinz, Torsten:** "Kommt der digitale Euro?", in: ZDF, 31.12.2022; https://www.zdf.de/nachrichten/digitales/digitaler-euro-ezb-100.html

18 Cf. **Bocksch, René:** "PayPal ist die Nummer Eins der Online-Bezahldienste". in: Statista, 10.6.2022; https://de.statista.com/infografik/23357/anteil-der-befragten-die-diese-online-bezahldienste-nutzen/#:~:text=In%20Deutschland%20ist%20die%20Nutzung,PayPal%20mit%20rund%2093%20Prozent.

19 **Ahrens, Sandra:** "Welche mobile Bezahllösung nutzen Sie?", in: Statista, 3.2.2022; https://de.statista.com/statistik/daten/studie/1166076/umfrage/mobilen-bezahlen-nutzung-nach-anbieter/

20 At the beginning of 2018, the American magazine *Wired* was already amused by the example of Facebook, which is "a company that dominates the media but doesn't want to be a media company" and always defiantly responds to queries: "Platform, platform, platform—for regulatory, financial and possibly even emotional reasons" **Guy, Eddie:** "Inside the Two Years That Shook Facebook—and the World. How a confused, defensive social media giant steered itself into a disaster, and how Mark Zuckerberg is trying to fix it all.", in: Wired, 12.2.2018; https://www.wired.com/story/inside-facebook-mark-zuckerberg-2-years-of-hell/; cf. on the many statements made by Mark Zuckerberg, e.g. **Castillo, Michelle:** "Zuckerberg tells Congress Facebook is not a media company: 'I consider us to be a technology company'", in: CNBC, 11.4.2018; https://www.cnbc.com/2018/04/11/mark-zuckerberg-facebook-is-a-technology-company-not-media-company.html

21 Cf. "Elon Musk's $44bn education on free speech. He has had a crash course in the trade-offs in protecting free expression", in: The Economist, 19.12.2022; https://www.economist.com/leaders/2022/12/19/elon-musks-44bn-education-on-free-speech

22 **Getahun, Hannah,** and **Erin Snodgrass:** "Elon Musk drohte Twitter-Mitarbeitern mit Kündigung, wenn sie seine Tweets nicht erfolgreicher als die von Joe Biden machen würden", in: Business Insider, 15.2.2023; https://www.businessinsider.de/wirtschaft/twitter-musk-drohte-mit-kuendigung-wenn-seine-tweets-nicht-sichtbarer-werden/; Mark Zuckerberg is also known to make erratic decisions; cf. **Mac, Ryan,** and **Craig Silverman:** Mark Changed The Rules: How Facebook Went Easy On Alex Jones And Other Right-Wing Figures", in: BuzzFeed, 22.2.2021; https://www.buzzfeednews.com/article/ryanmac/mark-zuckerberg-jo-el-kaplan-facebook-alex-jones

23 Cf. on Facebook, for example **Lecher, Colin,** and **Leon Yin:** "One Year After the Capitol Riot, Americans Still See Two Very Different Facebooks. Data from The Markup's Citizen Browser shows the platform's partisan divide continues", in: The Markup, 6.1.2022; https://themarkup.org/citizen-browser/2022/01/06/one-year-after-the-capitol-riot-americans-still-see-two-very-different-facebooks

24 Cf. **Hanfeld, Michael:** "Was sagen die 'Twitter-Files'? Das Geheimnis von Twitter", in: FAZ, 6.1.2023; https://www.faz.net/aktuell/feuilleton/medien/twitter-files-elon-musk-veroeffentlicht-bisher-geheime-dateien-18581277.html

25 Cf. **Eckert, Svea** et al.: "TikTok schränkt Meinungsfreiheit ein", in: Tagesschau, 5.10.2022; https://www.tagesschau.de/investigativ/ndr/tik-tok-begriffe-101.html;

26 **Weiss, Bari, Abigail Shrier, Michael Shellenberger,** and **Nellie Bowles:** "Twitters geheime schwarze Listen", in: Die Welt, 20.12.2022; https://www.welt.de/debatte/kommentare/plus242776401/Meinungs-Steuerung-Twitters-geheime-schwarze-Listen.html

27 Ibid.

28 **Kayser-Bril, Nicolas:** "AlgorithmWatch forced to shut down Instagram monitoring project after threats from Facebook", in: AlgorithWatch, 13.8.2021; https://algorithmwatch.org/en/instagram-research-shut-down-by-facebook/

29 **Baker-White, Emily:** "TikTok's Secret 'Heating' Button Can Make Anyone Go Viral", in: Forbes, 20.1.2023; https://www.forbes.com/sites/emilybaker-white/2023/01/20/tiktoks-secret-heating-button-can-make-anyone-go-viral/?sh=1181bd136bfd

30 **Dorsey, Jack:** "A native internet protocol for social media"; Statement zu den Twitter Files vom 13.12.2022; zugänglich unter https://www.getrevue.co/profile/jackjack/issues/a-na-

tive-internet-protocol-for-social-media-1503112?utm_campaign=Issue&utm_content=view_in_browser&utm_medium=email&utm_source=jack%27s.

31 **Zuboff, Shoshana:** The Age of Surveillance Capitalism: The Fight for the Future at the New Frontier of Power. London: Profile Books, 2019, p. 89.

32 Cf. **Baker-White, Emily:** "TikTok Spied On Forbes Journalists", in: Forbes, 22.12.2022; https://www.forbes.com/sites/emilybaker-white/2022/12/22/tiktok-tracks-forbes-journalists-bytedance/?sh=39bb07f87da5; **Hall, Ellie:** "TikTok Owner ByteDance Said Employees Improperly Obtained Journalists' User Data", in: BuzzFeed, 22.12.2022; https://www.buzzfeednews.com/article/ellievhall/bytedance-tiktok-user-data-report

33 "TikTok admits using its app to spy on reporters in effort to track leaks", in: The Guardian, 23.12.2022; https://www.theguardian.com/technology/2022/dec/22/tiktok-bytedance-workers-fired-data-access-journalists; **Dampz, Nils:** "TikTok räumt Datenmissbrauch ein", in: Tagesschau, 23.12.2022; https://www.tagesschau.de/ausland/amerika/tiktok-usa-datenmissbrauch-101.html

34 "One current employee asked that a Wired reporter turn off his phone so the company would have a harder time tracking whether it had been near the phones of anyone from Facebook"; **Guy, Eddie:** "Inside the Two Years That Shook Facebook—and the World. How a confused, defensive social media giant steered itself into a disaster, and how Mark Zuckerberg is trying to fix it all", in: Wired, 12.2.2018; https://www.wired.com/story/inside-facebook-mark-zuckerberg-2-years-of-hell/

35 Cf. **Solon, Olivia:** "'They'll squash you like a bug': how Silicon Valley keeps a lid on leakers.", in: The Guardian, 16.3.2018; https://www.theguardian.com/technology/2018/mar/16/silicon-valley-internal-work-spying-surveillance-leakers; https://www.mercurynews.com/2018/03/16/zuckerbergs-secret-police-how-facebooks-rat-catching-team-spies-on-employees-report/, also **Baron,**

Ethan: "Zuckerberg's 'secret police'. How Facebook's 'rat-catching team' spies on employees.", in: Mercury News, 16.3.2018; https://www.mercurynews.com/2018/03/16/zuckerbergs-secret-police-how-facebooks-rat-catching-team-spies-on-employees-report/

36 **Siu, Antoinette:** "TikTok Can Circumvent Apple and Google Privacy Protections and Access Full User Data, 2 Studies Say", in: The Wrap, 14.2.2022; https://www.thewrap.com/tiktok-circumvent-privacy-protections-user-data/#:~:text=TikTok%20can%20circumvent%20security%20protections,longstanding%20concerns%20raised%20by%20privacy

37 **Dascalescu, Ana:** "Tiktok Tracking: How Much Data Tiktok Uses and How To Stop It Tracking You", in: Tech the Lead, 23.12.2022; https://techthelead.com/tiktok-tracking-how-much-data-tiktok-uses-and-how-to-stop-it-tracking-you/

38 Cf. **Klais, Brian:** "New Research Across 200 iOS Apps Hints that Surveillance Marketing is Still Going Strong", in: URL Genius, 20.1.2022; https://app.urlgeni.us/blog/new-research-across-200-ios-apps-hints-surveillance-marketing-may-still-be-going-strong

39 Cf. **Solomon, Daina Beth:** "Uber could track passengers after they leave car, privacy group claims". In: L. A. Times, 22. 6. 2015; https://www.latimes.com/business/technology/la-fi-tn-uber-privacy-20150622-story.html

40 Cf. **McCracken, Harry:** "10 Things I Know to Be True About This Microsoft Hotmail Privacy Case"; in: Time.com, 22.3.2014; https://time.com/34229/microsoft-hotmail-privacy/

41 Cf. also the excellent volume **Münker, Stefan,** and **Alexander Rösler (Ed.):** Was ist ein Medium? Frankfurt/M.: Suhrkamp 2008.

42 **Zuboff, Shoshana:** The Age of Surveillance Capitalism: The Fight for the Future at the New Frontier of Power. London: Profile Books, 2019, p. 138-140.

Chapter IV—MONOPOLIES, FAKE NEWS, HATE SPEECH

1 **Wu, Tim:** The Curse of Bigness. Antitrust in the New Gilded Age. New York: Columbia Global Reports 2018, p. 18.

2 Cite ibid., p. 31.

3 Admittedly, § 19a GWB enables ex-ante regulation for the first time if a basic ruling is issued in advance according to which market dominance is given. However, the current proceedings against Meta and Alphabet show how reluctantly the Federal Cartel Office is using these new instruments. In these cases, ex-ante regulation was avoided by referring to the responsibilities of the state media authorities or other specialized bodies, such as the Arbitration Board for Copyright Matters.

4 Various such cases are discussed in **Graef, Inge:** "When Data Evolves into Market Power. Data Concentration and Data Abuse under Competition Law.", in: Digital Dominance. The Power of Google, Amazon, Facebook, and Apple. Ed. von Martin Moore und Damian Tambini. Oxford: OUP 2018, p. 71-97.

5 Bundeskartellamt: "Fusion bei Zeitungsverlagen untersagt"; 28.9.2021; Download unter https://www.bundeskartellamt.de/SharedDocs/Meldung/DE/Meldungen%20News%20Karussell/2021/28_09_2021_Funke_OTZ.html

6 **Fanta, Alexander:** "Peter Thiel, Monopoly's fiercest advocate"; https://netzpolitik.org/2021/peter-thiel-monopolys-fiercest-advocate/#:~:text=Spun%20out%20of%20a%20course,as%20he%20later%20summarized%20it

7 **Thiel, Peter:** Zero to One. Wie Innovation unsere Gesellschaft rettet. Frankfurt/M.: Campus 2014, p. 28.

8 Ibid., p. 30.

9 Ibid., p. 34.

10 **Hindman, Matthew:** The Internet Trap. How the Digital Economy Builds Monopolies and Undermines Democracy. Princeton, Oxford: PUP 2018, p. 9.

11 **Kim, Eugene:** "Jeff Bezos to employees: 'One day, Amazon will fail' but our job is to delay it as long as possible", in: CNBC, 15.11.2018; https://www.cnbc.com/2018/11/15/bezos-tells-employees-one-day-amazon-will-fail-and-to-stay-hungry.html

12 For overviews of sales and background information, see www.bigtechmustgo.com

13 Cf. http://www.cobbles.com/simpp_archive/paramount-doc_1938list.htm

14 Cf. the statement of the judgment at the time: "United States v. Paramount Pictures, Inc., 334 U.p. 131 (1948)", in: supreme.justia.com; https://supreme.justia.com/cases/federal/us/334/131/#167

15 "Although digital advertising is growing at a double-digit rate, this is mainly to the advantage of the large American platforms Google, Facebook, Amazon and Apple, which, according to industry estimates, now dominate 80 percent of the digital advertising market." **Scheppe, Michael:** "69 Prozent mehr Umsatz: Google und Co. gewinnen am Werbemarkt – Klassische Medien fallen zurück", in: Handelsblatt, 11.11.2021; https://www.handelsblatt.com/unternehmen/it-medien/werbewirtschaft-69-prozent-mehr-umsatz-google-und-co-gewinnen-am-werbemarkt-klassische-medien-fallen-zurueck/27787322.html

16 Bundeskartellamt: "Sektor-Untersuchung Online-Werbung. Diskussionsbericht." August 2022; p. 31f.; Download unter https://www.bundeskartellamt.de/SharedDocs/Publikation/DE/Sektoruntersuchungen/Sektoruntersuchung_Online_Werbung_Diskussionsbericht_lang.pdf?__blob=publicationFile&v=4

17 **Fechner, Frank:** Medienrecht. 21. Aufl. Tübingen: Mohr Siebeck 2021, p. 14f.

18 Ibid., p. 388.

19 KEK, Ed. (2022): 23. Jahresbericht 2021. Download unter: https://www.kek-online.de/fileadmin/user_upload/KEK/Publikationen/Jahresberichte/23._Jahresbericht.pdf, p. 19f.

20 KEK, Ed. (2022): Zukunftsorientierte Vielfaltssicherung im Gesamtmarkt der Medien. Bericht der Kommission zur Ermittlung der

Konzentration im Medienbereich (KEK); https://www.kek-online.de/publikationen/medienkonzentrationsberichte/siebter-konzentrationsbericht-2021, p. 31.

21 To describe it in more detail: Although the platforms will have to delete obviously illegal statements in future under the NetzDG and Digital Services Act, this will only be done using the "notice and takedown" procedure. However, because this content is usually used online within a few hours of being posted, such deletions always come too late and the damage to society has already been done.

22 Cf. on these values, e.g **Silberling, Amanda:** "YouTube's ad revenue is declining, but creator economy experts aren't worried"; in: TechCrunch, 27.10.2022; https://techcrunch.com/2022/10/27/youtubes-ad-revenue-is-declining-but-creator-economy-experts-arent-worried/. Facebook zahlt für Video Creator denselben Prozentsatz aus; cf. **Holla, Aravinda:** "Facebook Video Ad Revenue Sharing Model—What It Means For Content Creators"; in: Vidooly, https://vidooly.com/blog/facebook-video-ads-revenue-sharing-model-creators/. Bei YouTube Shorts sind es angeblich 45 %; cf. **Elias, Jennifer:** "YouTube will start sharing ad revenue with Shorts creators as the company tries to catch TikTok"; in: CNBC, 20.9.2022; https://www.cnbc.com/2022/09/20/youtube-will-share-revenue-with-shorts-creators-as-tiktok-surges.html.

23 The text of the famous law is available at https://www.law.cornell.edu/uscode/text/47/230

24 **Krempl, Stefan:** "Google und Section 230", in: Heise Online, 14.1.2023; https://www.heise.de/news/Google-und-Section-230-US-Gerichtsurteil-koennte-Internet-auf-den-Kopf-stellen-7459343.html

25 Cf. e.g. the overview in https://www.allaboutmarketresearch.com/internet.htm

26 **Peifer, Karl-Nikolaus:** "Konvergenz in der Störer- und Verbreiterhaftung: Vom Störer zum Verbreiter?", in: AfP – Zeitschrift für Medien- und Kommunikationsrecht 1/2014, p. 18–23.

27 Ibid.

28 Cf. **Biblin, Rebecca,** and **Cory Doctorow:** "Chokepoint Capitalism", Boston: Beacon 2022, p. 81.

29 **Gärtner, Markus:** "Sechs Millionen Marktplatz-Händler verkaufen bei Amazon", in: Amazon Watchblog, 25. 3. 2021; https://www.amazon-watchblog.de/unternehmen/2571-amazon-haendler-zahl.html

30 **Sanz Grossón, Ulrike:** "Amazon – Wie man sich gegen die Sperrung des Händleraccounts wehren kann", in: Etailment, 21.2.2020; https://etailment.de/news/stories/Amazon-Sperrung-H%C3%A4ndlerkonto-22150

31 Although there are restrictions to this unilateral relationship in German general terms and conditions law that could protect users in an emergency, these cannot usually be applied because the tech giants can play the extraterritorial card here too. The assessment of legal expert Friedrich Graf von Westphalen is clear: "The contractual relationships between the 'big players' and users in the online platform business never follow German law, but rather Luxembourg, Dutch or Irish law. None of these laws has a regulatory framework in favor of users that can be used to control general terms and conditions as in German law. Rather, we find an almost unrestricted principle of freedom to draft contracts. However, if foreign law is applicable to the contractual relationship between the online intermediary and its commercial user, then German law no longer has any say. The unilaterally determining freedom of contract prevails and can be utilized by the big players"; **Westphalen, Friedrich Graf von:** "Widerstand gegen GAFA", in: FAZ, 3.12.2020; https://www.faz.net/aktuell/feuilleton/medien/die-neue-europaeische-plattform-verordnung-reicht-nicht-aus-17082029.html?printPagedArticle=true#pageIndex_2. Nevertheless, there are current movements that impose restrictions on GAFAM here—for example, Facebook must specify the reasons and legal protection options for blocking or deleting an account (Federal Court of Justice, judgment III ZR 179/20 and III ZR 192/20). The Digital Services Act will also stipulate more transparent T&C rules from 2024, although it remains to be seen to what extent these rules will be enforced.

32 **Hasenbrink, Uwe:** "Meinungsbildung und Kontrolle der Medien", in: Bundesamt für politische Bildung 9.12.2016; https://www.bpb.de/themen/medien-journalismus/medienpolitik/172240/meinungsbildung-und-kontrolle-der-medien/

33 Background on www.bigtechmustgo.com

34 BVerfGE 73, 118.

35 BVerfGE 12, 205.

36 **Rushe, Dominic:** "Facebook and Google insist they did not know of Prism surveillance program", in: The Guardian, 8.6.2013; https://www.theguardian.com/world/2013/jun/07/google-facebook-prism-surveillance-program

37 **Friedrich, Benjamin:** "Datenspionage: Internetgiganten kassierten Millionen von NSA", in: Focus, 21.1.2014; https://www.focus.de/digital/internet/facebook-yahoo-microsoft-und-google-datenspionage-internetgiganten-kassierten-millionen-von-nsa_id_3113424.html; **Pakalski, Ingo:** "NSA zahlte Facebook, Google und Microsoft Millionenbeträge", in: Golem, 24.8.2013; https://www.golem.de/news/prism-skandal-nsa-zahlte-facebook-google-und-microsoft-millionenbetraege-1308-101177.html

38 **Rushe, Dominic:** "Facebook and Google insist they did not know of Prism surveillance program", in: The Guardian, 8.6.2013; https://www.theguardian.com/world/2013/jun/07/google-facebook-prism-surveillance-program

39 **Lindner, Roland:** "Ein Erdbeben namens 'Prism'", in: FAZ, 6.6.2014; https://www.faz.net/aktuell/wirtschaft/unternehmen/nsa-skandal-ein-erdbeben-namens-prism-12974896.html

40 Source: https://www.washingtonpost.com/wp-srv/special/politics/prism-collection-documents/

41 **Lischka, Konrad:** "Die scheinheilige Transparenz-Botschaft der Internetriesen", in: Der Spiegel, 18.7.2013; https://www.spiegel.de/netzwelt/netzpolitik/prism-scheinheilige-botschaft-von-apple-facebook-google-microsoft-a-911817.html

42 **Zuboff, Shoshana:** Das Zeitalter des Überwachungskapitalismus. Frankfurt/M.: Campus 2018, p. 142.

43 **Hanfeld, Michael:** "Was sagen die 'Twitter-Files'? Das Geheimnis von Twitter", in: FAZ, 6.1.2023; https://www.faz.net/aktuell/feuilleton/medien/twitter-files-elon-musk-veroeffentlicht-bisher-geheime-dateien-18581277.html

44 Ibid.

45 Cite in **Zhou, Li, Nancy Scola,** und **Ashley Gold:** "Senators to Facebook, Google, Twitter: Wake up to Russian threat", in: Politico, 11.1.2017; https://www.politico.com/story/2017/11/01/google-facebook-twitter-russia-meddling-244412

46 **Guy, Eddie:** "Inside the Two Years That Shook Facebook—and the World.", in: Wired, 12.2.2018; https://www.wired.com/story/inside-facebook-mark-zuckerberg-2-years-of-hell/

47 Cf. **Marquardt, Alex:** "Musk's SpaceX says it can no longer pay for critical satellite services in Ukraine", in: CNN, 14.10.2022; https://edition.cnn.com/2022/10/13/politics/elon-musk-spacex-starlink-ukraine/index.html

48 **Schmieder, Jürgen:** "Der Cyberwar-Minister", 1.12.2022; https://www.sueddeutsche.de/wirtschaft/ukraine-digitalisierung-re-invent-las-vegas-1.5707252

49 Ibid.

50 https://www.microsoft.com/en-us/securityengineering/gsp; cf. **Bremmer, Manfred:** "Microsoft stellt sichere Behörden-Cloud vor"; in: Computerwoche, 20.7.2022; https://www.computerwoche.de/a/microsoft-stellt-sichere-behoerden-cloud-vor,3553785

51 Cf. **Greif, Björn:** "Microsoft schließt Sicherheitsabkommen mit NATO", in: ZDNet, 15.9.2015; https://www.zdnet.de/88246500/microsoft-schliesst-sicherheitsabkommen-mit-nato/

52 Cf. **Wölbert, Christian:** "Wie Microsoft europäische Regierungen in die Cloud lockt"; in: Heise online, 21.6.2021; https://www.heise.de/hintergrund/Wie-Microsoft-europaeische-Regierungen-in-die-Cloud-lockt-6069702.html

53 Cf. **Speed, Richard:** "Microsoft floats Cloud for Sovereignty", in: The Register, 20.7.2022; https://www.theregister.com/2022/07/20/microsoft_cloud_for_sovereignty/

54 Cf. **Schumann, Harald,** und **Elisa Simantke:** "Cyber-Attacken auf staatliche IT: Europas fatale Abhängigkeit von Microsoft"; in: Tagesspiegel, 13.5.2017; https://www.tagesspiegel.de/gesellschaft/europas-fatale-abhangigkeit-von-microsoft-3821812.html

55 Cf. **Mayer, Maximilian,** and **Yen-Chi Lu:** "Auf dem Weg zur

digitalen Selbstbestimmung?", in: Konrad-Adenauer-Stiftung; 3.5.2022; https://www.kas.de/de/einzeltitel/-/content/auf-dem-weg-zur-digitalen-selbstbestimmung

56 Cf. e.g. **Breithut, Jörg:** "Microsoft greift in Cyberattacke gegen die Ukraine ein", in: Spiegel, 8.4.2022; https://www.spiegel.de/netzwelt/microsoft-greift-in-cyberattacke-gegen-die-ukraine-ein-a-a97df1af-5561-4ad1-8fb9-6d0b79e952d4

57 **Gralla, Preston:** "So hilft Microsoft der Ukraine im Cyberkrieg mit Russland", in: Computerwoche, 25.1.2023; https://www.computerwoche.de/a/so-hilft-microsoft-der-ukraine-im-cyberkrieg-mit-russland,3613694

58 Cf. **Krempl, Stefan:** "Google: Microsoft-Monokultur ist in US-Verwaltung ein Sicherheitsproblem", in: Heise online, 4.4.2022; https://www.heise.de/news/Google-Microsoft-Monokultur-ist-in-US-Verwaltung-ein-Sicherheitsproblem-6662388.html

59 Cf. "Microsoft beschwert sich über Milliardendeal für Amazon", in: Manager Magazin, 13.8.2021; https://www.manager-magazin.de/unternehmen/tech/cloud-auftrag-der-us-regierung-microsoft-beschwert-sich-gegen-milliardenzuschlag-fuer-amazon-a-6746519f-9d47-4898-ad6a-f7a7cee28ffd

60 **Wilkens, Andreas:** "Cybersicherheit: Microsoft, Google und Amazon kooperieren mit neuer US-Behörde", in: Heise online, 6.8.2021; https://www.heise.de/news/Cybersicherheit-Microsoft-Google-und-Amazon-kooperieren-mit-neuer-US-Behoerde-6157115.html

61 **Cantrill, Aggi:** "Big Tech Descends on Munich Conference in Support of Ukraine", in: Bloomberg, 19.2.2023; https://www.bloomberg.com/news/articles/2023-02-19/big-tech-descends-on-munich-conference-in-support-of-ukraine#xj4y7vzkg

62 Cf. Deutscher Bundestag, Wissenschaftliche Dienste: "Die rechtlichen Grundlagen des öffentlich-rechtlichen Rundfunks (ARD, ZDF, Deutschlandradio) im Grundgesetz, dem Rundfunkstaatsvertrag der Länder und gemäß höchstrichterlicher Rechtsprechung", in: 21.9.2016; https://www.bundestag.de/resource/blob/481528/af7bf6460dd9f7c07e51917f1ce9ff96/WD-10-046-16-pdf-data.pdf

63 Cf. BVerfGE 83, 238 (296): "Article 5,2 of the German Constitution obliges the State to guarantee the basic supply that falls to public service broadcasting in a dual broadcasting system"; see also BVerfGE 73, 118 (157f.): "For the control by the (external) bodies and the courts created to ensure diversity, a basic standard is decisive that encompasses the essential prerequisites of diversity of opinion: the possibility for all varieties of thought—including those of minorities—to be expressed in private broadcasting, and the exclusion of one-sided, highly unbalanced influence of individual providers or programs on the formation of public opinion, namely the prevention of the emergence of predominant power of opinion. It is the legislator's task to ensure strict enforcement of this basic standard by means of material, organizational and procedural regulations." Cf. also BVerfGE 87, 181 (197); BVerfGE 95, 220 (236); BVerfGE 57, 295 (319 ff.), 1774; BVerfGE 97, 228 (266 f.); BVerfGE NVwZ-RR 1999, 376; BVerfGE 74, 297 (324 f.), 2987; BVerfGE 136, 9 – ZDF-Staatsvertrag; BVerfGE 83, 238 (296 f.).

64 MStV, Preamble.

65 **Fanta, Alexander:** "ARD und ZDF auf Social Media. Von Algorithmen und Metriken verleitet", in: Netzpolitik.org, 7.6.2022; https://netzpolitik.org/2022/ard-und-zdf-auf-social-media-von-algorithmen-und-metriken-verleitet/; die Originalstudie der Otto Brenner Stiftung lautet **Eichler, Henning:** Journalismus in sozialen Netzwerken. ARD und ZDF im Bann der Algorithmen? Frankfurt 2022; https://www.otto-brenner-stiftung.de/journalismus-in-sozialen-netzwerken/

66 After all, the Bavarian State Media Authority has lodged a complaint with Twitter about the manipulation of traffic. It will be interesting to see what happens and, above all, whether Elon Musk cares. Cf. https://www.blm.de/infothek/pressemitteilungen/2023.cfm?object_ID=18618

67 Cf. **Dörr, Dieter, Johannes Kreile,** and Mark D. Cole (Ed.): Handbuch Medienrecht. Recht der elektronischen Medien. Frankfurt/M. 2008, p. 133f.; **Fechner, Frank:** Medienrecht. 21. Aufl. Tübingen: Mohr Siebeck 2021, p. 15; KEK, Ed. (2022): Zukunftsorientierte Vielfaltssicherung im Gesamtmarkt der Medien. Bericht der Kommission zur Ermittlung der Konzentration im Medienbereich (KEK). https://www.kek-online.de/publikationen/medienkonzentrationsberichte/siebter-konzentrationsbericht-2021

68 **Habermas, Jürgen:** Ein neuer Strukturwandel der Öffentlichkeit und die deliberative Öffentlichkeit. Frankfurt/M.: Suhrmamp 2022, p. 67.

69 It is actually the headline to this initiative, in the original: "ensuring fair and open markets"; cf. https://commission.europa.eu/strategy-and-policy/priorities-2019-2024/europe-fit-digital-age/digital-markets-act-ensuring-fair-and-open-digital-markets_en

Chapter V—ACCEPT HERE

1 Cf. https://news.stanford.edu/2005/06/12/youve-got-find-love-jobs-says/

2 **Brand, Steward (Ed.):** The Whole Earth Catalogue. Access to Tools. Herbst 1968; Download verfügbar unter https://monoskop.org/images/0/09/Brand_Stewart_Whole_Earth_Catalog_Fall_1968.pdf

3 "But he who must be a creator in good and evil: verily, he must first be a destroyer and break values. Thus the highest evil belongs to the highest goodness: but this is the creative force ...", it says in Thus Spoke Zarathustra (Part II, "Von der Selbst-Ueberwindung"); cf. also passages from The Gay Science: "The strongest and most evil spirits have so far brought mankind forward the most [...]. But the new is under all circumstances evil, as that which wants to conquer, to overthrow the old boundary stones and the old pieties"; or: "Life - that means being cruel and relentless against everything that becomes weak and old in us, and not only in us." or: "Only as creators we can destroy!"; **Nietzsche, Friedrich:** Sämtliche Werke. Kritische Studienausgabe. Ed. von Giorgio Colli und Mazzino Montinari. Bd. 1–15. München et al.: dtv 1988; Bd. 4, p. 149; Bd. 3, p. 376, p. 400, p. 422.

4 Cf. above all **Turner, Fred:** From counterculture to cyberculture. Stewart Brand, the Whole Earth Network, and the rise of digital utopianism. Chicago et al.: Univ. of Chicago Press 2006.

5 Cf. **Steven Levy:** Hackers. Heroes of the Computer Revolution. Doubleday, 1984;

6 **Blankenship, Loyd:** The Hacker's Manifesto. 1986; Download unter https://github.com/greyscalepress/manifestos/blob/master/content/manifestos/1986-hacker-manifesto.txt

7 Cf. on such metaphors of the digital also **Bickenbach, Matthias,** and **Harun Maye:** Metapher Internet. Literarische Bildung und Surfen. Berlin: Kadmos 2009.

8 **Negroponte, Nicholas:** Being Digital. London: Hodder & Stoughton 1995; **Rifkin, Jeremy:** The Age of Access. The new culture of hypercapitalism, where all of life is a paid-for experience. New York: Jeremy P. Tarcher/Putnam 2001 [2000]; **Tapscott, Don** und **Anthony D. Williams:** Wikinomics. How Mass Collaboration Changes Everything. New York et al.: Portfolio, 2008; **Jarvis, Jeff:** What would Google Do? New York: Harper Business 2011 [2009]; **Anderson, Chris:** The Long Tail. Why the Future of Business Is Selling Less of More. New York: Hyperion, 2006.

9 **Schmidt, Eric** und **Jared Cohen:** Die Vernetzung der Welt. Ein Blick in unsere Zukunft. Reinbek: Rowohlt 2013, p. 368.

10 **Beckedahl, Markus:** "Twitter-Übernahme wird zum Präzedenzfall für Plattformregulierung", in: Netzpolitik.org, 28.10.2022; https://netzpolitik.org/2022/elon-musk-twitter-uebernahme-wird-zum-praezedenzfall-fuer-plattformregulierung/

11 Cf. Corporate Europe Observatory und LobbyControl (Ed.): Die Lobbymacht von Big Tech. Wie Google & Co. die EU beeinflussen. Brüssel, Köln, 2021; Pdf-Download under https://www.lobbycontrol.de/wp-content/uploads/Studie_de_Lobbymacht-Big-Tech_31.8.21.pdf

12 Cf. **Ritzer, Uwe:** "Gefährliche Übermacht", in: sueddeutsche.de, 1.9.2021; https://www.sueddeutsche.de/wirtschaft/eu-lobbyisten-lobbycontrol-facebook-google-amazon-1.5397505?reduced=true Abgerufen am: 08.02.2023

13 **Krempl, Stefan:** "EU-Plattform-Regeln: Sozialdemokraten werfen Big Tech zwielichtiges Lobbying vor", in: Heise.de, 15.10.2022; https://www.heise.de/news/EU-Plattform-Regeln-Sozialdemokraten-werfen-Big-Tech-zwielichtiges-Lobbying-vor-7309644.html

14 **Taplin, Jonathan:** Move fast and break things. How Facebook, Google, and Amazon cornered culture and undermined democracy. New York: Little, Brown and Company 2017, p. 129f.

15 **Dachwitz, Ingo, and Alexander Fanta:** Medienmäzen Google. Wie der Datenkonzern den Journalismus umgarnt. Otto Brenner Stiftung, Frankfurt/M. 2020; Pdf-Download under https://www.otto-brenner-stiftung.de/wissenschaftsportal/informationsseiten-zu-studien/studien-2020/medienmaezen-google/

16 **Wiegand, Markus:** "So steht es im Kampf ums Google-Geld", in: kresspro 5, 2022, p. 18–22, hier p. 20.

17 Ibid.

18 The articles are available digitally at https://about.google/intl/de_ZZ/stories/aufbruch/—this is all about improving the world.

19 Cf. **Simon, Ulrike:** "Springer sahnt bei Facebook gleich doppelt ab", in: Horizont, 17.5.2021; https://www.horizont.net/medien/nachrichten/folgen-bald-google-microsoft--apple-springer-sahnt-bei-facebook-gleich-doppelt-ab-191598

20 **Meier, Christian:** "Warum Influencer für Facebook jetzt wichtiger sind als Journalisten", in: Die Welt, 21.11.2022; https://www.welt.de/kultur/medien/article242183183/Facebook-Warum-Journalisten-jetzt-weniger-wichtig-sind.html

21 Cf. "Die Gates-Millionen und der 'Spiegel'", in: Newsroom.de, 11.1.2022; https://www.newsroom.de/news/aktuelle-meldungen/unternehmen-11/die-gates-millionen-und-der-spiegel-und-die-frage-der-unabhaengigkeit-930751/

22 **Stadler, Rainer:** "Gates-Stiftung: eine potente Medienförderin", in: Info Sperber, 5.4.2022; https://www.infosperber.ch/medien/gates-stiftung-eine-potente-medienfoerderin/

23 Cf. author: "Medien bewerben Medien. Eine datenbasierte Annäherung", in: Medienwirtschaft 20, 1 (2023), p. 74-78.

24 **Dachwitz, Ingo,** und **Alexander Fanta:** Medienmäzen Google; Pdf-Download unter https://www.otto-brenner-stiftung.de/wissenschaftsportal/informationsseiten-zu-studien/studien-2020/medienmaezen-google/, p. 67.

25 **Hanfeld, Michael:** "Dreißig Prozent von nichts", in: FAZ, 21.12.2022; https://www.faz.net/aktuell/feuilleton/medien/kartellamt-stellt-verfahren-gegen-google-ein-18551196.html

26 **Mullins, Brody, Jack Nicas:** "Paying Professors. Inside Google's Academic Influence Campaign", in: Wall Street Journal, 14.7.2017; https://www.wsj.com/articles/paying-professors-inside-googles-academic-influence-campaign-1499785286

27 **Vogel, Kenneth P.:** "Google Critic Ousted From Think Tank Funded by the Tech Giant", in: New York Times, 30.8.2017; https://www.nytimes.com/2017/08/30/us/politics/eric-schmidt-google-new-america.html

28 **Hatmaker, Taylor:** "Facebook cuts off NYU researcher access, prompting rebuke from lawmakers", in: Techcrunch, 4.8.2021; https://techcrunch.com/2021/08/04/facebook-ad-observatory-nyu-researchers/

29 **Kayser-Bril, Nicolas:** "AlgorithmWatch forced to shut down Instagram monitoring project after threats from Facebook", in: AlgorithmWatch, 13.8.2021; https://algorithmwatch.org/en/instagram-research-shut-down-by-facebook/

30 **Beuth, Patrick,** and **Marcel Rosenbach:** "Ärger um Instagram-Studie. Facebook drohte kritischer NGO wegen Forschungsprojekt", in: Spiegel, 13.8.2021; https://www.spiegel.de/netzwelt/apps/instagram-studie-facebook-drohte-kritischer-ngo-wegen-forschungsprojekt-a-e2ca1d84-0002-0001-0000-000178784932

31 Cf. **Schneider, Johannes:** "Hochschulsponsoring in Berlin: Google eröffnet Institut an der Humboldt-Uni", in: Tagesspiegel, 26.10.2011; https://www.tagesspiegel.de/wissen/google-eroffnet-institut-an-der-humboldt-uni-6684754.html; "Google", in: lobbypedia.de, 18.12.2022; https://lobbypedia.de/wiki/Google

32 **Krone, Tobias** and **Thekla Jahn:** "Wenn Facebook der Forschung den Geldhahn zudreht", in: deutschlandfunk.de, 17.12.2019; https://www.deutschlandfunk.de/drittmittelfinanzierung-wenn-facebook-der-forschung-den-100.html

33 **Kästner, Sven:** "Warum Amazon deutsche Forschungsinstitute mitfinanziert", in: br.de, 14.6.2022; https://www.br.de/nachrichten/wissen/warum-amazon-deutsche-forschungsinstitute-mitfinanziert,T7hOPMb

Chapter VI—COUNTDOWN 2029

1 Nationally representative online study, AMP Digital Research, 1001 respondents (age 16-65, 50 % women, 50 % men), Germany, March 2023, 6-point rating scale from "I don't agree at all" to "I fully agree".

2 **Schoen, Douglas E.:** "Polling shows both sides of the aisle support reining in Big Tech", in: The Hill, 5.1.2022; https://thehill.com/opinion/technology/3471908-polling-shows-both-sides-of-the-aisle-support-reining-in-big-tech/

3 Mark Zuckerberg even says in his own manifesto The Hacker Way: "The Hacker Way—often called the hacker ethic—has nothing to do with politics or criminal activities. It is the philosophy of the computer age.. […] In reality, hacking just means building something quickly or testing the boundaries of what can be done". https://www.facebook.com/HackerWayPhilosophy/posts/hacker-way-focus-on-impact-be-fast-be-boldthe-hacker-way-often-called-the-hacker/1838301603165221/

4 Ibid.

5 Cf. https://www.allaboutmarketresearch.com/internet.htm

6 Manifestos for the Internet. Greyscale Press 2015, p. 38. Available under https://www.eff.org/de/cyberspace-independence

7 Otfried Jarren also criticizes the lack of co-determination in current initiatives: **Jarren, Otfried:** "Europäische Harmonisierung? Initiativen zur Regulierung des Medienmarkts", in: epd medien 42/43, 21.10.2022, p. 5-12, hier p. 10.

8 **McKinnon, John D., Ryan Tracy,** and **Chad Day:** "Big Tech Has Spent $36 Million on Ads to Torpedo Antitrust Bill", in: Wall Street Journal, 9.6.2022; https://www.wsj.com/articles/big-tech-has-spent-36-million-on-ads-to-torpedo-antitrust-bill-11654767000

9 **Zakrzewski, Cat** and **Elizabeth Dwoskin:** "Facebook quietly bankrolled small, grass-roots groups to fight its battles in Washington", in: Washington Post, 17.5.2022; https://www.washingtonpost.com/technology/2022/05/17/american-edge-facebook-regulation/

10 Cf., for example **Schoen, Douglas E.:** "Polling shows both sides of the aisle support reining in Big Tech", in: The Hill, 5.1.2022; https://thehill.com/opinion/technology/3471908-polling-shows-both-sides-of-the-aisle-support-reining-in-big-tech/